A CENTUR[Y OF]
ANGLO-BOE[R WAR]
STORIES

A Century of Anglo-Boer War Stories

Selected and introduced by

Chris N van der Merwe
and
Michael Rice

JONATHAN BALL PUBLISHERS
Johannesburg

Although every effort has been made to trace the copyright holders, this has not always been possible. Should any infringement have occurred, the publisher apologises and undertakes to amend the omissions in the event of a reprint.

All rights reserved.
No part of this publication may be reproduced or transmitted, in any form or by any means, without the permission of the publisher and copyright holders.

© This selection Chris N van der Merwe and Michael Rice, 1999

Published in 1999 by
JONATHAN BALL PUBLISHERS (PTY) LTD
P O Box 33977
Jeppestown
2043

Reprinted 2000

ISBN 1 86842 093 0

Cover design by Annelize van Rooyen
Typesetting by Anna-Marie Petzer, Alinea Studio, Cape Town
Printed and bound by NBD, Drukkery Street, Goodwood, Western Cape

Contents

Introduction   9

Rudyard Kipling
The Way that He Took   32

Gustav Preller
Lettie   51

Sol T. Plaatje
Mafeking Diary   58

Olive Schreiner:
The Cry of South Africa   65

Olive Schreiner
Eighteen-Ninety-Nine   66

C. Louis Leipoldt
Oom Gert's Story   99

Rudyard Kipling
A Sahib's War   110

Rudyard Kipling
Bridge-Guard in the Karroo   129

F. W. Reitz
Gods of the Jingo   132

Gustav Preller
Outnumbered   134

M. Grover
I Killed a Man at Graspan   154

Thomas Hardy
Drummer Hodge   157

Jan F.E. Celliers
The Camp Sister   158

Totius
Forgive and Forget   160

William Plomer
The Boer War   162

Eugène N. Marais
Afrikander Cattle   163

C.R. Prance
A Transvaal Ulysses   182

J. van Melle
Revenge   190

Toon van den Heever
The Shield of Old Sem   199

Stuart Cloete
Always Light   209

Sampie de Wet
Concentration Camp   228

J.C. Steyn
Peace   236

Elsa Joubert
THE BRUNT OF THE WAR ... 245

Herman Charles Bosman
THE ROOINEK 253

Michael Rice
THE BLACK CAT 270

Herman Charles Bosman
THE TRAITOR'S WIFE 277

Etienne Leroux
THE FLOOD 283

Herman Charles Bosman
MAFEKING ROAD 298

Pieter Wagener
THE BOERS OF SUNDAYS RIVER 304

Peter Wilhelm
HOMECOMING 312

Christoffel Coetzee
THREE PAIRS OF YELLOW EYES 321

A.H.M. Scholtz
POJO'S CHILD 328

Herman Charles Bosman
THE AFFAIR AT YSTERSPRUIT 331

Karel Schoeman
MISS GODBY AND THE MAGISTRATE 337

CHRIS VAN DER MERWE is Associate Professor in Afrikaans and Dutch Literature at the University of Cape Town. He has written various academic articles on literature, and is the author of, amongst others, *Breaking Barriers: Stereotypes and the changing of values in Afrikaans writing, 1875-1990*. His main field of study is South African fiction, and he is especially interested in the moral values underlying fiction and in the relationship between history and fiction.

MICHAEL RICE currently works as an independent education and development consultant. His doctorate *From Dolly Gray to Sarie Marais* was a survey of over 100 years of literature associated with the Anglo-Boer conflict in which he examined the ways popular fiction both reflects and shapes perceptions of historical events. His short story "The Black Cat", included in this collection and modelled on Kipling, is an example of his practical application of academic insights and opportunities.

Introduction

The Anglo-Boer War saw the end of a century, a reign and a way of life. It was in many respects the curtain-raiser to the twentieth century, providing a foretaste of what have become all too familiar horrors over the last hundred years: the mass involvement of civilian populations in war, concentration camps, and guerrilla warfare. The war also saw the demise of the fledgling Boer Republics and the end of agrarian politics based on the Old Testament.

This anthology contains English and translated Afrikaans stories and poems about the Anglo-Boer War. Texts were in the first place selected on grounds of quality, but sometimes their political and ideological significance also played a part. They are primarily arranged in chronological order; however, thematic links and developments also determine the sequence. The selected works illustrate the contrasting war experience of Afrikaners and English as well as the common ground between them, increasingly discovered in the course of time. The stories by Plaatje, Kipling and Preller, at the beginning of the anthology, for instance, show the differences between the views of the pro-English black person, the British imperialist and the Afrikaner nationalist during and immediately after the war. With the passing of time, shared themes of general human interest were explored: the atrocities of war, the pangs of moral guilt and the meaning of suffering. The anthology is concluded by an extract from Karel Schoeman's novel *Verliesfontein*, containing moral statements profoundly relevant to all people. Taken together, the tales in the anthology reveal the painful working through of a profound national trauma.

Like most modern wars, the Boer War spawned its own brand of escapist English fiction. More than 250 novels in English have appeared in the last one hundred years, few of them worth more than a passing glance except insofar as they reveal popular perceptions and prejudices; in other words, as trawling grounds for social and literary historians.

The number of short stories has been much more limited. In English, barely forty have appeared. However, without doubt, the best and to date the most enduring fiction in English about the war is in this form. Few English writers of lasting reputation have written novels about the Anglo-Boer conflict. Douglas Blackburn (*A Burgher Quixote,* 1903) and C. Louis Leipoldt (*Stormwrack,* 1980) are two exceptions. Though, it must be admitted that Blackburn's reputation outside of a small coterie of academics is hardly known, while Leipoldt's continued standing as a writer is not likely to depend on *Stormwrack*. On the other hand, the short story has been somewhat better served by the likes of Olive Schreiner, Herman Charles Bosman, C.R. Prance and Rudyard Kipling. Many of their tales have stood the test of time and make compulsive reading today, as this anthology attests.

One of the most common features of the South African short story is the personality of the teller of the tale. The best known of these raconteurs is, of course, Bosman's Oom Schalk Lourens. His function is not only to tell the tale and describe the world in which it is acted out, but also to reveal, albeit unwittingly, much about himself that must influence the way his story is received. Oom Schalk appears in this volume in "The Traitor's Wife" and "Mafeking Road", nor is he the only representative of his kind. Kipling's Umr Singh performs the same function in "A Sahib's War" as does the anonymous observer in "The Black Cat", the most recent of the stories to appear in this collection.

Afrikaans fiction on the war is relatively scarce. Directly after the war, numerous historical accounts, biographies and factual reports about Anglo-Boer War suffering and heroism were published in Afrikaans – 22 of these between 1900 and 1905. On the literary side, poets like Leipoldt, Celliers and Totius poured out anger and bitterness about the war; but we find a surprising sparseness of Anglo-Boer War fictional writing. Over the years, the Great Trek has provided Afrikaans novelists with far more historical material; perhaps because it contains more data fitting for the creation of a nationalistic myth – an exodus with Biblical connotations. Directly after the Peace of Vereeniging, the remembrance of the realities of war was probably still too agonising to be used for the creation of imagined stories; the most urgent need was to tell directly, without imaginative "embellishment", about the experience of war. And yet it is surprising that, over the past century, a history which had such a profound effect on the Afrikaner psyche has produced relatively little fiction in Afrikaans.

One of the reasons for the scarcity might be that many people feared that the remembrance of the war could have a divisive effect on society. For many years, a debate continued between Afrikaners who wanted to "forgive and forget" and those who wanted to remember. One of the books intended to keep the memory of the past alive, was Gustav Preller's *Oorlogsoormag en ander sketse en verhale* (Outnumbered and Other Sketches and Stories). The first story, "Lettie", commences with the following words: ". . . (I) thought it should be noted down now, otherwise it might be completely lost. The whole war is slowly but surely fading from our memories . . . to please colourless politics" (translated by Madeleine van Biljon).

It is often difficult to distinguish fact from fiction in Preller's book; and it is clear that the stories are at least partly connected to the author's own experiences. P.C. Schoonees, in his *Die Prosa van die Tweede Afrikaanse Beweging* (The Prose of the Second Afrikaans Movement) remarks that the stories are told with the authenticity of someone who experienced the war; but that the historical events are recreated by the imagination, to emphasise the human side of the war. Preller's stories indeed have the stamp of authenticity; they do not idealise the Boer soldiers and the experience of war. In the title story, for instance, the Boer soldiers' heroism and ingenuity are balanced with their feelings of despondency despite their achievements; the war experience is permeated by gloom and despair.

The stories in English collected together for this volume represent three phases of literary production associated with the conflict. However, it must be asserted that such divisions are purely for the sake of convenience and should be regarded as nothing more than a heuristic device. The first phase then, the imperial phase, coincides roughly with the conflict and extends up to the First World War. The second phase is roughly between the two world wars and the third phase extends more or less from 1948 to the present day. Each phase is characterised by a different ideological view of the conflict. In Afrikaans fiction, on the other hand, it is impossible to distinguish the same three phases. Between the two world wars, for instance, conventional as well as unconventional Afrikaans stories on the war were produced.

As might be expected, the first phase in English fiction is dominated by the experience of Empire. This is the literature of imperialism, either in support of or in reaction to it. Most of the novels about the war were written at this time. Some of their titles give a flavour of the age: B. Ronan, *The Passing of the Boer* (1899); E. Ames, *The Tremendous Twins, or How the Boers Were Beaten* (1900); C.D. Haskim, *For the Queen in South Africa* (1900); F. Russell, *The Boer's Blunder* (1900); H. Nisbet, *For Right and England* (1900) and *The Empire Makers* (1900).

As products of past ideologies the stories often reveal the attitudes and prejudices of a bygone age, and sometimes use language that is no longer acceptable. All of which might be a salutary reminder that political correctness is as much subject to fashion as anything else.

The first phase was a period of high imperialism when most

writers saw it as their bounded duty to sing the glories and responsibilities of Empire. There were, of course, doubters, and not all of them were Boers or members of the Socialist International. Although Kipling was a convinced imperialist, he was aware of the dangers it concealed:

> If, drunk with sight of power, we loose
> Wild tongues that have not Thee in awe,
> Such boastings as the Gentiles use,
> Or lesser breeds without the Law –
> Lord God of Hosts, be with us yet,
> Lest we forget – lest we forget!

Rudyard Kipling was the most famous literary figure of his time to visit South Africa during the war, though there was no shortage of literary figures out here doing their bit for the Empire. Conan Doyle, Rider Haggard, John Buchan, Edgar Wallace, Sir Percy Fitzpatrick and Winston Churchill all played a part. Conan Doyle came out to South Africa as a doctor and played a major role improving hospital facilities for the troops. Rider Haggard already had a long experience of the country. It was he who ran up the Union Jack in Church Square in Pretoria when Shepstone annexed the Transvaal in 1877. Buchan was attached to Milner's "kindergarten" immediately after the war. Edgar Wallace came as a journalist to cover the war and subsequently became the first editor of the *Rand Daily Mail*. Fitzpatrick was one of the original conspirators implicated in the Jameson Raid, and Churchill covered the war for *The Morning Post*.

It may come as a surprise to Kipling's admirers to learn that the bard of Empire had never seen war at first hand before he arrived in South Africa in February 1900. Kipling's first experience of war was at Modder River, itself the scene of heavy fighting some weeks earlier, when he saw the wounded returning from the Battle of Paardeberg which was then still in progress. A few months later he was to see his first battle at Karree Siding. Shortly thereafter, he wrote "A Sahib's War".

The Boer War was fought in two distinct phases. The first was a conventional affair of set battles and sieges. The second was dominated by guerrilla action, farm burning and the concentration camps. It was the outbreak of guerrilla war that exposed the limitations of the British army. Kipling's views on the inadequate training of the British soldiers is well illustrated in his story "The Comprehension of Private Copper":

> Private Copper crawled up the side of a bluish rock-strewn hill thinly fringed with brush a-top, and remembering how he had peered at Sussex conies through the edge of furze-clumps, cautiously parted the dry stems before his face. At the foot of the long slope sat three farmers smoking. To his natural lust for tobacco was added personal wrath because spiky plants were pricking his belly, and Private Copper slid the backsight up to fifteen hundred yards . . .
>
> "Good evening Khaki. Please don't move," said a voice on his left, and as he jerked his head round he saw entirely down the barrel of a well-kept Lee-Metford protruding from an insignificant tuft of thorn. Very few graven images have moved less than did Private Copper through the next ten seconds.
>
> "It's nearer seventeen hundred than fifteen hundred," said a young man in an obviously ready-made suit of grey tweed, possessing himself of Private Copper's rifle. "Thank you. We've got a post of thirty-seven men out yonder. You've eleven – eh? We don't want to kill 'em. We have no quarrel with poor uneducated khakis, and we do not want prisoners we do not keep. It's demoralising for both sides – eh?"

The Karroo is not Sussex. Clearly, all Private Copper's experience poaching rabbits on the Downs has not provided him with the veldcraft he needs to spy on the Boers. Kipling is, of course, making a point about how badly trained the British Tommies are. They have none of the skills that make the Boers so observant, adaptable and dangerous. One of the major criticisms levelled at the British training programme after the war was the inordinate amount of time devoted to "spit and polish". Musketry was given hardly any attention at all. Most of the troops who arrived in South Africa, like Private Copper, were incapable of setting their rifle sights properly.

Kipling enjoyed his war. While in Bloemfontein, he helped edit *The Friend* for two weeks, an experience he was to look back on with delight: "Never again will there be such a paper. Never again such a staff. Never such fine larks." For all the accusations of jingoism that can be levelled against him, he had a grudging respect for the Boers in the field, which he expressed in a poem entitled "Piet":

> I do not love my Empire's foes,
> Nor call 'em angel; still,
> What is the sense of 'ating those
> 'Oom, you are paid to kill?
> So, barrin' all that foreign lot
> Which only joined for spite,
> Myself, I'll just as soon as not
> Respect the man I fight.
> Ah there, Piet! – 'is trousies to 'is knees,
> 'Is coat-tails lyin' level in the bullet-sprinkled breeze;
> 'E does not lose 'is rifle an' 'e does not lose 'is seat,
> I've known a lot of people ride a dam' sight worse than
> Piet.

Kipling was the first British author to describe the life of the ordinary Tommy, and his insights into their suffering made him popular with the rank and file. The success of *The Friend* was largely due to his "Fables for the Staff", in which he delighted in showing up the limitations of the military mind and the staff officers:

> A General, having offered libations to Fortuna, went out to fight a Battle in the course of which his Frontal Attack developed into a Rear Guard action, and his left Flank became a Modulous of varying Elasticity for several hours, owing to his right Flank having wandered towards the Equator.
>
> The Enemy seeing these inexplicable Evolutions, were so overcome with Amazement that they retired in large Numbers and left the General a complete Victory.
>
> A week later, the General, learning from the Reports of his Staff that he was a Heaven-born strategist, diligently read a Book and gave Battle upon the lines therein laid down.
>
> After this he was never seen to smile but frequently heard to murmur: "If I had only trusted my bally Luck instead of a bally Book, I should not now be travelling first-class to Stellenbosch."
>
> MORAL. – Invention is a good servant, but the Letter killeth.

Fashions in humour have changed. Kipling's heavy-handed satire has much in common with the laboured captions of contemporary cartoons. Nonetheless, acknowledged as the Bard of Empire he occupied a privileged position from which he could aim his barbs with impunity. Kipling continued to champion the cause of the common soldier throughout the war in poetry, short stories and journalistic pieces, while keeping up unfaltering criticism of the British high command's lack of initiative and imagination.

The Anglo-Boer War was known as the last of the gentlemen's

wars. It was also described as a white man's war. In fact, the number of blacks who perished during the war far exceeded the total white fatalities. But as has so often happened in South African history, their existence has not even been acknowledged in official celebrations of the conflict. The publication some years ago of Sol Plaatje's account of the siege of Mafeking cast a wholly new light on Baden Powell and the part played by the Tswana as pawns in the British strategy. Apart from Kipling there are very few references in the fiction even mentioning the existence of "non-whites". Where they are acknowledged, it is usually as the "good kaffir" who proves his loyalty by remaining behind on the abandoned farm to protect his master's property, as in Stuart Cloete's "Always Light". "A Sahib's War" is unique in the fiction for telling the story through the eyes of a dead British officer's Sikh batman, though Oom Schalk Lourens in Bosman's "Peaches Ripening in the Sun" does admit that: "a regiment of Indian troops was fighting on that (Natal) front, and we were anxious that an Eastern race should see white men at . . . a disadvantage." Although Kipling's attitudes to "lesser breeds without the law" appear racist and patronising today, there is no doubt in this story about whom he sees as degenerate. The description of the Boers responsible for ambushing the young British officer under the protection of a white flag is little short of virulent propaganda.

Olive Schreiner, the other writer in this collection who wrote at the time of the conflict, stood at the opposite end of the ideological spectrum. Whereas Kipling had a profound belief in the imperial cause, Schreiner wrote in reaction to it. Schreiner never had any doubt about the true effects of war. It was never for her the "Great Game" as it was for Kipling. War for Schreiner was a squalid affair in which men died for dubious causes and women were left in the ruins simply to endure. This is the theme of her short story "Eighteen-Ninety-Nine". Her poem "The Cry of South Africa" expresses her anguish:

> Give back my dead!
> They who by kop and fountain
> First saw the light upon my rocky breast!
> Give back my dead,
> The sons who played upon me
> When childhood's dews still rested on their heads.
> Give back my dead
> Whom thou hast riven from me
> By arms of men loud called from earth's farthest bound
> To wet my bosom with, my children's blood!
> Give back my dead,
> The dead who grew up on me!

Olive Schreiner's portrait of women as the victims of war in "Eighteen-Ninety-Nine" is most sensitive and perceptive, very different from her portrait of Tant' Sannie in *The Story of an African Farm*. The two female characters in "Eighteen-Ninety-Nine" stand for all women in times of war. Schreiner uses their anonymity to suggest the universality of their situation. Like the women of Troy, their fate is to endure. Their only solace is a bitter one. The mother tries to rationalise her grief by dwelling on her son's heroic death. The wife is mute. She is left with a void. She does not even have a child through whom she could contemplate the future. Schreiner was the first English writer to see in the Afrikaner woman a universal symbol of suffering womanhood. Fortunately, she goes beyond that and invests her characters with a vitality that saves them from becoming bloodless metaphors. Most remarkably, Schreiner predicts the birth of the new South Africa. The grandmother teaches her grandson, destined to die in the Boer War: "'This land will be a great land one day with one people from the sea to the north – but we shall not live to see it.' He said to her: 'But how can that be when we are all of different races?' She said: 'The land will make us one. Were not our fathers of more than one race?'"

The second phase of English writing about the war, from the end of the First to the end of the Second World War, is considerably less chauvinistic than that which preceded it. The dominant feature of the English fiction written at this time is an implicit ideological commitment to the Union of South Africa. There is no longer the certitude about the momentum of historical progress that typified the earlier fiction. The First World War had destroyed all that. In place of confidence, there is now an anxiety about the future; an anxiety given all the more emphasis by the new problem areas of the Poor White, the 1914 Rebellion, the 1922 Strike and ultimately the Depression. The solution to South Africa's problems is seen in the union of the two white groups. The conflict is depicted essentially as a civil war in which the members of the same (white) family have fought on opposite sides but must now for their common good make peace.

From the 1930s onwards there is a diminishing concern with depicting the causes and consequences of the Anglo-Boer War as dogmatic assertions to be attacked or defended. Coincidentally, there is a tendency to describe the struggle from the Boer point of view as in C.R. Prance's *Tante Rebella's Saga*. His "A Transvaal Ulysses", written from a perspective of time which has mediated the passions and patriotism that drove the Boers to defend their way of life, describes the ultimate stupidity and waste of the war. The idealism that drove men to take on the greatest empire of the day is seen to be no more worthwhile than that of the jingoes. In the end no one cares. A new generation has its own concerns and those who were once heroes and stood on principle become no more than a bureaucratic nuisance. In this second phase then, the emphasis shifts to a focus on individuals caught up by events they do not understand, trying to work out their personal destinies against a backdrop of cataclysmic events. Writers have fewer ideological axes to grind.

In contrast, Afrikaans fiction in the thirties is coupled with a revival of Afrikaner nationalism and a confirmation of conventional Afrikaner thinking. An increase in the publication of war diaries is noticable as well as a (slight) revival of the war theme in Afrikaans fiction. War novels published in the thirties include: *'n Wiel binne 'n wiel* (A Wheel Within a Wheel) by Miemie Louw-Theron (1935), T.C. Pienaar's *'n Merk vir die eeue* (A Mark for the Centuries, 1937), J.R.L. van Bruggen's *Bittereinders* ("Bitter-enders", or hardliners), an early Afrikaans example of "faction"; furthermore the "Oorlogstories" (War Stories) by the foremost Afrikaans poet, N.P. van Wyk Louw, published in *Die Jongspan* of 4 March 1938, and the short story "Jaap kan nie verstaan nie" (Jaap Cannot Understand) in *Steiltes* by G. J. Joubert (1938). These stories have little literary merit, like the following which were published before the thirties: *Die tweede Grieta* (The Second Grieta) by J.H.H. de Waal (1912), *Deur die smeltkroes* (Through the Melting-pot) by Gordon Tomlinson (1917) and *Wraak* (Revenge) by Joubert Reitz.

A recurring pattern in these stories is that of the villainous "joiner" (turncoat) and the heroic bitter-ender competing for the favour of the lovely Boer girl; the bitter-ender ultimately gets the girl as just reward for his loyalty to his people. Innocence and guilt are totally and simplistically contrasted; the stories are indictments against the injustices of the war and especially focus on the hardships in the concentration camps. Such a novel is *Helkampe* (Hell Camps) by Ewald Steenkamp, published during the Second World War (in 1941), and banned by the government for reasons of state security.

The above-mentioned stereotypical writings reveal and confirm traditional Afrikaner views on the war, on moral right and wrong and on Afrikaner heroism. Some Afrikaner writers have reacted against these conventional views and portrayals.

Johannes van Melle is such an unconventional writer; his lengthy short story "Wraak" (Revenge), included in his collection of short stories *Begeestering* (Inspiration, 1943), is especially relevant here. It deals with the struggle of the farmer Berend Viviers to forgive his "bywoner" (subfarmer) who was a joiner in the war and who killed Berend's son.

Typical of Van Melle's stories, we do not find a simplistic contrast of hero and villain here. The bitter-ender Berend as well as the joiner are depicted with empathy, showing their strengths and weaknesses. The "bywoner" betrayed the cause during the war, but acknowledges and confesses his sins afterwards and truly regrets his moral failure. Berend, on the other hand, is an exemplary Christian and Afrikaner, but in his attempt to forgive his son's killer, he is driven to reach the humanly impossible. In his striving, he is fundamentally motivated by pride, and through his hubris he brings a catastrophe on himself and others. The sins of the traitor and murderer are, in this story, linked to the spiritual pride of an "exemplary Christian" to depict the theme of universal human guilt.

Although Eugène Marais has for many years primarily been honoured as pioneer poet, his contribution to Afrikaans prose is now receiving more recognition. Marais published a number of stories about the Anglo-Boer War. In these stories he does not focus on typical issues like the suffering of the Afrikaners, the injustices and cruelties committed by the English, or the maintenance of Afrikaner group identity. He writes as a journalist, for entertainment. The stories deal with exceptional events; what he presents as the truth, often looks like fantasy. The ideological "neutrality" of his stories might in reality be an ideological position: an anti-nationalistic one. For example: the story "Afrikanerbeeste" (Afrikander Cattle) from *Die leeus van Magoeba* (The Lions of Magoeba, 1934), describes an exceptionally competent Boer scout, Gool Winterbach; but he is not the focal point of the story. The role of main character is shared by the Bushman Hendrik, who knows the veld even better than Gool, and the clever Afrikaner cattle that follow Hendrik's commands. The Boer hero is marginalised to give the central position to the Bushman; and the narrator is more interested in Afrikaner cattle than Afrikaner heroes.

As a young man, C. Louis Leipoldt wrote two stories in Dutch, strongly condemning the English war effort: *De rebel* (The Rebel) and *Bambinelino* (name of a person). Both were published in the Dutch magazine *Elseviers Geïllustreerd Maandblad*; in volume X no 12 (December 1900) and volume XI no 11 (November 1901) respectively. During the war he attended, as reporter, a number of court cases in which Cape rebels were tried. He was deeply moved by their fate, which forms the central theme in his narrative poem "Oom Gert vertel" (Oom Gert's Story, 1911) as well as in his English novel *Stormwrack,* written in the thirties and posthumously discovered and edited by Stephen Gray.

Leipoldt was a supporter of Louis Botha's policy of reconciliation with England. Later in life he avoided the theme of war with its nationalistic connotations – and when he really felt the need to recount a war story, he chose English as his medium. In his Afrikaans writing, even more than in that of Marais, the silence about the war is a significant one.

It is clear that a wide variety of attitudes is reflected in Afrikaans writing between the two world wars; between those who wanted to forget the past for the sake of reconciliation, and those who wanted to remember the injustices.

Since 1948, the third phase in the English fiction, there has been a greater interest in addressing such vexed questions as the concentration camps, the effects of martial law, the "hensoppers" (Boer soldiers who surrendered to the British) and the results of the scorched earth policy. Sampie de Wet's "Concentration Camp" reflects this change of attitude. For while it is unremitting in its descriptions of the suffering endured by the women and children in the Middlebult camp, it is essentially a story about tolerance and reconciliation.

With the passage of time, writers have been more willing to address the skeletons in the cupboards of Boer and Brit alike. Exposing the hidden sins of the past is a dominant feature of recent Afrikaans stories, e.g. those of Pieter Wagener, Christoffel Coetzee and

Karel Schoeman. Before them, Herman Charles Bosman touched upon sensitive issues such as the theme of betrayal. The question of betrayal by the "hensoppers" and the "joiners" was, of course, one of the skeletons in the Afrikaner cupboard left over from the war. The fact that Bosman returned to this theme in four of his short stories: "The Affair at Ysterspruit", "The Traitor's Wife", "Mafeking Road", and "Peaches Ripening in the Sun" probably accounts to some extent for his lack of popular appeal for many years in the Afrikaner community. Bosman's interest was not in political oversimplifications but in the complexity of human motives. The myths of national solidarity held no attractions for him. Hence it is "With a queer jumble of inarticulate feelings" that the schoolmaster leaves Ouma Engelbrecht in "The Affair at Ysterspruit" after realising that the son she worshipped and who had died at Ysterspruit, had been a National Scout and had fought for the British.

In the following extract from "The Traitor's Wife", the narrator – Bosman's other persona, Oom Schalk Lourens – remembers Serfina Roux. Her husband had been an admired leader of the commando to which Oom Schalk belonged but, for reasons never disclosed, had surrendered to the English. Leendert Roux and his wife know that his life is forfeit. The scene is set just after Serfina has betrayed Leendert to the commando and he has been captured and shot:

> Serfina looked even more shadowy than she had done in my dream when she set off back to the homestead along the footpath through the thorns. The sun was just beginning to rise. And I understood how right Jurie Bekker had been when he said that she was just like the Transvaal, with the dawn wind fluttering her skirts about her ankles as it rippled the grass. And I remembered it was the Boer women that kept on when their menfolk recoiled before the steepness of the Drakensberge and spoke of turning back.

I also thought of how strange it was that Serfina should have come walking over to our camp, in the middle of the night, just as she had done in my dream. But where my dream was different was that she had reported not to me but to our veldkornet where Leendert Roux was.

For Oom Schalk, there is something about Serfina that defies definition. However, it is with the image of the Boer women inexorably encouraging their menfolk to cross the Drakensberge that much of her quality comes into focus. It was they who had the vision to see the possibilities of the world beyond the mountains, and it was they who drove their men to seek freedom in a new land. The end justified the means. So it is with Serfina. Though the story hints that Serfina's motives may not be entirely based on patriotism. What is left unclear is the exact nature of her relationship with the man who takes over as commandant when Leendert surrenders to the English. Things are not as they seem. Serfina remains for Oom Schalk, to the end of the story, dreamlike, illusive and uncanny.

Stuart Cloete's ability to tell a rattling good yarn is well illustrated by "Always Light". From the point of view of the other stories in this collection, this story is little more than well-executed entertainment, and as such it reflects a parallel shift in the novels of the same period. For most writers of fiction, the Anglo-Boer conflict has ceased to be anything more than an excuse to tell a tale of high adventure against the background of the war. Cloete avoids any of the tricky issues regarding the rights and wrongs of the conflict or the vexed questions concerning honour, patriotism and motive. Nonetheless, he tells a gripping adventure and he tells it well.

The specific events of the war are less important in the third stage than the universally human themes embodied in the stories about the war. This can be well illustrated by two stories by Toon van den Heever: "Die beukelaar van outa Sem" (The Shield of Old

Sem) and "Outa Sem en Vader Krismis" (Old Sem and Father Christmas), both from the collection of short stories *Gerwe uit die erfpag van Skoppensboer* (Sheaves from the Grim Reaper's Tenure, 1948). Both stories are about a child staying on the farm while his father and older brothers are on the battlefield. His mother has died and two faithful Griqua characters, Sem and his wife, Koema, look after him. Through the Griqua characters, the author portrays the suffering of black people in the war and their loyalty to their masters; he reminds us that the war did not affect whites only.

Historical facts are less important here than issues of general human relevance. In "Die beukelaar van outa Sem", Sem combines "Lord Roberts" and "God" to form his often-repeated exclamation "God Roberts" – a symbol of everything in life that is frightening. In his imagination, Sem deals easily with the threatening "God Roberts"; but when the English soldiers appear at the farm, imagination has no chance against this stark reality, and Sem takes to his heels.

In "Outa Sem en Vader Krismis", Sem tells the story of how he helped Father Christmas with his transport problems with a "brilliant" suggestion: a wagon pulled through the air by dung-beetles. The rise and fall of the wagon graphically represent the central theme: a flight of fancy followed by disillusion. And yet, disillusion does not have the last word, for Sem's little presents given to the child, and above all his enchanting story, turn the drab wartime Christmas into something special.

The role of religion, almost nonexistent in English fiction about the war, plays a prominent role in Afrikaans war fiction. Linked to religious faith is the question of unjust suffering; the loss of independence at the Peace of Vereeniging, even more than the trials of the war, raised questions about God's will. Why did God not support the Boers' just cause? Was all the suffering in vain, now that independence had been lost? In the already-mentioned *'n Wiel binne 'n wiel* (1935) by Miemie Louw-Theron, it is concluded that human beings cannot fully grasp the complexities of God's will. Yet, through the Afrikaner's tribulations one thing became clear – the need to help and support one another.

In his first published prose work, the novelette *Veldslag* (Battle, 1965), Karel Schoeman is concerned with the search for meaning. The widow Esther Naudé finds meaning by caring for the wounded Boer soldier Frans; and Frans, when he has recovered, finds meaning in the continuation of the struggle for the Boer cause. He is killed on the battlefield, but after his death he becomes an inspiring symbol of the heroic Boer struggle. As always in Schoeman's work, there is a strong moral content. The author is more concerned with the general questions of moral right and wrong than with the particular war against England.

The meaning of suffering is dealt with in the short story "Vrede" (Peace) by J.C. Steyn, from *Op pad na die grens* (On the Way to the Border, 1976). The experiences during the war and finally the loss of independence fill the young narrator with a sense of hopelessness, and he becomes pessimistic and cynical. His teacher, a clever and knowledgeable man, supports his views. In contrast, the narrator's parents accept in faith what has happened and are able to find peace in the midst of their adversity. The title "Peace" could be interpreted in many ways: peace has come at last to the country, but the Peace of Vereeniging has brought no inner peace to the Afrikaners. The narrator has no experience of peace, but of unrest. However, the narrator's parents have a lasting peace, independent of outward circumstances.

The narrator presents two contrasting views without taking sides. Yet he changes significantly during the story. In the end he suggests the possibility that God might grant human beings an inner peace, and pleads for God's mercy. Although he does not possess the inner peace his parents have achieved, he strives to find it.

In Elsa Joubert's masterly novel, *Die reise van Isobelle* (The Journeys of Isobelle, 1995), the hardships of the war are also linked to the meaning of suffering. The reverend Josias van Velden, the main character in part one of the novel, visits the concentration camp at Springfontein and is deeply moved by the suffering of the women and children. And yet he also finds the visit an enriching experience, because he learns to feel genuine sympathy for the afflicted and is moved to an almost mystical feeling of unity with the suffering:

"He finds the experience in the camp . . . more beautiful and holy than anything previously experienced. Together we form the body of Christ, the suffering humanity for which he felt so much sympathy" (translated by Chris van der Merwe).

The death of the pious Hester Prinsloo also becomes a meaningful event to him. When she dies, the smell of tuberoses fills her tent, and Hester has a vision of a multitude of angels gathered around her. This episode seems to confirm what is suggested elsewhere in the book, that suffering is the price for a mystical union with God:

"Is suffering the price of the awareness of God? he thought as he walked to his tent. Is it true, then, that suffering is the instrument with which God brings his children to Him?"

Another notable point about *Die reise van Isobelle* is that the Anglo-Boer War is linked to the subsequent rise of Afrikaner nationalism. Although the author is critical of the exclusive and racist Afrikaner nationalism developing in the thirties, part of the blame by implication is laid on the past oppressors of the Afrikaner, who forced them into a laager mentality to fend for themselves effectively. It is suggested that the roots of apartheid are partly to be found in the war lost against Britain.

One of the most imaginative novels about the war is *Magersfontein, o Magersfontein!* (1976) by Etienne Leroux. It describes a foreign team of film makers who come to South Africa to produce a film about the historic battle of Magersfontein. Leroux uses the story to depict the archetypical battle between what is personified as the "white clown" and the "black clown" in the human psyche as well as in society at large. That is, between the orderly, rational side and the irrational, spontaneous "dark side" of human nature.

The conflict in the novel is not between the Boers and the British but between the opposing forces of rationality and creativity; between as they are depicted, the white clowns General Cronjé and Lord Methuen, and the black clowns Generals De la Rey and Wauchope. Neither side has a monopoly of rationality or spontaneity. By and large the author's sympathy seems to be on the side of the often suppressed dark side of human nature: the black clown. Leroux suggests that the Boers won at Magersfontein because under De la Rey they were able to exploit the creative and unconventional, whereas the English were locked into conventional ways of regarding warfare, with fatal results. Wauchope is the innocent scapegoat of the superficial order of the white clown.

The Coloured character Gert Garries is a modern equivalent of Wauchope and De la Rey. In crises, he reveals something of De la Rey's unconventional brilliance. Garries is pragmatic and has learnt to devise practical solutions for the problems caused by the caprices of fate. He changes roles easily as circumstances dictate. He fights gallantly and effectively when threatened, but knows when it is futile to continue fighting.

In all his eleven novels, Leroux has been searching for a life-giving "myth" that could revitalise the disintegrating modern Western world. With Garries he comes closest to this ideal. Garries is neither white clown nor black clown, but a pragmatic and spontaneous combination of both; he is neither black man nor white man, but a South African who genuinely loves his country.

Magersfontein, o Magersfontein! was Leroux's second-last novel. In his last novel, *Onse Hymie* (Our Hymie, 1982), we find another Garries figure, a clear parallel with the Garries of *Magersfontein*. In *Onse Hymie* Garries survives catastrophe, unlike in *Magersfontein*. In *Magersfontein* he is primarily a Wauchope, a victim of the white clown; in *Onse Hymie* he becomes a De la Rey, a brilliant sign of hope amidst the destruction of racial conflict.

The advent of the war centenary has stimulated many new Afrikaans works of fiction about the Anglo-Boer War. The first was published in April 1998 – an amazing debut titled *Op soek na generaal Mannetjies Mentz* (In Search of General Mannetjies Mentz), written by Christoffel Coetzee. In his portrayal of the war, Coetzee turns many Afrikaner myths on their head. There is no romanticising of the valour of the Boer soldiers; although no "Boer bashing" either. The real "villain" of the story is war itself. The violence of the war is shown to spread, ultimately involving everyone in the country. The women characters become hardened and merciless in order to survive. The Witsies, a group of black people who seemingly had nothing to do with the war, become as ruthless as the members of Mentz's commando, in order to drive them away. There is clearly no such thing as "a gentleman's war".

It is apparent that the war was not only fought between white men, but that white women and black people were also affected. Sometimes the real war heroes on the Boer side were the women. The women felt much more strongly about the continuation of the war, and brilliant war strategies were sometimes planned by the women, not the men. The myth of the Afrikaner patriarchal society, with strong men and subservient women, is clearly exposed.

Another myth that is exposed, is that of the traditional "apartheid" of whites and blacks. There are a number of scenes depicting sexual relations across the colour lines. Furthermore, white and black women were friends at the outbreak of the war; they danced together and prayed together. A strong bond of friendship exists between an Afrikaner farmer and his black confidant, Jan Witsie. Together they fought against the English at Majuba, and together they go on hunting expeditions. However, the war changes everything. The first signs of change appear when, in a most dramatic scene, the farmer's wife orders Jan Witsie to burn down their farm.

She denies the English soldiers the pleasure of burning it down, but she is unable to do it herself; Jan Witsie has to do the dirty work.

The strong historical basis of the novel suggests that the author wants to comment on history. And yet the book is not "merely" history. The fictional element provides the author with an opportunity to move from the specific war to the universals of human existence. *Op soek na generaal Mannetjies Mentz* is, in many ways, a study in evil, which is always present but manifests itself more clearly in times of war as cruel, senseless violence and unrestrained sexuality.

Not restricted to history, and focusing on the essence of human nature and existence, Coetzee's novel has a relevance which transcends a specific time and place. The activities of the Mentz commando have a clear parallel to the "couvert activities" undertaken in South Africa during the eighties. The book has just as much to say about the present trauma of working through the recent past as it has about the history of the Anglo-Boer War. The natural tendency, today as in the past, is to dissociate oneself completely from the "rogues" of history, just as the Mentz's whom the author interviewed denied any family relationship to General Mentz. We are today still "in search of Mannetjies Mentz", and Christoffel Coetzee shows where to find him as a first step in being reconciled with our past and with ourselves.

Coetzee started the fictional remembrance of the war in Afrikaans; a number of other books have followed. In some of them Afrikaner self-confrontation and moral guilt are apparent, as in the moving novel by Karel Schoeman, set in the Cape Colony during 1900-1901: *Verliesfontein* (Fountain of Loss) tells the story of the pro-English Coloured man Adam Balie, who was martyred and shot by the Boers. It is reminiscent of Bill Nasson's historical study *Abraham Esau's War.* The first major Afrikaans "Coloured" novelist, A.H.M. Scholtz, published a novel titled *Afdraai* (Turn-off) which deals partly with the war and focuses on the tragedy of racism. In a more traditional vein are the war novels *Kus van die winterskerpioen* (Coast of the Winter Scorpion) by Johnita le Roux and *Groot duiwels dood* (Big Devils Kill) by Eleanor Baker. Furthermore, Van Schaik Publishers has published an anthology of new Afrikaans short stories about the war. Surely other war stories will follow. The Anglo-Boer War is a tragic, fascinating and complex historical event. It will most probably recapture the interest of historical and fictional writers, to be interpreted and reinterpreted by every new generation.

Chris N. van der Merwe
Michael Rice

November 1998

The Way that He Took

Rudyard Kipling

The guns of the field-battery were hidden behind white-thorned mimosas, scarcely taller than their wheels, that marked the line of a dry nullah; and the camp pretended to find shade under a clump of gums planted as an experiment by some Minister of Agriculture. One small hut, reddish stone with a tin roof, stood where the single track of the railway split into a siding. A rolling plain of red earth, speckled with loose stones and sugar-bush, ran northward to the scarps and spurs of a range of little hills – all barren and exaggerated in the heat-haze. Southward, the level lost itself in a tangle of scrub-furred hillocks, upheaved without purpose or order, seared and blackened by the strokes of the careless lightning, seamed down their sides with spent watercourses, and peppered from base to summit with stones – riven, piled, scattered stones. Far away, to the eastward, a line of blue-grey mountains, peaked and horned, lifted itself over the huddle of the tortured earth. It was the only thing that held steady through the liquid mirage. The nearer hills detached themselves from the plain, and swam forward like islands in a milky ocean. While the major stared through puckered eyelids, Leviathan himself waded through the far shallows of it – a black and formless beast.

"That," said the major, "must be the guns coming back." He had sent out two guns, nominally for exercise – actually to show that there was artillery near the railway if any patriot thought fit to tamper with it. Chocolate smears, looking as though they had been swept with a besom through the raffle of stones, wandered across the earth – unbridged, ungraded, unmetalled. They were the roads to the brown mud huts, one in each valley, that were officially styled farm-houses. At very long intervals a dusty Cape-cart or a tilted wagon would move along them, and men would come to sell fruit or scraggy sheep. At night the farm-houses were lighted up in a style out of all keeping with Dutch economy; the scrub would light itself on some far headland, and the house-lights twinkled in reply. Three or four days later the major would read bad news in the Cape Town papers thrown to him from the passing troop trains.

The guns and their escort changed from Leviathan to the likeness of wrecked boats, their crews struggling beside them. Presently they took on their true shape, and lurched into camp amid clouds of dust.

The mounted infantry escort set about its evening meal; the hot air filled with the scent of burning wood; sweating men rough-dried sweating horses with wisps of precious forage; the sun dipped behind the hills, and they heard the whistle of a train from the south.

"What's that?" said the major, slipping into his coat. The decencies had not yet left him.

"Ambulance train," said the captain of Mounted Infantry, raising his glasses. "I'd like to talk to a woman again, but it won't stop here. . . . it *is* stopping, though, and making a beastly noise. Let's look."

The engine had sprung a leaky tube, and ran lamely into the siding. It would be two or three hours at least before she could be patched up.

Two doctors and a couple of nursing sisters stood on the rear platform of a carriage. The major explained the situation, and invited them to tea.

"We were just going to ask *you*," said the medical major of the ambulance train.

"No, come to our camp. Let the men see a woman again!" he pleaded.

Sister Dorothy, old in the needs of war, for all her twenty-four years, gathered up a tin of biscuits and some bread and butter new cut by the orderlies. Sister Margaret picked up the teapot, the spirit-lamp, and a waterbottle.

"Cape Town water," she said with a nod. "Filtered too. *I* know Karoo water." She jumped down lightly on to the ballast.

"What do you know about the Karoo, Sister?" said the captain of Mounted Infantry, indulgently as a veteran of a month's standing.

She laughed. "This is my home. I was born out there – just behind that big range of hills – out Oudtshoorn way. It's only sixty miles from here. Oh, how good it is!"

She slipped the nurse's cap from her hair, tossed it through the open car-window, and drew a breath of deep content. With the sinking of the sun the dry hills had taken life and glowed against the green of the horizon. They rose up like jewels in the utterly clear air, while the valleys between flooded with purple shadow. A mile away, stark-clear, withered rocks showed as though one could touch them with the hand, and the voice of a herdboy in charge of a flock of sheep came in clear and sharp over twice that distance. Sister Margaret devoured the huge spaces with eyes unused to shorter ranges, snuffed again the air that has no equal under God's skies, and, turning to her companion, said: "What do *you* think of it?"

"I am afraid I'm rather singular," he replied. "Most of us hate the Karoo. I used to, but it grows on one somehow. I suppose it's the lack of fences and roads that's so fascinating. And when one gets back from the railway . . ."

"You're quite right," she said, with an emphatic stamp of her foot. "People come to Matjiesfontein – ugh! – with their lungs, and they live opposite the railway station and that new hotel, and they think *that's* the Karoo. They say there isn't anything in it. It's *full* of life when you really get into it. You see that? I'm *so* glad. D'you know, you're the first English officer I've heard who has spoken a good word for my country?"

"I'm glad I pleased you," said the captain, looking into Sister Margaret's black-lashed grey eyes under the heavy brown hair shot with grey where it rolled back from the tanned forehead. This kind of nurse was new in his experience. The average sister did not lightly stride over rolling stones, and – was it possible that her easy pace up-hill was beginning to pump him? As she walked, she hummed joyously to herself, a queer catchy tune of one line several times repeated:

Vat jou goed en trek, Ferreira,
Vat jou goed en trek.

It ran off with a little trill that sounded like:

Swaar dra, al aan die een kant;
Jannie met die hoepelbeen!

"Listen!" she said, suddenly. "What was that?"

"It must be a wagon on the road. I heard the whip, I think."

"Yes, but you didn't hear the wheels, did you? It's a little bird that makes just that noise, 'Whe-ew'!" she duplicated it perfectly. "We call it" – she gave the Afrikaans name, which did not, of course, abide with the captain. "We must have given him a scare! You hear him in the early mornings when you are sleeping in the wagons. It's just like the noise of a whiplash, isn't it?"

They entered the major's tent a little behind the others, who were discussing the scanty news of the campaign.

"Oh, no," said Sister Margaret coolly, bending over the spirit-lamp, "the Transvalers will stay around Kimberley and try to put Rhodes in a cage. But, of course, if a commando gets through to De Aar they will all rise –"

"You think so, Sister?" said the medical major, deferentially.

"I know so. They will rise anywhere in the Colony if a commando comes actually to them. Presently they will rise in Prieska – if it is only to steal the forage at Van Wyk's Vlei. Why not?"

"We get most of our opinions of the war from Sister Margaret," said the civilian doctor of the train. "It's all new to me, but, so far, all her prophecies have come true."

A few months ago that doctor had retired from practice to a country-house in rainy England, his fortune made and, as he tried to believe, his life-work done. Then the bugles blew, and, rejoicing at the change, he found himself, his experience, and his fine bedside manner, buttoned up in a black-tabbed khaki coat, on a hospital train that covered eleven hundred miles a week, carried a hundred wounded each trip and dealt him more experience in a month than he had ever gained in a year of home practice.

Sister Margaret and the captain of Mounted Infantry took their cups outside the tent. The captain wished to know something more about her. Till that day he had believed South Africa to be populated by sullen men and slack-waisted women; and in some clumsy fashion betrayed the belief.

"Of course, you don't see any others where you are," said Sister Margaret, leniently, from her camp-chair. "They are all at the war. I have two brothers and a nephew, my sister's son, and – oh, I can't count my cousins." She flung her hands outward with a curiously un-English gesture. "And then, too, you have never been off the railway. You have only seen Cape Town? All the *ske* – all the useless people are there. You should see *our* country beyond the ranges – out Oudtshoorn way. We grow fruit and vines. It is much prettier, *I* think, than Paarl."

"I'd like to very much. I may be stationed in Africa after the war is over. What a night it is, Sister!" He dwelt lovingly on the last word, as men did in South Africa.

The soft darkness had shut upon them unawares and the world had vanished. There was not so much breeze as a slow motion of the whole dry air under the vault of the immeasurably deep heavens. "Look up," said the captain; "doesn't it make you feel as if we were tumbling down into the stars – all upside down?"

"Yes," said Sister Margaret, tilting her head back. "It is always like that. I know. And those are *our* stars."

They burned with a great glory, large as the eyes of cattle by lamp-light; planet after planet of the mild southern sky. As the captain said, one seemed to be falling from out the hidden earth sheer through space, between them.

"Now, when I was little," Sister Margaret began very softly, "there was one day in the week at home that was all our own. We could get up as soon as we liked after midnight, and there was the basket in the kitchen – our food. We used to go out at three o'clock sometimes, my two brothers, my sisters and the two little ones – out into the Karoo for all the day. All-the-long-day. First we built a fire, and then we made a kraal for the two little ones – a kraal of thorn-bushes so that they should not be bitten by anything. You see? Often we made the kraal before morning – when those" – she jerked her firm chin at the stars – "were just going out. Then we old ones went hunting lizards – and snakes and birds and centipedes, and all that sort of nice thing. Our father collected them. He gave us half-a-crown for a *spoegslang* – a kind of snake. You see?"

"How old were you?" Snake-hunting did not strike the captain as a safe amusement for the young.

"I was eleven then – or ten, perhaps, and the little ones were two and three. Why? Then we came back to eat, and we sat under a rock all afternoon. It was hot, you see, and we played – we played with the stones and the flowers. You should see our Karoo in spring! All flowers! All our flowers! Then we came home, carrying the little ones on our backs asleep – came home through the dark – just like this night. That was our own day! Oh, the good days! We used to watch the meerkats playing, too, and the little buck. When I was at Guy's, learning to nurse, how home-sick that made me!"

"But what a splendid open-air life!" said the captain.

"Where else *is* there to live except the open air?" said Sister Margaret, looking off into twenty-thousand square miles of it with eyes that burned.

"You're quite right."

"I'm sorry to interrupt you two," said Sister Dorothy, who had been talking to the gunner major; "but the guard says we shall be ready to go in a few minutes. Major Devine and Dr Johnson have gone down already."

"Very good, Sister. We'll follow." The captain rose unwillingly and made for the worn path from the camp to the rail.

"Isn't there another way?" said Sister Margaret. Her grey nursing gown glimmered like some big moth's wing.

"No. I'll bring a lantern. It's quite safe."

"I did not think of *that*," she said with a laugh; "only *we* never come home by the way we left it when we live in the Karoo. If any one – suppose you had dismissed a servant, or got him sjamboked, and he saw you go out? He would wait for you to come back on a tired horse, and the . . . You see? But, of course, in England where the road is all walled, it is different. How funny! Even when we were little we learned never to come home by the way we went out."

"Very good," said the captain, obediently. It made the walk longer, and he approved of that.

"That's curious sort of woman," said the captain to the major, as they smoked a lonely pipe together when the train had gone.

"*You* seemed to think so."

"Well – I couldn't monopolise Sister Dorothy in the presence of my senior officer. What was she like?"

"Oh, it came out that she knew a lot of my people in London. She's the daughter of a chap in the next county to us, too."

The general's flag still flew before his unstuck tent to amuse Boer binoculars. But the general himself had gone to join an army a hundred miles away; drawing off, from time to time, every squadron, gun and company that he dared. His last words to the few troops he left behind covered the entire situation.

"If you can bluff 'em till we get round 'em up north to tread on their tails, it's all right. If you can't they'll probably eat you up. Hold 'em as long as you can."

So the skeleton remnant of the brigade lay close among the koppies till the Boers, not seeing them in force on the sky-line, feared that they might have learned the rudiments of war. They rarely disclosed a gun, for the reason that they had so few; they scouted by fours and fives instead of clattering troops and chattering companies, and, where they saw a too obvious way opened to attack they, lacking force to drive it home, looked elsewhere. Great was the anger in the Boer commando across the river – the anger and unease.

"The reason is they have so few men," the farmer reported, all fresh from selling melons to the camp, and drinking Queen Victoria's health in good whisky. "They have no horses – only what they call Mounted Infantry. Come on and shoot them. Then you will see us rise and cut the line."

"Yes, we know how you rise, you Colonials," said the Boer commandant above his pipe. "We know what has come to all your promises from Beaufort West, and even from De Aar. *We* do the work – all the work – and you kneel down with your parsons and pray for our success. What good is that? The president has told you a hundred times God is on our side. Why do you worry Him? We did not send you Mausers and ammunition for *that*."

"We kept our commando horses ready for six months – and forage is very dear. We sent all our young men," said an honoured member of local society.

"A few here and a few servants there. What is that? You should have risen down to the sea all together."

"But you were so quick. Why did not you wait the year? We were not ready, Jan."

"That is a lie. You want to save your cattle and your farms. Wait till *our* flag flies from here to Port Elizabeth and you shall see what you will save when the president learns how you have risen."

The saddle-coloured sons of the soil looked down their noses. "Yes – it is true. Some of our farms are close to the line. They say at Worcester and in the Paarl that many soldiers are always coming in from the sea. One must think of that – at least till they are shot. But we know there are very few in front of you here. Give them what you gave the fools at Stormberg, and you will see how we can shoot rooineks."

"Yes. I know that cow. She is always going to calve. Get away. I am answerable to the president – not to the Cape."

But the information stayed in his mind, and, not being a student of military works, he made a plan to suit. The tall koppie on which the English had planted their helio-station commanded the more or less open plain to the northward, but did not command the five-mile belt of broken country between that and the utmost English pickets, some three miles from camp. The Boers had established themselves very comfortably among these rock-ridges and scrub-patches, and the "great war" drizzled down to long shots and longer stalking. The young bloods wanted rooineks to shoot, and said so.

"See here," quoth the experienced Jan van Staden that evening to as many of his commando as cared to listen. "You youngsters from the Colony talk a lot. Go and turn the rooineks out of their koppies to-night. Eh? Go and take their bayonets from them and stick them into them. Eh? You don't go!"

"Jan – Jan," said one young man appealingly, "don't make mock of us."

"I thought that was what you wanted so badly. No? Then listen to me. Behind us the grazing is bad. We have too many cattle here. To-morrow, by the sky's look, it will blow a good wind. So, to-morrow early I shall send all our cattle north to the new grazing. That will make a great dust for the English to see from their helio yonder." He pointed to a winking night-lamp stabbing the darkness with orders to any outlying picket. "With the cattle we will send all our women. Yes, all the women and the wagons we can spare, and the lame ponies and the broken carts we took from Andersen's farm. That will make a big dust – the dust of our retreat. Do you see?"

They saw and approved, and said so.

"Good. There are many men here who want to go home to their wives. I shall let thirty of them away for a week. Men who wish to do this will speak to me to-night. These men will look after the cattle and see that they make a great dust for a long way. They will run about behind the cattle showing their guns, too. So *that*, if the wind blows well, will be our retreat. The cattle will feed beyond Koopman's Kop."

"No good water there," growled a farmer who knew that section. "Better to go on to Zwartpan. It is always sweet at Zwartpan."

The commando discussed the point for twenty minutes. It was much more serious than shooting rooineks. Then Jan went on:

"When the rooineks see our retreat they may all come into our koppies together. If so, good. But it is tempting God to expect such a favour. *I* think they will first send some men to scout." He grinned broadly, twisting the English word. "Almighty! To scout! They have none of that sort of rooinek that they used at Sunnyside." (Jan meant incomprehensible men from a place called Australia across the southern seas who played what they knew of the war game to kill.) "They have only some mounted infantry," – again he used the English words. "They were once a red-jacket regiment, so their scouts will stand up bravely to be shot at."

"Good – good, we will shoot them," said a youngster from Stellenbosch, who had come up on a free pass as a Cape Town excursionist just before the war to a farm on the border, where his aunt was taking care of his horse and rifle.

"But if you shoot their scouts I will sjambok you myself," said Jan, amid roars of laughter. "We must let them *all* come into the koppies to look for us; and I pray God will not allow any of us to be tempted to shoot them. They will cross the ford in front of their camp. They will come along the road – so!" he imitated with ponderous arms the army style of riding. "They will trot up the road this way and that way" – here he snaked his hard finger in the dust – "between koppies, till they come here, where they can see the plain and all our cattle going away. Then they will *all* come in close together. Perhaps they will even fix their bayonets. *We* shall be up here behind the rock – there and there." He pointed to two flat-topped koppies, one on either side of the road, some eight hundred yards away. "That is our place. We will go there before sunrise. Remember we must be careful to let the very last of the rooineks pass before we begin shooting. They will come along a little careful at first. But we do not shoot. Then they will see our fires and the fresh horse-dung, so they will know we have gone on. They will run together and talk and point and shout in this nice open place. Then we begin shooting them from above."

"Yes, uncle, but if the scouts see nothing and there are no shots and we let them go back quite quiet, they will think it was a trick. Perhaps the main body may never come here at all. Even rooineks learn in time – and so we may lose even the scouts."

"I have thought of that too," said Jan, with slow contempt, as the Stellenbosch boy delivered his shot. "If you had been *my* son I should have sjamboked you more when you were a youngster. I shall put *you* and four or five more on the nek (the pass), where the road comes from their camp into these koppies. You go there before it is light. Let the scouts pass in or I will sjambok you myself. When the scouts come back after seeing nothing here, then you may shoot them, but not till they have passed the nek and are on the straight road back to their camp again. Do you understand? Repeat what I have said, so that I shall know."

The youth obediently repeated his orders.

"Kill their officers if you can. If not, no great matter, because the scouts will run to camp with the news that our koppies are empty. Their helio-station will see your party trying to hold the nek so hard – and all that time they will see our dust out yonder, and they will think you are the read-guard, and they will think *we* are escaping. They will be angry."

"Yes – yes, uncle, we see," from a dozen elderly voices.

"But this calf does not. Be silent! They will shoot at you, Nicholaas, on the nek, because they will think you are to cover our getting away. They will shell the nek. They will miss. You will then ride away. All the rooineks will come after you, hot and in a hurry – perhaps, even, with their cannon. They will pass our fires and our fresh horse-dung. They will come here as their scouts came. They will see the plain so full of our dust. They will say, 'The scouts spoke truth. It is a full retreat.' *Then* we up there on the rocks will shoot, and it will be like the fight at Stormberg in daytime. Do you understand *now*?"

Those of the commando directly interested lit new pipes and discussed the matter in detail till midnight.

Next morning the operations began with, if one may borrow the language of some official despatches, "the precision of well-oiled machinery".

The helio-station reported the dust of the wagons and the movements of armed men in full flight across the plain beyond the koppies. A colonel, newly appointed from England, by reason of his seniority, sent forth a dozen mounted infantry under command of a captain. Till a month ago they had been drilled by a cavalry instructor, who taught them "shock" tactics to the music of trumpets. They knew how to advance in echelon of squadrons, by cat's cradle of troops, in quarter column of stable-litter, how to trot, to gallop, and, above all, to charge. They knew how to sit their horses unremittingly, so that at the day's end they might boast how many hours they had been in the saddle without relief, and they learned to rejoice in the clatter and stamp of a troop audible five miles away.

They trotted out two and two along the farm road, that trailed lazily through the wind-driven dust; across the half-dried ford to a nek between low stony hills leading into the debatable land.

(Vrooman, of Emmaus, from his neatly bushed hole noted that one man carried a sporting Lee-Enfield rifle with a short fore-end. Vrooman, of Emmaus, argued that the owner of it was the officer to be killed on his return, and went to sleep.) They saw nothing except a small flock of sheep and a herdsman who spoke broken English with curious fluency. He had heard that the Boers had decided to retreat on account of their sick and wounded. The captain in charge of the detachment turned to look at the helio-station four miles away. "Hurry up," said the dazzling flash. "Retreat apparently continues, but suggest you make sure. Quick!"

"Ye-es," said the captain, a shade bitterly, as he wiped the sweat from a sun-skinned nose. "You want me to come back and report all clear. If anything happens it will be my fault. If they get away, it will be my fault for disregarding the signal. I love officers who suggest and advise, and want to make their reputations in twenty minutes."

"Don't see much 'ere, sir," said the sergeant, scanning the bare cup of the hollow where a dust-devil danced alone.

"No? We'll go on."

"If we get among these steep 'ills we lose touch of the 'elio."

"Very likely. Trot."

The rounded mounds grew to spiked koppies, heartbreaking to climb under a hot sun at four thousand feet above sea level. This is where the scouts found their spurs peculiarly useful.

Jan van Staden had thoughtfully allowed the invading force a front of two rifle-shots or four thousand yards, and they kept a thousand yards within his estimate. Ten men strung over two miles feel that they have explored all the round earth.

They saw stony slopes combing over in scrub, narrow valleys clothed with stone, low ridges of splintered stone, and tufts of brittle-stemmed bush. An irritating wind, split up by many rocky barriers, cuffed them over the ears and slapped them in the face at every turn. They came upon an abandoned camp fire, a little fresh horse-dung, and an empty ammunition-box splintered up for firewood, an old boot, and a stale bandage.

A few hundreds yards farther along the road a battered Mauser had been thrown into a bush. The glimmer of its barrel drew the scouts from the hillside, and here the road, after passing between two flat-topped koppies, entered a valley nearly half a mile wide, rose slightly, and over the nek of a ridge gave clear view across the windy plain northward.

"They're on the dead run, for sure," said a trooper. "Here's their fires and their litter and their guns, and that's where they're bolting to." He pointed over the ridge to the bellying dust cloud a mile long. A vulture high overhead flickered down, steadied herself, and hung motionless.

"See," said Jan van Staden from the rocks above the road, to his waiting commando. "It turns like a well-oiled wheel. They look where they need not look, but *here*, where they should look on both sides, they look at our retreat – straight before them. It is tempting our people too much. I pray God no one will shoot them."

"That's about the size of it," said the captain, rubbing the dust from his binoculars. "Boers on the run. I expect they find their main line of retreat to the north is threatened. We'll get back and tell the camp." He wheeled his pony and his eye traversed the flat-topped koppie commanding the road. The stones at its edge seemed to be piled with less than Nature's carelessness.

"That 'ud be a dashed ugly place if it were occupied – and that other one, too. Those rocks aren't five hundred yards from the road, either of 'em. Hold on, sergeant, I'll light a pipe." He bent over the bowl, and above his lighted match squinted at the koppie. A stone, a small roundish brown boulder on the lip of another one, seemed to move very slightly. The short hairs of his neck grated his collar. "I'll have another squint at their retreat," he cried to the sergeant, astonished at the steadiness of his own voice. He swept the plain, and, wheeling, let the glass rest for a moment on the koppie's top.

One cranny between the rocks was pinkish, where blue sky should have shown. His men, dotted down the valley, sat heavily on their horses – it never occurred to them to dismount. He could hear the squeak of the leathers as a man shifted. An impatient gust blew through the valley and rattled the bushes. On all sides the expectant hills stood still under the pale blue.

"And we passed within a quarter of a mile of 'em! We're done!" The thumping heart slowed down, and the captain began to think clearly – so clearly that the thoughts seemed solid things. "It's Pretoria gaol for us all. Perhaps that man's only a look-out, though. We'll have to bolt! And I led 'em into it! . . . You fool," said his other self, above the beat of the blood in his eardrums. "If they could snipe you all from up there, why haven't they begun already? Because you're the bait for the rest of the attack. They don't want you *now*. You're to go back and bring up the others to be killed. Go back! Don't detach a man or they'll suspect. Go back all together. Tell the sergeant you're going. Some of them up there will understand English. Tell it aloud! Then back you go with the news – the real news."

"The country's all clear, sergeant," he shouted. "We'll go back and tell the colonel." With an idiotic giggle he added, "It's a good road for guns, don't you think?"

"Hear you that?" said Jan van Staden, gripping a burgher's arm. "God is on our side to-day. They *will* bring their little canons after all!"

"Go easy. No good bucketing the horses to pieces. We'll need 'em for the pursuit later," said the captain. "Hullo, there's a vulture! How far would you make him?"

"Can't tell, sir, in this dry air."

The bird swooped towards the second flat-topped koppie, but suddenly shivered sideways, and wheeled off again, followed intently by the captain's glance.

"And that koppie's simply full of 'em too," he said, flushing.

"Perfectly confident they are, that we'd take this road – and then they'll scupper the whole boiling of us! They'll let us through to fetch up the others. But I mustn't let 'em know we know. By Jove, they do *not* think much of us! Don't blame 'em." The cunning of the trap did not impress him until later.

Down the track jolted a dozen well-equipped men, laughing and talking – a mark to make a pious burgher's mouth water. Thrice had their captain explicitly said that they were to march easy, so a trooper began to hum a tune that he had picked up in Cape Town streets:

Vat jou goed en trek, Ferreira,
Vat jou goed en trek;
Jannie met die hoepelbeen, Ferreira,
Jannie met die hoepelbeen!

Then with a whistle:

Swaar dra – al aan die een kant –

The captain, thinking, furiously, found his mind turn to a camp in the Karoo, months before; an engine that had halted in that waste, and a woman with brown hair, early grizzled – an extraordinary woman . . . Yes, but as soon as they had dropped the flat-topped koppie behind its neighbour he must hurry back and report: . . . A woman with grey eyes and black eye-lashes . . . The Boers would probably be massed on those two koppies. How soon dare he break into a canter? . . . A woman with a queer cadence in her speech . . . It was not more than five miles home by the straight road –

"Even when we were children we learned not to go back by the way we had come."

The sentence came back to him, self-shouted, so clearly that he almost turned to see if the scouts had heard. The two flat-topped koppies behind him were covered by a long ridge. The camp lay due south. He had only to follow the road to the nek – a notch, unscouted as he recalled now, between the two hills.

He wheeled his men up a long valley.

"Excuse me, sir, that ain't our road!" said the sergeant. "Once we get over this rise, straight on, we come into direct touch with the 'elio, on that flat bit o' road there they 'elioed us goin' out."

"But we aren't going to get in touch with them just now. Come along, and come quick."

"What's the meaning of this?" said a private in the rear. "What's 'e doin' this detour for? We sha'n't get in for hours an' hours."

"Come on, men. Flog a canter our of your brutes, somehow," the captain called back.

For two throat-parched hours he held west by south, away from the nek, puzzling over a compass already demented by the ironstone in the hills, and then turned south-east through an eruption of low hills that ran far into the re-entering bend of the river that circled the left bank of the camp.

Eight miles to eastward that student from Stellenbosch had wriggled out on the rocks above the nek to have a word with Vrooman of Emmaus. The bottom seemed to have dropped out of at least one portion of their programme; for the scouting party were not to be seen.

"Jan is a clever man," he said to his companion, "but he does not think that even rooineks may learn. Perhaps those scouts will have seen Jan's commando, and perhaps they will come back to warn the rooineks. That is why I think he should have shot them *before* they came to the nek, and made quite sure that only one or two got away. It would have made the English angry, and they would have come out across the open in hundreds to be shot. Then when we ran away they would have come after us without thinking. If you can make the English hurry, they never think. Jan is wrong this time."

"Lie down, and pray you have not shown yourself to their heliostation," growled Vrooman, of Emmaus. "You throw with your arms and kick with your legs like a rooinek. When we get back I will tell Jan and he will sjambok you. All will yet come right. They will go and warn the rest, and the rest will hurry out by this very nek. Then we can shoot. Now you lie still and wait."

"'Ere's a rummy picnic. We left camp, as it were, by the front door. 'E 'as given us a giddy-go-round, an' no mistake," said a dripping private as he dismounted behind the infantry lines.

"Did you see our helio?" This was the colonel, hot from racing down from the helio-station. "There were a lot of Boers waiting for you on the nek. We saw 'em. We tried to get at you with the helio, and tell you we were coming out to help you. Then we saw you didn't come over that flat bit of road where we had signalled you going out, and we wondered why. We didn't hear any shots."

"I turned off, sir, and came in by another road," said the captain.

"By another road!" The colonel lifted his eyebrows. "Perhaps you're not aware, sir, that the Boers have been in full retreat for the last three hours, and that those men on the nek were simply a rearguard put out to delay us for a little. We could see that much from here. Your duty, sir, was to have taken them in the rear, and then we could have brushed them aside. The Boer retreat has been going on all morning, sir – all morning. You were despatched to see the front clear and to return at once. The whole camp has been under arms for three hours; and instead of doing your work you wander all about Africa with your scouts to avoid a handful of skulking Boers! You should have sent a man back at once – you should have – "

The captain got off his horse stiffly.

"As a matter of fact," said he, "I didn't know for sure that there were any Boers on the nek, but I went round it in case it was so. But I *do* know that the koppies beyond the nek are simply crawling with Boers."

"Nonsense. We can see the whole lot of 'em retreating out yonder."

"Of course you can. That's part of their game, sir. I saw 'em lying on the top of a couple of koppies commanding the road, where it goes into the plain on the far side. They let us come in to see, and they let us go out to report the country clear and bring you up. Now they are waiting for *you*. The whole thing is a trap."

"D'you expect any officer of my experience to believe that?"

"As you please, sir," said the captain hopelessly. "My responsibility ends with my report."

Source:
Rudyard Kipling. *Land and Sea Tales for Scouts and Guides.* London: Macmillan: 1923, written c. 1904.

Lettie

Gustav Preller

The story of Lettie and the English officer happened a long time ago, the finer details are already fading from memory but precisely because of that, I thought it should be noted down now, otherwise it might be completely lost. The whole war is slowly but surely fading from our memories, like an unfixed portrait in sunlight. The great moments which we should all remember, we forget for the sake of a historical researcher; the small things which hurt in small circles, we erase to please colourless politics. Colenso, Magersfontein, Spion Kop are becoming mere names amongst small groups of English and small groups of Boers who shot and shot; the droning of bullets and the groaning of those who were hurt; the hunger and the thirst and the distress – everything disappears from memory like the teacher's homework when we were children. Merebank, Irene, St Helena – we erase it ourselves. But Lettie . . .

She was a pretty thing, Lettie, fresh and delicate and wholesome like the bedewed *vygies* on the garden wall in the morning, now home, unspoilt, for a year or two from our old girls' school with just enough worldly wisdom to realise more or less how little she knew and to be glad that she had a nation of her own to belong to.

And she was the only one available that day at Rietpol's old homestead, below Slangampies, when the Khaki officer came riding up, accompanied by a few others and a national scout guide. Ma was ill in bed, her father and her eldest brother were on commando and the smaller ones were with the workers in the fields.

Stiff from riding a long distance, the officer lifted himself heavily out of the saddle, struggled to get his foot out of the stirrup and threw the reins to his orderly after which he strolled, stride-legged, up the garden path towards the door: yellow leggings, wide riding breeches, khaki helmet and a monocle.

The scout wanted to follow him but he made a forestalling gesture indicating that he should stay with the horse.

He knocked on the door with the head of his riding crop, cleared his throat a few times and Let came to the door.

Were there any men at home? he asked Let, after he had rather superciliously made a vague gesture with his riding crop in the direction of his helmet.

"No," was the reply.

"Where is the owner of the farm?"

"On commando."

"Ha . . . where is the commando?"

"That you should know better than me."

"Come, come, don't be . . . ha-hm . . . cheeky; it's not sensible for such a pretty girl, especially," he added with another hm-ha and an idiotic laugh, "if her father is on commando and she's alone at home!"

Let was deeply offended but she merely shrugged and gazed uneasily for a moment in the direction of the fields.

"You might invite me in."

"If your were an ordinary visitor, yes, but under the circumstances, no."

"But I'll have to search the house for weapons?"

"Then you'll do so without any invitation."

"Are there any weapons here?"

"Yes."

"Ha! . . . hm . . . well then," he decided, "would you be so kind as to hand them over?"

Without a word Let turned and entered the house.

The officer gestured to his subordinates and two soldiers with loaded rifles approached; he unholstered his own revolver and entered the house.

The girl returned almost immediately with two guns and a few cartridges which she put down on a table: an old Martini without a sight and a bright new small Mauser hunting rifle.

"That's it," she said and despite her earlier resolute attitude, she nevertheless cast a sad glance at the little Mauser. It was a gift from her brother and she had learnt to shoot with it.

He picked up the little Mauser.

"Ah . . . hm . . . I'll take this little toy . . ."

"Would you be kind enough to send the soldiers out?"

Two Tommies, the officer's retinue, stood with their rifles at the ready in the living room and Let was getting huffy.

The officer put his revolver down on a table and looked more closely at the two guns. The Martini he gave to the soldiers with orders to smash it and then go back.

They saluted and moved away to the camp which was just across the hill.

"This toy," he continued with the Mauser in his hands, "I'll look after myself for you; perhaps it will give me the . . . a . . . hm . . . ha . . . the opportunity to come again one day!"

He opened the bolt and a cartridge fell out, a snub-nosed lead-pointed one.

"Ha . . . a . . . !"

"It's only for game," Lettie remarked a trifle uneasily.

"Hm . . . but also for . . . English?"

"If they're game, certainly."

One after another he pulled all the other cartridges out of the magazine onto the table, looked at the fine bead of the rifle and after a while spelt out the girl's name on the silver plate on the stock.

"Your father's name?"

"No."

"Your brother's?"

"No."

"Whose, then?"

"Mine."

"O . . . but what do you do with a rifle?"

"I really believe about the same that others do."

"Target shooting?"

"I can shoot . . . but, sir, why this catechism? Please take the rifle away and leave us in peace."

But it seemed the last thing the intruder wanted to do at that moment. And no wonder: months of commando life, gave the presence of a pretty, charming Boer girl with her cheeky attitude, a magnetic attraction against which the civilised man had no immunity. Her cool, polite attitude was in strong contrast to the militant attitude of most others with whom his work brought him into contact, apart from those who wept themselves into a stupor – which was totally lost on him. At the very least he wanted to tease her a bit longer.

"This," he said, pointing to the lead-pointed bullets, "would give me the right to set fire to the roof . . ."

"I didn't know that you had to have a reason for it; it's your work, isn't it?"

"Hm . . . it is my work, alas," he replied, "but . . . ha . . . if you play a tune for me on the . . . hm . . . harmonium, it won't be my duty in this case," with a grimace that was meant to be a smile.

Let was ready with a sharp retort when she remembered her mother, ill in a side room and the irresponsible rage was immediately replaced with fear. He had the power to burn down the house in their presence – he might well do it: it had been done so often! No, she would rather try to keep him going.

He noticed her embarrassment and spoke again:

"Or shall we do some target practice?"

Her mind still occupied, Let made an impatient gesture.

"I'll tell you what we'll do," he suggested, "we'll have a wager: each one has three shots; and if I win . . ."

"No," she said firmly, as if she had taken a sudden decision, "no, we each get one shot only and no conditions beforehand. Terms can be arranged later!"

"Ahem . . . excellent . . . ha!"

He picked up the rifle and put all the bullets back into the magazine.

Lettie put on her sunbonnet and went outside ahead of him.

She led the way across the threshing floor to a level place precisely in the direction of the English camp, and indicated the shooting range.

He couldn't keep his eyes off her and was much too taken with her to see where it was all leading. Talking away, he strolled next to her at a typical officer's pace with the least possible bending of the knees.

"Ah . . . what shall we put up . . . a . . . ha . . . an egg?"

"What distance?"

"Hundred yards . . . ha?"

"No," Lettie said, "at such a short distance, rather a matchbox . . . on its side!"

"Ha . . . a matchbox?"

He had suggested an egg as a joke, intending to put up his helmet. The matchbox on its side left him completely flabbergasted.

"Yes, put it down on that ant hill over there and then pace a hundred yards to here. No excessively long steps, hey!"

He rummaged in the pocket of his riding breeches and took out a box of matches. The ant hill was pointed out to him once more and he strolled towards it with wide-swinging arms.

"Pace from there," Let mischievously called after him, "not from here!"

He stopped and turned and then the meaning of what she had said, struck him.

"Ha . . . yes."

"Shall we draw lots for the first shot?" she asked when he was back and had the assurance that it was the correct ant hill.

"Hm . . . no . . . ladies first, and ha . . . you see, then I won't have to walk down again to set up the matchbox for myself!"

And he giggled excessively as though it was a great joke.

Lettie loaded the gun herself, looked at the sight, aimed and wanted at first to take aim on one knee but found that she was shaking too much. She got up and aimed offhandedly.

"Please cast a shadow over the bead."

He hung a purple handkerchief, smelling of lavender water, over his riding crop and held it between the sun and the bead.

A few breathless seconds followed.

She let the rifle drop again, suddenly aimed and almost simultaneously pulled the trigger . . .

A small cloud of dust rose far beyond the ant hill and the bullet sang over the hilltop towards the camp. The matchbox had disappeared.

"A direct hit!" the Englishman shouted . . . "Hip, hip . . ."

"Now set it up again," Let commanded, without waiting.

"Hm . . . ha . . . and if we both score a hit, we'll have to have a return match . . ."

"Yes."

When he was fifty yards away, Let pushed another cartridge into the breech and followed him softly. When he turned towards her at the ant hill, she lifted the Mauser . . .

"Hands up!" she ordered so firmly and resolutely that her intention was absolutely clear.

"Ha . . . ha!"

"Hands up!" it sounded again from behind the fine bead.

Both his hands went up and the monocle dropped.

"Now listen!" she ordered, the little rifle still pressed to her shoulder and aimed at him . . . "Take off your sabre!"

Mechanically he unbuckled the sabre belt with the revolver and cartridge case and dropped it against the ant hill.

"Take off your hat!"

He wanted to remonstrate, something about the heat of the sun but . . .

"Take off your hat or I'll shoot!"

He threw down the helmet and for the first time bared a gleaming skull to the sun's rays.

"Right about turn and run as fast as you can over that hill . . . run!"

Again he wanted to remonstrate, to discuss, but at fifty yards he was staring down the barrel of a loaded Mauser. He remembered the lead-pointed bullet . . . the matchbox and her determined attitude filled his heart with the fear that she might just tamper with the trigger . . .

He started running, first at a stiff little trot with his arms raised . . .

"Faster!" he heard from behind him, looked back and then he ran in such a way that one would never have guessed that his knees were so stiff. He ran directly to the camp.

The first shot had already caused alarm in the English camp behind the hill and at the same time that the diminishing shape of the senior officer was nearing the crest of the hill, about five or six other English appeared on the hilltop in front of him.

Let grabbed the broken matchbox with the matches – it was deep into the second year of the war – but left the Englishman's possessions where he had dropped them at the ant hill and returned home.

That same afternoon Rietpol's lovely old house was burnt to the ground and a few days later Lettie, her mother, and the little brothers were taken to Merebank's concentration camp.

But, as I've said, it all happened a long time ago, it's fading from memory.

Source:
Gustav Preller: *Oorlogsoormag en ander sketse en verhale.* Cape Town: Nasionale Pers: 1923.
Translated by Madeleine van Biljon

MAFEKING DIARY (Extract)

Sol T. Plaatje

The extract contains the first entry of Sol Plaatje's diary written in Mafeking during its siege by the Boers.

OCTOBER-NOVEMBER 1899

Sunday, 29th
Divine Services. No thunder. Haikonna[1] terror; and I have therefore got ample opportunity to sit down and think before I jot down anything about my experiences of the past week. I have discovered nearly everything about war and find that artillery in war is of no use. The Boers seem to have started hostilities, the whole of their reliance leaning on the strength and number of their cannons – and they are now surely discovering their mistake. I do not think that they will have more pluck to do anything better than what they did on Wednesday[2] and we can therefore expect that they will either go away or settle round us until the troops arrive.[3]

To give a short account of what I found war to be, I can say: no music is as thrilling and as immensely captivating as to listen to the firing of the guns on your own side. It is like enjoying supernatural melodies in a paradise to hear one or two shots fired off the armoured train; but no words can suitably depict the fascination of the music produced by the action of a Maxim, which to Boer ears, I am sure, is an exasperation which not only disturbs the ear but also disorganises the free circulation of the listener's blood. At the city of Kanya[4] they have been entertained (I learn from one just arrived) with the melodious tones of big guns, sounding the "Grand Jeu" of war,[5] like a gentle subterranean instrument, some thirty fathoms beneath their feet and not as remote as Mafeking; they have listened to it, I am told, with cheerful hearts, for they just mistook it for what it is not. Undoubtedly the enrapturing charm of this delectable music will give place to a most irritating discord when they have discovered that, so far from it being the action of the modern Britisher's workmanship going for the Dutch, it is the "boom" of the state artillerist[6] giving us thunder and lightning with his guns.

I was roaming along the river[7] at 12 o'clock with David[8] yesterday when we were disgusted by the incessant sounds and clappering of Mausers to the north of the town: and all of a sudden four or five "booms" from the armoured train quenched their metal. It was like a member of the Payne family[9] silencing a boisterous crowd with the prelude of a selection she is going to give on the violin. When their beastly fire "shut up" the Maxim began to play: it was like listening to the Kimberley R.C. choir with their organ, rendering one of their mellifluous carols on Christmas Eve; and its charm could justly be compared with that of the Jubilee Singers[10] performing one of their many quaint and classical oratories. But like everything desirable it ceased almost immediately. The Maxim is everybody's favourite here. Whenever there is an almost sickening rattle of Mausers you can hear them enquiring amongst themselves when "makasono" is going to "kgalema".[11] Boers are fond of shooting. They do not wait until they see anything but let go at the rate of 100 rounds per minute at the least provocation. I am afraid if they could somehow or other lay their hands on a Maxim they would simply shake it until there is not a single round left to mourn the loss of the others. One can almost fancy that prior to their leaving the State[12] their weapons were imprecated by empyrean authority – and the following are my reasons for believing that the State ammunition has been cursed: when I passed the gaol yesterday afternoon Phil[13] told me that while some prisoners were working in front of the gaol one of them was hit by a Mauser bullet (from the Boer lines) on the ribs. They expected the man to drop down dead, but the bullet dropped down (dead) instead. Immediately after, another hit a European's thigh. It penetrated the clothes but failed to pierce his skin; and just as if to verify this statement, another came round and struck the shoulder of a white man, who was shocked but stood as firm as though nothing had happened, when the bullet dropped down in front of him.

I have already mentioned that on Wednesday (the day of the all-round attack) I was surprised to find that on getting to town not one person was killed – while the Dutch ambulances were busy all the afternoon.

On Friday morning Teacher Samson[14] and 15 others crept along the river until they were very close to a party of Boers, who were busy sniping the location[15] from an ambush. They killed eight of them and wounded several; they were all going to return without a hitch – but they advanced to disarm the dead men, and Samson received a slight wound on the shoulder.

Yesterday 22 Fingoes[16] went out to the brickfields,[17] which may be said to be exactly on "disputed territory": they took shelter among the bricks and killed several of them, which vexed the latter to such an extent that they fetched one of their 7-pounders and cocked it right into the kilns. Our men lay flat against the bricks, 7-pounder shells crashing amongst them with the liberty of the elements. They went for the bricks, knocked spots out of the ground they lay on, and shattered the woodworks of their rifles between and alongside them; in fact they wrecked everything except the flesh of human beings. It affused several of its mortal discharges over them and when convinced that every one of them was dead, cleared away leaving the 22 men quite sound, but so badly armed that if the Boers had the courage to come near they would have led them away by the hands. The gunsmith is very busy mending their rifles, two of which are quite irreparable, and the men are having holidays in consequence.

Our ears cannot stand anything like the bang of a door: the rat-tat of some stones nearby shakes one inwardly. All of these things have assumed the attitude of death-dealing instruments and they almost invariably resemble Mausers or Dutch cannons. We often hear the alarm and run outside to find nothing wrong; and such alarm was often the motion of the pillow if one was lying down. David was yesterday grumbling: "Oh, what a restless life; if I knew that things were going to turn out this way I would never have left Aliwal North."

After I left Mr Mahlelebe yesterday I came through the gaol yard onto the Railway Reserve's fence. Mauser bullets were just like hail on the main road to our village. I had just left the fence when one flew close to my cap with a "ping" – giving me such a fright as caused me to sit down on the footpath. Someone behind me exclaimed that I was nearly killed and I looked round to see who my sympathiser was. When I did so another screeched through his legs with a "whiz-z-z-z" and dropped between the two of us. I continued my journey in company of this man, during which I heard a screech and a tap behind my ear: it was a Mauser bullet and as there can be no question about a fellow's death when it enters his brain through the lobe, I knew at the moment that I had been transmitted from this temporary life on to eternity. I imagined I held a nickel bullet in my heart. That was merely the faculty of the soul recognising (in ordinary post-mortal dream) who occasioned its departure – for I was dead! Dead, to rise no more. A few seconds elapsed after which I found myself scanning the bullet between my finger and thumb, to realise that it was but a horsefly.

Notes and References:
October-November 1899

1. Originally a Nguni term meaning (literally) "not there"; now a popular South African colloquialism, it simply means "no" when used thus. Its use in this context is interesting. Barolong, when speaking today of a vio-

lent man, often describe him as being Zulu; in the traditional world-view, the Zulu are associated with military strength – a notion that derives from perceived historical experience. Plaatje's use of a word that is commonly thought of in South Africa as being of Zulu origin, and its juxtaposition with "terror", is obviously meant to be ironic. This is a day of peace – in a white man's war. The thunder referred to immediately before is probably used here to mean shelling or artillery bombardment, though Barolong speaking English sometimes use "thunder" metaphorically to mean "death".

2. On 25 October, General Cronje (then head of the Boer forces) launched a heavy attack. The 94-pounder Creusot siege-gun – one of four bought from France – was set to work for the first time in earnest and was, with the rest of the Boer artillery, intended to pave the way for a two-pronged attack. Estimates of the number of attacks vary between 500 and 1 000. The force, however, was repelled. Altogether some 300 shells fell within the lines of investment.

3. The arrival of a relief-force was a constant subject of discussion. Any hopes at that time, however, must have been very remote as Colonel Plumer's regiment had been placed at Tuli near the Rhodesian border. Owing to the size and distance of his force, Plumer was in no position to attempt an attack on the besiegers. The arrival of troops from England had also been delayed.

4. Kanya (now officially spelt "Kanye") is the capital of the Bangwaketse chiefdom. It lies approximately sixty miles north-north-west of Mafeking, in what is now Botswana.

5. Plaatje was a keen music-lover and musician. In the diary this is reflected in his predilection for the use of musical metaphor.

6. The "Staats Artillerie" were responsible for the operation of Boer artillery. According to Grinnell-Milne (*Baden Powell at Mafeking*, 1957, p. 106), many of these gunners were Germans lent from the Kaiser's army.

7. The Molopo flows through the stadt. Plaatje resided in a homestead near the river bank.

8. David Phooko, a distant relative of Plaatje. Of Sotho origin, he was employed as a constable attached to the staff of the Inspector of Native Reserves at Mafeking from August 1899 to May 1900, and seems to have shared lodgings with Plaatje in the stadt. One survivor of the siege who knew Plaatje has proffered the information that David was the diarist's "cousin" (the exact genealogical relationship is unclear as Tshidi use this term to denote a variety of classificatory relationships), as well as his closest friend.

9. The Payne family were a popular musical group from Australia, consisting of vocalists, violinists, pianists, flautists and bell-ringers. Plaatje would probably have seen them in March 1895 or January 1897, when they gave a number of performances in Kimberley.

10. The Jubilee Singers were a black American choir, popular with black and white audiences alike, who toured southern Africa on several occasions during the 1890s. Plaatje's recollections of them probably date from their visit to Kimberley in July 1895 and May 1896.

11. *Makasono* is the Tswana rendering of "Maxim". *Kgalema* literally translated means "chide", "scold", "speak angrily" (J. Tom Brown, *Secwana-English Dictionary*, 1931). The use of the vernacular here is not arbitrary. It reflects a common Barolong linguistic practice. When speaking English, Tswana words which have – for the speaker – either an onomatopoeic quality or greater descriptive suitability are used. *Makosono* has a staccato quality that is missing from its less descriptive English equivalent, and the *kg-* (*kga-lema*) represents a hard sound (ejective velar fricative) which is appropriate when used to indicate the implied emotion.

12. This is often used by Plaatje as shorthand to denote the Transvaal and Orange Free State republics.

13. Philemon Mahlelebe Moshoeshoe, warder at the Mafeking gaol. Formerly with the Basotho Mounted Police, he settled in Mafeking in 1894 and served as the local turnkey until 1912. During his early years there he was known as Philemon Mahlelebe, but after the siege reverted to his original family name, Moshoeshoe. Of Sotho origin, he became a natu-

ralised member of the chiefdom in 1910. Plaatje refers to him as Philemon Mahlelebe.

14. Barnabas Samson was a well-known teacher, sometimes cited (erroneously) as the first African teacher in Mafeking. The Barolong predilection for nicknaming explains why he is referred to as "Teacher" rather than by his first name. Like Philemon Moshoeshoe, Samson was of Sotho origin, and became a naturalised member of the chiefdom in 1910.

15. This is used to denote an African township or village. The term subsequently became synonymous with African urban concentrations throughout South Africa. Here it refers to what was originally the Fingo village (see below).

16. These Fingoes came from a tribe which lives on the south-eastern plain of southern Africa. They had been recruited to travel north with Rhodes' Pioneer Column nine years earlier. However, on arriving at Mafeking, they chose to remain and establish a village outside the stadt. During the siege this settlement was known as the Fingo location. There was also an urban location outside Mafeking. This was populated by Africans of mixed ethnic origin (as opposed to the Barolong village which was almost exclusively Tswana). This location existed until 1967, when its population was moved into the newly constructed Montshiwa Township. Unless otherwise specified, "location" (in both text and notes) refers to the urban strangers' location and not the Fingo village.

Source:
Sol T. Plaatje: *Mafeking Diary: A Black Man's View of a White Man's War*, John L. Comaroff (ed). Johannesburg: Macmillan: 1973.

The Cry of South Africa

Olive Schreiner

Give back my dead!
They who by kop and fountain
First saw the light upon my rocky breast!
Give back my dead,
The sons who played upon me
When childhood's dews still rested on their heads.
Give back my dead
Whom thou hast riven from me
By arms of men loud called from earth's farthest bound
To wet my bosom with, my children's blood!
Give back my dead,
The dead who grew up on me!

Source:
Olive Schreiner: *Stories, Dreams and Allegories.* London: T. Fisher Unwin: 1923, written c. 1900.

Eighteen-Ninety-Nine

Olive Schreiner

"Thou fool, that which thou sowest is not quickened unless it die."

I

It was a warm night: the stars shone down through the thick soft air of the Northern Transvaal into the dark earth, where a little daub-and-wattle house of two rooms lay among the long, grassy slopes.

A light shone through the small window of the house, though it was past midnight. Presently the upper half of the door opened and then the lower, and the tall figure of a woman stepped out into the darkness. She closed the door behind her and walked towards the back of the house where a large round hut stood; beside it lay a pile of stumps and branches quite visible when once the eyes grew accustomed to the darkness. The woman stooped and broke off twigs till she had her apron full, and then returned slowly, and went into the house.

The room to which she returned was a small, bare room, with brown earthen walls and a mud floor; a naked deal table stood in the centre, and a few dark wooden chairs, home-made, with seats of undressed leather, stood round the walls. In the corner opposite the door was an open fireplace, and on the earthen hearth stood an iron three-foot, on which stood a large black kettle, under which coals were smouldering, though the night was hot and close. Against the wall on the left side of the room hung a gun-rack with three guns upon it, and below it a large hunting-watch hung from two nails by its silver chain.

In the corner by the fireplace was a little table with a coffee-pot upon it and a dish containing cups and saucers covered with water, and above it were a few shelves with crockery and a large Bible; but the dim light of the tallow candle which burnt on the table, with its wick of twisted rag, hardly made the corners visible. Beside the table sat a young woman, her head resting on her folded arms, the light of the tallow candle falling full on her head of pale flaxen hair, a little tumbled, and drawn behind into a large knot. The arms crossed on the table, from which the cotton sleeves had fallen back, were the full, rounded arms of one very young.

The older woman, who had just entered, walked to the fireplace, and kneeling down before it took from her apron the twigs and sticks she had gathered and heaped them under the kettle till a blaze sprang up which illumined the whole room. Then she rose up and sat down on a chair before the fire, but facing the table, with her hands crossed on her brown apron.

She was a woman of fifty, spare and broad-shouldered, with black hair, already slightly streaked with grey; from below high, arched eyebrows, and a high forehead, full dark eyes looked keenly, and a sharply cut aquiline nose gave strength to the face; but the mouth below was somewhat sensitive, and not over-full. She crossed and recrossed her knotted hands on her brown apron.

The woman at the table moaned and moved her head from side to side.

"What time is it?" she asked.

The older woman crossed the room to where the hunting-watch hung on the wall.

It showed a quarter-past one, she said, and went back to her seat before the fire, and sat watching the figure beside the table, the firelight bathing her strong upright form and sharp aquiline profile.

Nearly fifty years before her parents had left the Cape Colony, and had set out on the long trek northward, and she, a young child, had been brought with them. She had no remembrance of the colonial home. Her first dim memories were of travelling in an oxwagon; of dark nights when a fire was lighted in the open air, and people sat round it on the ground, and some faces seemed to stand out more than others in her memory which she thought must be those of her father and mother and of an old grandmother; she could remember lying awake in the back of the wagon while it was moving on, and the stars were shining down on her; and she had a vague memory of great wide plains with buck on them, which she thought must have been in the Free State. But the first thing which sprang out sharp and clear from the past was a day when she and another child, a little boy cousin of her own age, were playing among the bushes on the bank of a stream; she remembered how, suddenly, as they looked through the bushes, they saw black men leap out, and mount the ox-wagon outspanned under the trees; she remembered how they shouted and dragged people along, and stabbed them; she remembered how the blood gushed, and how they, the two young children among the bushes, lay flat on their stomachs and did not move or breathe, with that strange self-preserving instinct found in the young of animals or men who grow up in the open.

She remembered how black smoke came out of the back of the wagon and then red tongues of flame through the top; and even that some of the branches of the tree under which the wagon stood caught fire. She remembered later, when the black men had gone, and it was dark, that they were very hungry, and crept out to where the wagon had stood, and that they looked about on the ground for any scraps of food they might pick up, and that when they could not find any they cried. She remembered nothing clearly after that till some men with large beards and large hats rode up on horseback: it might have been next day or the day after. She remembered how they jumped off their horses and took them up in their arms, and how they cried; but that they, the children, did not cry, they only asked for food. She remembered how one man took a bit of thick cold roaster-cake out of his pocket, and gave it to her, and how nice it tasted. And she remembered that the men took them up before them on their horses, and that one man tied her close to him with a large red handkerchief.

In the years that came she learnt to know that that which she remembered so clearly was the great and terrible day when, at Weenen, and in the country round, hundreds of women and children and youths and old men fell before the Zulus, and the assegais of Dingaan's braves drank blood.

She learnt that on that day all of her house and name, from the grandmother to the baby in arms, fell, and that she only and the boy cousin, who had hidden with her among the bushes, were left of all her kin in that northern world. She learnt, too, that the man who tied her to him with the red handkerchief took them back to his wagon, and that he and his wife adopted them, and brought them up among their own children.

She remembered, though less clearly than the day of the fire, how a few years later they trekked away from Natal, and went through great mountain ranges, ranges in and near which lay those places the world was to know later as Laings Nek, and Amajuba, and Ingogo; Elands-laagte, Nicholson Nek, and Spion Kop. She remembered how at last after many wanderings they settled down near the Witwaters Rand where game was plentiful and wild beasts were dangerous, but there were no natives, and they were far from the English rule.

There the two children grew up among the children of those who had adopted them, and were kindly treated by them as though they were their own; it yet was but natural that these two of the same name and blood should grow up with a peculiar tenderness for each other. And so it came to pass that when they were both eighteen years old they asked consent of the old people, who gave it gladly, that they should marry. For a time the young couple lived on in the house with the old, but after three years they gathered together all their few goods and in their wagon, with their guns and ammunition and a few sheep and cattle, they moved away northwards to found their own home.

For a time they travelled here and travelled there, but at last they settled on a spot where game was plentiful and the soil good, and there among the low undulating slopes, near the bank of a dry sloot, the young man built at last, with his own hands, a little house of two rooms.

On the long slope across the sloot before the house, he ploughed a piece of land and enclosed it, and he built kraals for his stock and so struck root in the land and wandered no more. Those were brave, glad, free days to the young couple. They lived largely on the game which the gun brought down, antelope and wildebeest that wandered even past the doors at night; and now and again a lion was killed: one no farther than the door of the round hut behind the house where the meat and the milk were stored, and two were killed at the kraals. Sometimes, too, traders came with their wagons and in exchange for skins and fine horns sold sugar and coffee and print and tan cord, and such things as the little household had need of. The lands yielded richly to them, in maize, and pumpkins, and sweet-cane, and melons; and they had nothing to wish for. Then in time three little sons were born to them, who grew as strong and vigorous in the free life of the open veld as the young lions in the long grass and scrub near the river four miles away. Those were joyous, free years for the man and woman, in which disease, and carking care, and anxiety played no part.

Then came a day when their eldest son was ten years old, and the father went out a-hunting with his Kaffir servants: in the evening they brought him home with a wound eight inches long in his side where a lioness had torn him; they brought back her skin also, as he had shot her at last in the hand-to-throat struggle. He lingered for three days and then died. His wife buried him on the low slope to the left of the house; she and her Kaffir servants alone made the grave and put him in it, for there were no white men near. Then she and her sons lived on there; a new root driven deep into the soil and binding them to it through the grave on the hill-side. She hung her husband's large hunting-watch up on the wall, and put three of his guns over it on the rack, and the gun he had in his hand when he met his death she took down and polished up every day; but one gun she always kept loaded at the head of her bed in the inner room. She counted the stock every night and saw that the Kaffirs ploughed the lands, and she saw to the planting and watering of them herself.

Often as the years passed men of the country-side, and even from far off, heard of the young handsome widow who lived alone with her children and saw to her own stock and lands; and they came a-courting. But many of them were afraid to say anything when once they had come, and those who had spoken to her, when once she had answered them, never came again. About this time too the country-side began to fill in; and people came and settled as near as eight and ten miles away; and as people increased the game began to vanish, and with the game the lions, so that the one her husband killed was almost the last ever seen there. But there was still game enough for food, and when her eldest son was twelve years old, and she gave him his father's smallest gun to go out hunting with, he returned home almost every day with meat enough for the household tied behind his saddle. And as time passed she came also to be known through the country-side as a "wise woman". People came to her to ask advice about their illnesses, or to ask her to dress old wounds that would not heal; and when they questioned her whether she thought the rains would be early, or the game plentiful that year, she was nearly always right. So they called her a "wise woman" because neither she nor they knew any word in that up-country speech of theirs for the thing called "genius". So all things went well till the eldest son was eighteen, and the dark beard was beginning to sprout on his face, and his mother began to think that soon there might be a daughter in the house; for on Saturday evenings, when his work was done, he put on his best clothes and rode off to the next farm eight miles away, where was a young daughter. His mother always saw that he had a freshly ironed shirt waiting for him on his bed, when he came home from the kraals on Saturday nights, and she made plans as to how they would build on two rooms for the new daughter. At this time he was training young horses to have them ready to sell when the traders came round: he was a fine rider and it was always his work. One afternoon he mounted a young horse before the door and it bucked and threw him. He had often fallen before, but this time his neck was broken. He lay dead with his head two feet from his mother's doorstep. They took up his tall, strong body and the next day the neighbours came from the next farm and they buried him beside his father, on the hill-side, and another root was struck into the soil. Then the three who were left in the little farm-house lived and worked on as before, for a year and more.

Then a small native war broke out, and the young burghers of the district were called out to help. The second son was very young, but he was the best shot in the district, so he went away with the others. Three months after the men came back, but among the few who did not return was her son. On a hot sunny afternoon, walking through a mealie field which they thought was deserted and where the dried yellow stalks stood thick, an assegai thrown from an unseen hand found him, and he fell there. His comrades took him and buried him under a large thorn tree, and scraped the earth smooth over him, that his grave might not be found by others. So he was not laid on the rise to the left of the house with his kindred, but his mother's heart went often to that thorn tree in the far north.

And now again there were only two in the little mud-house; as there had been years before when the young man and wife first settled there. She and her young lad were always together night and day, and did all that they did together, as though they were mother and daughter. He was a fair lad, tall and gentle as his father had been before him, not huge and dark as his two elder brothers; but he seemed to ripen towards manhood early. When he was only sixteen the thick white down was already gathering heavy on his upper lip; his mother watched him narrowly, and had many thoughts in her heart. One evening as they sat twisting wicks for the candles together, she said to him, "You will be eighteen on your next birthday, my son, that was your father's age when he married me." He said, "Yes," and they spoke no more then. But later in the evening when they sat before the door she said to him: "We are very lonely here. I often long to hear the feet of a little child about the house, and to see one with your father's blood in it play before the door as you and your brothers played. Have you ever thought that you are the last of your father's name and blood left here in the north; that if you died there would be none left?" He said he had thought of it. Then she told him she thought it would be well if he went away, to the part of the country where the people lived who had brought her up: several of the sons and daughters who had grown up with her had now grown-up children. He might go down and from among them seek out a young girl whom he liked and who liked him; and if he found her, bring her back as a wife. The lad thought very well of his mother's plan. And when three months were passed, and the ploughing season was over, he rode away one day, on the best black horse they had, his Kaffir boy riding behind him on another, and his mother stood at the gable watching them ride away. For three months she heard nothing of him, for trains were not in those days, and letters came rarely and by chance, and neither he nor she could read or write. One afternoon she stood at the gable end as she always stood when her work was done, looking out along the road that came over the rise, and she saw a large tent-wagon coming along it, and her son walking beside it. She walked to meet it. When she had greeted her son and climbed into the wagon she found there a girl of fifteen with pale flaxen hair and large blue eyes whom he had brought home as his wife. Her father had given her the wagon and oxen as her wedding portion. The older woman's heart wrapt itself about the girl as though she had been the daughter she had dreamed to bear of her own body, and had never borne.

The three lived joyfully at the little house as though they were one person. The young wife had been accustomed to live in a larger house, and down south, where they had things they had not here. She had been to school, and learned to read and write, and she could even talk a little English; but she longed for none of the things which she had had; the little brown house was home enough for her.

After a year a child came, but, whether it were that the mother was too young, it only opened its eyes for an hour on the world and closed them again. The young mother wept bitterly, but her husband folded his arms about her, and the mother comforted both. "You are young, my children, but we shall yet hear the sound of children's voices in the house," she said; and after a little while the young mother was well again and things went on peacefully as before in the little home.

But in the land things were not going on peacefully. That was the time that the flag to escape from which the people had left their old homes in the Colony, and had again left Natal when it followed them there, and had chosen to face the spear of the savage, and the conflict with wild beasts, and death by hunger and thirst in the wilderness rather than live under, had by force and fraud unfurled itself over them again. For the moment a great sullen silence brooded over the land. The people, slow of thought, slow of speech, determined in action, and unforgetting, sat still and waited. It was like the silence that rests over the land before an up-country thunderstorm breaks.

Then words came, "They have not even given us the free government they promised" – then acts – the people rose. Even in that remote country-side the men began to mount their horses, and with their guns ride away to help. In the little mud-house the young wife wept much when he said that he too was going. But when his mother helped him pack his saddle-bags she helped too; and on the day when the men from the next farm went, he rode away also with his gun by his side.

No direct news of the one they had sent away came to the waiting women at the farm-house; then came fleet reports of the victories of Ingogo and Amajuba. Then came an afternoon after he had been gone two months. They had both been to the gable end to look out at the road, as they did continually amid their work, and they had just come in to drink their afternoon coffee when the Kaffir maid ran in to say she saw someone coming along the road who looked like her master. The women ran out. It was the white horse on which he had ridden away, but they almost doubted if it were he. He rode bending on his saddle, with his chin on his breast and his arm hanging at his side. At first they thought he had been wounded, but when they had helped him from his horse and brought him into the house they found it was only a deadly fever which was upon him. He had crept home to them by small stages. Hardly had he any spirit left to tell them of Ingogo, Laings Nek, and Amajuba. For fourteen days he grew worse and on the fifteenth day he died. And the two women buried him where the rest of his kin lay on the hill-side.

And so it came to pass that on that warm starlight night the two women were alone in the little mud-house with the stillness of the veld about them; even their Kaffir servants asleep in their huts beyond the kraals; and the very sheep lying silent in the starlight. The two were alone in the little house, but they knew that before morning they would not be alone, they were awaiting the coming of the dead man's child.

The young woman with her head on the table groaned. "If only my husband were here still," she wailed. The old woman rose and stood beside her, passing her hard, work-worn hand gently over her shoulder as if she were a little child. At last she induced her to go and lie down in the inner room. When she had grown quieter and seemed to have fallen into a light sleep the old woman came to the front room again. It was almost two o'clock and the fire had burned low under the large kettle. She scraped the coals together and went out of the front door to fetch more wood, and closed the door behind her. The night air struck cool and fresh upon her face after the close air of the house, the stars seemed to be growing lighter as the night advanced, they shot down their light as from a million polished steel points. She walked to the back of the house where, beyond the round hut that served as a store-room, the wood-pile lay. She bent down gathering sticks and chips till her apron was full, then slowly she raised herself and stood still. She looked upwards. It was a wonderful night. The white band of the Milky Way crossed the sky overhead, and from every side stars threw down their light, sharp as barbed spears, from the velvety blue-black of the sky. The woman raised her hand to her forehead as if pushing the hair farther off it; and stood motionless, looking up. After a long time she dropped her hand and began walking slowly towards the house. Yet once or twice on the way she paused and stood looking up. When she went into the house the woman in the inner room was again moving and moaning. She laid the sticks down before the fire and went into the next room. She bent down over the bed where the younger woman lay, and put her hand upon her. "My daughter," she said slowly, "be comforted. A wonderful thing has happened to me. As I stood out in the starlight it was as though a voice came down to me and spoke. The child which will be born of you tonight will be a man-child and he will live to do great things for his land and for his people."

Before morning there was the sound of a little wail in the mud-house; and the child who was to do great things for his land and for his people was born.

II

Six years passed, and all was as it had been at the little house among the slopes. Only a new piece of land had been ploughed up and added to the land before the house, so that the ploughed land now almost reached to the ridge.

The young mother had grown stouter, and lost her pink and white; she had become a working-woman, but she still had the large knot of flaxen hair behind her head and the large wondering eyes. She had many suitors in those six years, but she sent them all away. She said the old woman looked after the farm as well as any man might, and her son would be grown up by and by. The grandmother's hair was a little more streaked with grey, but it was as thick as ever, and her shoulders as upright; only some of her front teeth had fallen out, which made her lips close more softly.

The great change was that wherever the women went there was the flaxen-haired child to walk beside them holding on to their skirts or clasping their hands.

The neighbours said they were ruining the child: they let his hair grow long, like a girl's, because it curled; and they never let him wear velschoens like other children but always shop boots; and his mother sat up at night to iron his pinafores as if the next day were always a Sunday.

But the women cared nothing for what was said; to them he was not as any other child. He asked them strange questions they could not answer, and he never troubled them by wishing to go and play with the little Kaffirs as other children trouble. When neighbours came over and brought their children with them he ran away and hid in the sloot to play by himself till they were gone. No, he was not like other children!

When the women went to lie down on hot days after dinner sometimes, he would say that he did not want to sleep; but he would not run about and make a noise like other children – he would go and sit outside in the shade of the house, on the front doorstep, quite still, with his little hands resting on his knees, and stare far away at the ploughed lands on the slope, or the shadows nearer; the women would open the bedroom window, and peep out to look at him as he sat there.

The child loved his mother and followed her about to the milk house, and to the kraals; but he loved his grandmother best.

She told him stories.

When she went to the lands to see how the Kaffirs were ploughing he would run at her side holding her dress; when they had gone a short way he would tug gently at it and say, "Grandmother, tell me things!"

And long before day broke, when it was yet quite dark, he would often creep from the bed where he slept with his mother into his grandmother's bed in the corner; he would put his arms round her neck and stroke her face till she woke, and then whisper softly, "Tell me stories!" and she would tell them to him in a low voice not to wake the mother, till the cock crowed and it was time to get up and light the candle and the fire.

But what he liked best of all were the hot, still summer nights, when the women put their chairs before the door because it was too warm to go to sleep; and he would sit on the stoof at his grandmother's feet and lean his head against her knees, and she would tell him on and on of the things he liked to hear; and he would watch the stars as they slowly set along the ridge, or the moonlight, casting bright-edged shadows from the gable as she talked. Often after the mother had got sleepy and gone in to bed the two sat there together.

The stories she told him were always true stories of the things she had seen or of things she had heard. Sometimes they were stories of her own childhood: of the day when she and his grandfather hid among the bushes, and saw the wagon burnt; sometimes they were of the long trek from Natal to the Transvaal; sometimes of the things which happened to her and his grandfather when first they came to that spot among the ridges, of how there was no house there nor lands, only two bare grassy slopes when they outspanned their wagon there the first night; she told of a lion she once found when she opened the door in the morning, sitting, with paws crossed, upon the threshold, and how the grandfather jumped out of bed and re-opened the door two inches, and shot it through the opening; the skin was kept in the round storehouse still, very old and mangy.

Sometimes she told him of the two uncles who were dead, and of his own father, and of all they had been and done. But sometimes she told him of things much farther off: the old Colony where she had been born, but which she could not remember, and of the things which happened there in the old days. She told him of how the British had taken the Cape over, and of how the English had hanged their men at the "Slachters Nek" for resisting the English Government, and of how the friends and relations had been made to stand round to see them hanged whether they would or no, and of how the scaffold broke down as they were being hanged, and the people looking on cried aloud, "It is the finger of God! They are saved!" but how the British hanged them up again. She told him of the great trek in which her parents had taken part to escape from under the British flag; of the great battles with Moselikatse; and of the murder of Retief and his men by Dingaan, and of Dingaan's Day. She told him how the British Government followed them into Natal, and of how they trekked north and east to escape from it again; and she told him of the later things, of the fight at Laings Nek, and Ingogo, and Amajuba, where his father had been. Always she told the same story in exactly the same words over and over again, till the child knew them all by heart, and would ask for this and then that.

The story he loved best, and asked for more often than all the others, made his grandmother wonder, because it did not seem to her the story a child would like best; it was not a story of lion-hunting, or wars, or adventures. Continually when she asked what she should tell him, he said, "About the mountains!"

It was the story of how the Boer women in Natal when the English Commissioner came to annex their country, collected to meet him and pointing towards the Drakens Berg Mountains said, "We go across those mountains to freedom or to death!"

More than once, when she was telling him the story, she saw him stretch out his little arm and raise his hand, as though he were speaking.

One evening as he and his mother were coming home from the milking kraals, and it was getting dark, and he was very tired, having romped about shouting among the young calves and kids all the evening, he held her hand tightly.

"Mother," he said suddenly, "when I am grown up, I am going to Natal."

"Why, my child?" she asked him; "there are none of our family living there now."

He waited a little, then said, very slowly, "I am going to go and try to get our land back!"

His mother started; if there were one thing she was more firmly resolved on in her own mind than any other it was that he should never go to the wars. She began to talk quickly of the old white cow who had kicked the pail over as she was milked, and when she got to the house she did not even mention to the grandmother what had happened; it seemed better to forget.

One night in the rainy season when it was damp and chilly they sat round the large fireplace in the front room.

Outside the rain was pouring in torrents and you could hear the water rushing in the great dry sloot before the door. His grandmother, to amuse him, had sprung some dried mealies in the great black pot and sprinkled them with sugar, and now he sat on the stoof at her feet with a large lump of the sticky sweetmeat in his hand, watching the fire. His grandmother from above him was watching it also, and his mother in her elbow-chair on the other side of the fire had her eyes half closed and was nodding already with the warmth of the room and her long day's work. The child sat so quiet, the hand with the lump of sweetmeat resting on his knee, that his grandmother thought he had gone to sleep too. Suddenly he said without looking up, "Grandmother?"

"Yes."

He waited rather a long time, then said slowly, "Grandmother, did God make the English too?"

She also waited for a while, then said slowly, "Yes, my child; He made all things."

They were silent again, and there was no sound but of the rain falling and the fire cracking and the sloot rushing outside. Then he threw his head backwards on to his grandmother's knee and looking up into her face, said, "But, grandmother, why did He make them?"

Then she too was silent for a long time. "My child," at last she said, "we cannot judge the ways of the Almighty. He does that which seems good in His own eyes."

The child sat up and looked back at the fire. Slowly he tapped his knee with the lump of sweetmeat once or twice; then he began to munch it; and soon the mother started wide awake and said it was time for all to go to bed.

The next morning his grandmother sat on the front doorstep cutting beans in an iron basin; he sat beside her on the step pretending to cut too, with a short, broken knife. Presently he left off and rested his hands on his knees, looking away at the hedge beyond, with his small forehead knit tight between the eyes.

"Grandmother," he said suddenly, in a small, almost shrill voice, "do the English want *all* the lands of *all* the people?"

The handle of his grandmother's knife as she cut clinked against the iron side of the basin. "All they can get," she said.

After a while he made a little movement almost like a sigh, and took up his little knife again and went on cutting.

Some time after that, when a trader came by, his grandmother bought him a spelling-book and a slate and pencils, and his mother began to teach him to read and write. When she had taught him for a year he knew all she did. Sometimes when she was setting him a copy and left a letter out in a word, he would quietly take the pencil when she set it down and put the letter in, not with any idea of correcting her, but simply because it must be there.

Often at night when the child had gone to bed early, tired out with his long day's play, and the two women were left in the front room with the tallow candle burning on the table between them, then they talked of his future.

Ever since he had been born everything they had earned had been put away in the wagon chest under the grandmother's bed. When the traders with their wagons came round the women bought nothing except a few groceries and clothes for the child; even before they bought a yard of cotton print for a new apron they talked long and solemnly as to whether the old one might not be made to do by repatching; and they mixed much more dry pumpkin and corn with their coffee than before he was born. It was to earn more money that the large new piece of land had been added to the lands before the house.

They were going to have him educated. First he was to be taught all they could at home, then to be sent away to a great school in the old colony, and then he was to go over the sea to Europe and come back an advocate or a doctor or a parson. The grandmother had made a long journey to the next town, to find out from the minister just how much it would cost to do it all.

In the evenings when they sat talking it over the mother generally inclined to his becoming a parson. She never told the grandmother why, but the real reason was because parsons do not go to the wars. The grandmother generally favoured his becoming an advocate, because he might become a judge. Sometimes they sat discussing these matters till the candle almost burnt out.

"Perhaps, one day," the mother would at last say, "he may yet become President!"

Then the grandmother would slowly refold her hands across her apron and say softly, "Who knows? – who knows?"

Often they would get the box out from under the bed (looking carefully across to the corner to see he was fast asleep) and would count out all the money, though each knew to a farthing how much was there; then they would make it into little heaps, so much for this, so much for that, and they would count on their fingers how many good seasons it would take to make the rest, and how old he would be.

When he was eight and had learnt all his mother could teach him, they sent him to school every day on an adjoining farm six miles off, where the people had a schoolmaster. Every day he rode over on the great white horse his father went to the wars with; his mother was afraid to let him ride alone at first, but his grandmother said he must learn to do everything alone. At four o'clock when he came back one or other of the women was always looking out to see the little figure on the tall horse coming over the ridge.

When he was eleven they gave him his father's smallest gun; and one day not long after he came back with his first small buck. His mother had the skin dressed and bound with red, and she laid it as a mat under the table, and even the horns she did not throw away, and saved them in the round house, because it was his first.

When he was fourteen the schoolmaster said he could teach him no more; that he ought to go to some larger school where they taught Latin and other difficult things; they had not yet money enough and he was not quite old enough to go to the Colony, so they sent him first to the High-veld, where his mother's relations lived and where there were good schools, where they taught the difficult things; he could live with his mother's relations and come back once a year for the holidays.

They were great times when he came.

His mother made him koekies and sasarties and nice things every day; and he used to sit on the stoof at her feet and let her play with his hair like when he was quite small. With his grandmother he talked. He tried to explain to her all he was learning, and he read the English newspapers to her (she could neither read in English nor Dutch), translating them. Most of all she liked his atlas. They would sometimes sit over it for half an hour in the evening tracing the different lands and talking of them. On the warm nights he used still to sit outside on the stoof at her feet with his head against her knee, and they used to discuss things that were happening in other lands and in South Africa; and sometimes they sat there quite still together.

It was now he who had the most stories to tell; he had seen Krugersdorp, and Johannesburg, and Pretoria; he knew the world; he was at Krugersdorp when Dr Jameson made his raid. Sometimes he sat for an hour, telling her of things, and she sat quietly listening.

When he was seventeen, nearly eighteen, there was money enough in the box to pay for his going to the Colony and then to Europe; and he came home to spend a few months with them before he went.

He was very handsome now; not tall, and very slight, but with fair hair that curled close to his head, and white hands like a town's man. All the girls in the country-side were in love with him. They all wished he would come and see them. But he seldom rode from home except to go to the next farm where he had been at school. There lived little Aletta, who was the daughter of the woman his uncle had loved before he went to the Kaffir war and got killed. She was only fifteen years old, but they had always been great friends. She netted him a purse of green silk. He said he would take it with him to Europe, and would show it her when he came back and was an advocate; and he gave her a book with her name written in it, which she was to show to him.

These were the days when the land was full of talk; it was said the English were landing troops in South Africa, and wanted to have war. Often the neighbours from the nearest farms would come to talk about it (there were more farms now, the country was filling in, and the nearest railway station was only a day's journey off), and they discussed matters. Some said they thought there would be war; others again laughed, and said it would be only Jameson and his white flag again. But the grandmother shook her head, and if they asked her, "Why," she said, "it will not be the war of a week, nor of a month; if it comes it will be the war of years," but she would say nothing more.

Yet sometimes when she and her grandson were talking alone together in the lands she would talk.

Once she said: "It is as if a great heavy cloud hung just above my head, as though I wished to press it back with my hands and could not. It will be a great war – a great war. Perhaps the English government will take the land for a time, but they will not keep it. The gold they have fought for will divide them, till they slay one another over it."

Another day she said: "This land will be a great land one day with one people from the sea to the north – but we shall not live to see it."

He said to her: "But how can that be when we are all of different races?"

She said: "The land will make us one. Were not our fathers of more than one race?"

Another day, when she and he were sitting by the table after dinner, she pointed to a sheet of exercise paper, on which he had been working out a problem and which was covered with algebraical symbols, and said, "In fifteen years' time the Government of England will not have one piece of land in all South Africa as large as that sheet of paper."

One night when the milking had been late and she and he were walking down together from the kraals in the starlight she said to him: "If this war comes let no man go to it lightly, thinking he will surely return home, nor let him go expecting victory on the next day. It will come at last, but not at first."

"Sometimes," she said, "I wake at night and it is as though the whole house were filled with smoke – and I have to get up and go outside to breathe. It is as though I saw my whole land blackened and desolate. But when I look up it is as though a voice cried out to me, 'Have no fear!'"

They were getting his things ready for him to go away after Christmas. His mother was making him shirts and his grandmother was having a kaross of jackals' skin made that he might take with him to Europe where it was so cold. But his mother noticed that whenever the grandmother was in the room with him and he was not looking at her, her eyes were always curiously fixed on him as though they were questioning something. The hair was growing white and a little thin over her temples now, but her eyes were as bright as ever, and she could do a day's work with any man.

One day when the youth was at the kraals helping the Kaffir boys to mend a wall, and the mother was kneading bread in the front room, and the grandmother washing up the breakfast things, the son of the Field-Cornet came riding over from his father's farm, which was about twelve miles off. He stopped at the kraal and Jan and he stood talking for some time, then they walked down to the farm-house, the Kaffir boy leading the horse behind them. Jan stopped at the round store, but the Field-Cornet's son went to the front door. The grandmother asked him in, and handed him some coffee, and the mother, her hands still in the dough, asked him how things were going at his father's farm, and if his mother's young turkeys had come out well, and she asked if he had met Jan at the kraals. He answered the questions slowly, and sipped his coffee. Then he put the cup down on the table; and said suddenly in the same measured voice, staring at the wall in front of him, that war had broken out, and his father had sent him round to call out all fighting burghers.

The mother took her hands out of the dough and stood upright beside the trough as though paralysed. Then she cried in a high, hard voice, unlike her own, "Yes, but Jan cannot go! He is hardly eighteen! He's got to go and be educated in other lands! You can't take the only son of a widow!"

"Aunt," said the young man slowly, "no one will make him go."

The grandmother stood resting the knuckles of both hands on the table, her eyes fixed on the young man. "He shall decide himself," she said.

The mother wiped her hands from the dough and rushed past them and out at the door; the grandmother followed slowly.

They found him in the shade at the back of the house, sitting on a stump; he was cleaning the belt of his new Mauser which lay across his knees.

"Jan," his mother cried, grasping his shoulder, "you are not going away? You can't go! You must stay. You can go by Delagoa Bay if there is fighting on the other side! There is plenty of money!"

He looked softly up into her face with his blue eyes. "We have all to be at the Field-Cornet's at nine o'clock to-morrow morning," he said. She wept aloud and argued.

His grandmother turned slowly without speaking, and went back into the house. When she had given the Field-Cornet's son another cup of coffee, and shaken hands with him, she went into the bedroom and opened the box in which her grandson's clothes were kept, to see which things he should take with him. After a time the mother came back too. He had kissed her and talked to her until she too had at last said it was right he should go.

All day they were busy. His mother baked him biscuits to take in his bag, and his grandmother made a belt of two strips of leather; she sewed them together herself and put a few sovereigns between the stitching. She said some of his comrades might need the money if he did not.

The next morning early he was ready. There were two saddlebags tied to his saddle and before it was strapped the kaross his grandmother had made; she said it would be useful when he had to sleep on damp ground. When he had greeted them, he rode away towards the rise; and the women stood at the gable of the house to watch him.

When he had gone a little way he turned in his saddle, and they could see he was smiling; he took off his hat and waved it in the air; the early morning sunshine made his hair as yellow as the tassels that hang from the head of ripening mealies. His mother covered her face with the sides of her kappie and wept aloud; but the grandmother shaded her eyes with both her hands and stood watching him till the figure passed out of sight over the ridge; and when it was gone the mother returned to the house crying, she still stood watching the line against the sky.

The two women were very quiet during the next days, they worked hard, and seldom spoke. After eight days there came a long letter from him (there was now a post once a week from the station to the Field-Cornet's). He said he was well and in very good spirits. He had been to Krugersdorp, and Johannesburg, and Pretoria; all the family living there were well and sent greetings. He had joined a corps that was leaving for the front the next day. He sent also a long message to Aletta, asking them to tell her he was sorry to go away without saying good-bye; and he told his mother how good the biscuits and biltong were she had put into his saddle-bag; and he sent her a piece of "vierkleur" ribbon in the letter, to wear on her breast.

The women talked a great deal for a day or two after this letter came. Eight days after there was a short note from him, written in pencil in the train on his way to the front. He said all was going well, and if he did not write soon they were not to be anxious; he would write as often as he could.

For some days the women discussed that note too.

Then came two weeks without a letter, the two women became

very silent. Every day they sent the Kaffir boy over to the Field-Cornet's, even on the days when there was no post, to hear if there was any news.

Many reports were flying about the country-side. Some said that an English armoured train had been taken on the western border; that there had been fighting at Albertina, and in Natal. But nothing seemed quite certain.

Another week passed . . . Then the two women became very quiet.

The grandmother, when she saw her daughter-in-law left the food untouched on her plate, said there was no need to be anxious; men at the front could not always find paper and pencils to write with and might be far from any post office. Yet night after night she herself would rise from her bed saying she felt the house close, and go and walk up and down outside.

Then one day suddenly all their servants left them except one Kaffir and his wife, whom they had had for years, and the servants from the farms about went also, which was a sign there had been news of much fighting; for the Kaffirs hear things long before the white man knows them.

Three days after, as the women were clearing off the breakfast things, the youngest son of the Field-Cornet, who was only fifteen and had not gone to the war with the others, rode up. He hitched his horse to the post, and came towards the door. The mother stepped forward to meet him and shook hands in the doorway.

"I suppose you have come for the carrot seed I promised your mother? I was not able to send it, as our servants ran away," she said, as she shook his hand. "There isn't a letter from Jan, is there?" The lad said no, there was no letter from him, and shook hands with the grandmother. He stood by the table instead of sitting down.

The mother turned to the fireplace to get coals to put under the coffee to rewarm it; but the grandmother stood leaning forward with her eyes fixed on him from across the table. He felt uneasily in his breast pocket.

"Is there no news?" the mother said without looking round, as she bent over the fire.

"Yes, there is news, Aunt."

She rose quickly and turned towards him, putting down the brazier on the table. He took a letter out of his breast pocket. "Aunt, my father said I must bring this to you. It came inside one to him and they asked him to send one of us over with it."

The mother took the letter; she held it, examining the address.

"It looks to me like the writing of Sister Annie's Paul," she said. "Perhaps there is news of Jan in it" – she turned to them with a half-nervous smile – "they were always such friends."

"All is as God wills, Aunt," the young man said, looking down fixedly at the top of his riding-whip.

But the grandmother leaned forward motionless, watching her daughter-in-law as she opened the letter.

She began to read to herself, her lips moving slowly as she deciphered it word by word.

Then a piercing cry rang through the roof of the little mud-farm-house.

"He is dead! My boy is dead!"

She flung the letter on the table and ran out at the front door.

Far out across the quiet ploughed lands and over the veld to where the kraals lay the cry rang. The Kaffir woman who sat outside her hut beyond the kraals nursing her baby heard it and came down with her child across her hip to see what was the matter. At the side of the round house she stood motionless and open-mouthed, watching the woman, who paced up and down behind the house with her apron thrown over her head and her hands folded above it, crying aloud.

In the front room the grandmother, who had not spoken since he came, took up the letter and put it in the lad's hands. "Read," she whispered.

And slowly the lad spelled it out.

"My Dear Aunt,

"I hope this letter finds you well. The Commandant has asked me to write it.

"We had a great fight four days ago, and Jan is dead. The Commandant says I must tell you how it happened. Aunt, there were five of us first in a position on that koppie, but two got killed, and then there were only three of us – Jan, and I, and Uncle Peter's Frikkie. Aunt, the khakies were coming on all round just like locusts, and the bullets were coming just like hail. It was bare on that side of the koppie where we were, but we had plenty of cartridges. We three took up a position where there were some small stones and we fought, Aunt; we had to. One bullet took off the top of my ear, and Jan got two bullets, one through the flesh in the left leg and one through his arm, but he could still fire his gun. Then we three meant to go to the top of the koppie, but a bullet took Jan right through his chest. We knew he couldn't go any farther. The khakies were right at the foot of the koppie just coming up. He told us to lay him down, Aunt. We said we would stay by him, but he said we must go. I put my jacket under his head and Frikkie put his over his feet. We threw his gun far away from him that they might see how it was with him. He said he hadn't much pain. He was full of blood from his arm, but there wasn't much from his chest, only a little out of the corners of his mouth. He said we must make haste or the khakies would catch us; he said he wasn't afraid to be left there.

"Aunt, when we got to the top, it was full of khakies like the sea on the other side, all among the koppies and on our koppie too. We were surrounded, Aunt; the last I saw of Frikkie he was sitting on a stone with the blood running down his face, but he got under a rock and hid there; some of our men found him next morning and brought him to camp. Aunt, there was a khakie's horse standing just below where I was, with no one on it. I jumped on and rode. The bullets went this way and the bullets went that, but I rode! Aunt, the khakies were sometimes as near me as that tentpole, only the Grace of God saved me. It was dark in the night when I got back to where our people were, because I had to go round all the koppies to get away from the khakies.

"Aunt, the next day we went to look for him. We found him where we left him; but he was turned over on to his face; they had taken all his things, his belt and his watch, and the pugaree from his hat, even his boots. The little green silk purse he used to carry we found on the ground by him, but nothing in it. I will send it back to you whenever I get an opportunity.

"Aunt, when we turned him over on his back there were four bayonet stabs in his body. The doctor says it was only the first three while he was alive; the last one was through his heart and killed him at once.

"We gave him Christian burial, Aunt; we took him to the camp.

"The Commandant was there, and all of the family who are with the Commando were there, and they all said they hoped God would comfort you . . ."

The old woman leaned forward and grasped the boy's arm. "Read it over again," she said, "from where they found him." He turned back and re-read slowly. She gazed at the page as though she were reading also. Then, suddenly, she slipped out at the front door.

At the back of the house she found her daughter-in-law still walking up and down, and the Kaffir woman with a red handkerchief bound round her head and the child sitting across her hip, sucking from her long, pendulous breast, looking on.

The old woman walked up to her daughter-in-law and grasped her firmly by the arm.

"He's dead! You know, my boy's dead!" she cried, drawing the apron down with her right hand and disclosing her swollen and bleared face. "O, his beautiful hair – Oh, his beautiful hair!"

The old woman held her arm tighter with both hands; the younger opened her half-closed eyes, and looked into the keen, clear eyes fixed on hers, and stood arrested.

The old woman drew her face closer to hers. "You . . . do . . . not . . . know . . . what . . . has . . . happened!" she spoke slowly, her tongue striking her front gum, the jaw moving stiffly, as though partly paralysed. She loosed her left hand and held up the curved work-worn fingers before her daughter-in-law's face. "Was it not told me . . . The night he was born . . . here . . . at this spot . . . That he would do great things . . . great things . . . for his land and his people?" She bent forward till her lips almost touched the other's. "Three . . . bullet . . . wounds . . . and four . . . bayonet . . . stabs!" She raised her left hand high in the air. "Three . . . bullet . . . wounds . . . and four . . . bayonet . . . stabs! . . . Is it given to many to die so for their land and their people!"

The younger woman gazed into her eyes, her own growing larger and larger. She let the old woman lead her by the arm in silence into the house.

The Field-Cornet's son was gone, feeling there was nothing more to be done; and the Kaffir woman went back with her baby to her hut beyond the kraals. All day the house was very silent. The Kaffir woman wondered that no smoke rose from the farm-house chimney, and that she was not called to churn, or wash the pots. At three o'clock she went down to the house. As she passed the grated window of the round out-house she saw the buckets of milk still standing unsifted on the floor as they had been set down at breakfast time, and under the great soap-pot beside the wood pile the fire had died out. She went round to the front of the house and saw the door and window shutters still closed, as though her mistresses were still sleeping. So she rebuilt the fire under the soap-pot and went back to her hut.

It was four o'clock when the grandmother came out from the dark inner room where she and her daughter-in-law had been lying down; she opened the top of the front door, and lit the fire with twigs, and set the large black kettle over it. When it boiled she made coffee, and poured out two cups and set them on the table with a plate of biscuits, and then called her daughter-in-law from their inner room.

The two women sat down one on each side of the table, with their coffee cups before them, and the biscuits between them, but for a time they said nothing, but sat silent, looking out through the open door as the shadow of the house in the afternoon sunshine beyond it. At last the older woman motioned that the younger should drink her coffee. She took a little, and then folding her arms on the table rested her head on them, and sat motionless as if asleep.

The older woman broke up a biscuit into her own cup, and stirred it round and round; and then, without tasting, sat gazing out into the afternoon's sunshine till it grew cold beside her.

It was five, and the heat was quickly dying; the glorious golden colouring of the late afternoon was creeping over everything when she rose from her chair. She moved to the door and took from behind it two large white calico bags hanging there, and from nails on the wall she took down two large brown cotton kappies. She walked round the table and laid her hand gently on her daughter-in-law's arm. The younger woman raised her head slowly and looked up into her mother-in-law's face; and then, suddenly, she knew that her mother-in-law was an old, old woman. The little shrivelled face that looked down at her was hardly larger than a child's, the eyelids were half closed and the lips worked at the corners and the bones cut out through the skin in the temples.

"I am going out to sow – the ground will be getting too dry tomorrow; will you come with me?" she said gently.

The younger woman made a movement with her hand, as though she said "What's the use?" and redropped her hand on the table.

"It may go on for long, our burghers must have food," the old woman said gently.

The younger woman looked into her face, then she rose slowly and taking one of the brown kappies from her hand, put it on, and hung one of the bags over her left arm; the old woman did the same and together they passed out of the door. As the older woman stepped down the younger caught her and saved her from falling.

"Take my arm, mother," she said.

But the old woman drew her shoulders up. "I only stumbled a little!" she said quickly. "That step has been always too high;" but before she reached the plank over the sloot the shoulders had drooped again, and the neck fallen forward.

The mould in the lands was black and soft; it lay in long ridges, as it had been ploughed up a week before, but the last night's rain had softened it and made it moist and ready for putting in the seed.

The bags which the women carried on their arms were full of the seed of pumpkins and mealies. They began to walk up the lands, keeping parallel with the low hedge of dried bushes that ran up along the side of the sloot almost up to the top of the ridge. At every few paces they stopped and bent down to press into the earth, now one and then the other kind of seed from their bags. Slowly they walked up and down till they reached the top of the land almost on the horizon line; and then they turned, and walked down, sowing as they went. When they had reached the bottom of the land before the farm-house it was almost sunset, and their bags were nearly empty; but they turned to go up once more. The light of the setting sun cast long, gaunt shadows from their figures across the ploughed land, over the low hedge and the sloot, into the bare veld beyond; shadows that grew longer and longer as they passed slowly on pressing in the seeds . . . The seeds! . . . that were to lie in the dank, dark, earth, and rot there, seemingly, to die, till their outer covering had split and fallen from them . . . and then, when the rains had fallen, and the sun had shone, to come up above the earth again, and high in the clear air to lift their feathery plumes and hang out their pointed leaves and silken tassels! To cover the ground with a mantle of green and gold through which sunlight quivered, over which the insects hung by thousands, carrying yellow pollen on their legs and wings and making the air alive with their hum and stir, while grain and fruit ripened surely . . . for the next season's harvest!

When the sun had set, the two women with their empty bags turned and walked silently home into the dark to the farm-house.

NINETEEN HUNDRED AND ONE

Near one of the camps in the Northern Transvaal are the graves of two women. The older one died first, on the twenty-third of the month, from hunger and want; the younger woman tended her with ceaseless care and devotion till the end. A week later when the British Superintendent came round to inspect the tents, she was found lying on her blanket on the mud-floor dead, with the rations of bread and meat she had got four days before untouched on a box beside her. Whether she died of disease, or from inability to eat the food, no one could say. Some who had seen her said she hardly seemed to care to live after the old woman died; they buried them side by side.

There is no stone and no name upon either grave to say who lies there . . . our unknown . . . our unnamed . . . our forgotten dead.

IN THE YEAR NINETEEN HUNDRED AND FOUR

If you look for the little farm-house among the ridges you will not find it there to-day.

The English soldiers burnt it down. You can only see where the farm-house once stood, because the stramonia and weeds grow high and very strong there; and where the ploughed lands were you can only tell, because the veld never grows quite the same on land that has once been ploughed. Only a brown patch among the long grass on the ridge shows where the kraals and huts once were.

In a country house in the north of England the owner has upon his wall an old flint-lock gun. He takes it down to show his friends. It is a small thing he picked up in the war in South Africa, he says. It must be at least eighty years old and is very valuable. He shows how curiously it is constructed; he says it must have been kept in such perfect repair by continual polishing for the steel shines as if it were silver. He does not tell that he took it from the wall of the little mud house before he burnt it down.

It was the grandfather's gun, which the women have kept polished on the wall.

In a London drawing-room the descendant of a long line of titled forefathers entertains her guests. It is a fair room, and all that money can buy to make life soft and beautiful is there.

On the carpet stands a little dark wooden stoof. When one of her guests notices it, she says it is a small curiosity which her son brought home to her from South Africa when he was out in the war there; and how good it was of him to think of her when he was away in the back country. And when they ask what it is, she says it is a thing Boer women have as a footstool and to keep their feet warm; and she shows the hole at the side where they put the coals in, and the little holes at the top where the heat comes out.

And the other woman puts her foot out and rests it on the stoof just to try how it feels, and drawls. "How f-u-n-n-y!"

It is grandmother's stoof, that the child used to sit on.

The wagon chest was found and broken open just before the thatch caught fire, by three private soldiers, and they divided the money between them; one spent his share in drink, another had his stolen from him, but the third sent his home to England to a girl in the East End of London. With part of it she bought a gold brooch and ear-rings, and the rest she saved to buy a silk wedding-dress when he came home.

A syndicate of Jews in Johannesburg and London have bought the farm. They purchased it from the English Government, because they think to find gold on it. They have purchased it and paid for it ... but they do not possess it.

Only the men who lie in their quiet graves upon the hill-side, who lived on it, and loved it, possess it; and the piles of stones above them, from among the long waving grasses, keep watch over the land.

Source:
Olive Schreiner: *Stories, Dreams and Allegories.* London: T. Fisher Unwin: 1923, written c. 1906.

Oom[1] Gert's Story

C. Louis Leipoldt

My boy, what do you think that I can tell you?
You want to hear the story of our death?
All right!
   It never is too late to learn
More about that, if you can use the knowledge,
Especially for you youngsters. Just hold tight
To what we have, stand on your feet and take
Your part in this our nation.
                        But you've come
To the wrong man; there must be many others
Who'd tell the story straight, in the right order
And with a moral too, and better grasp
Of all the politics than I could have:
My only knowledge comes out of my soul,
I can delve only into my own heart,
And it is very old and almost dead –
My heart, I mean. Truly, if you yourself
Had been through what I've been through, seen as much,
And struggled as I've struggled – what's more, seen
So many things that you would rather not have –
Your heart would also not be free of cracks.
But come – let's see what I can tell you of.
It's a long story! And a sad one, too,
Shot through with tears and sobs, my boy. All right?
You want to hear it? Good!
                        But sit, man, sit.
How can I talk while you stay standing up?
Sit there. (And, Gerrie, fetch something to drink!

Your Dad could use a cup of coffee, too.)
Right. Now, you know, my boy, that when our people
Round here were all dumbfounded by the war,
A troop of khakis occupied the town
And "Martjie Louw",[2] as usual, was proclaimed.
Old Smith, the magistrate – he is a man
For whom I have respect although he's English:
He always acted like a gentleman
And got on with our people very well;
But he was quietly removed from office
And sent off to East London. This because
He wouldn't glibly dance to all their tunes.
And in his place a colonel was appointed,
His name – say Gerrie, now, what was his name?
Jones? No, child, *he* was just an underling,
You know, that ape with chevrons on his sleeve.
Ah! that's it, Wilson, that was the chap's name –
A big, fat bloke with yellow-grey moustaches,
And great, long eye-teeth and a bright red face;
They said he drank; I must say, though, I never
Saw him the worse for drink and don't now want
To slander him behind his back. Although
He was indeed a swine, one must be fair.
He really ground us down; his hand was hard:
We weren't allowed to light the lamps at night,
And had to be indoors by eight o'clock.
He kept us under constant watch and even
Came nosing through our houses to make sure
That none of us were hiding arms or powder,
Cartridges, caps or anything like that.
He thought we had collected stocks of food
In order to supply the Boer Commandos.
Yes, he was hard all right! (Sweatheart, pass back

The sugar, please! Two lumps are not enough:
You know Dad likes his coffee sweet.)
                                          And we
Were all confused and in a state of panic,
And not one of us knew from day to day
What to expect or what was going to happen.
The town was seething with rebellious murmurs,
Like dough in which the yeast has been well kneaded;
You've seen it rise? Well, we were just like that!
Yes, all our people. But, what could we do?
The younger ones, especially, were so restive
That we could hardly keep them all in check,
And, without warning, two of them cut loose.
(Young Klaas's cup is empty again, sweetheart.)

One evening Bennie Bêrends came to me,
With him was Johnnie Hendriks, old Saarl's son.
They'd skipped across the street so quietly,
The sentry didn't even get a glimpse –
Else Saarl and I would have known all about it!
And had to pay a fine into the bargain! –
Old Saarl and I had always been good friends;
But that same month, alas, he died of cancer –
A cancer of the stomach – God's hand there,
For thus he didn't live to see the day . . .
But wait, I go too fast, we'll come to that.
Yes, I was sitting here in my own chair
And Bennie sat right there where you are now,
And Johnnie there. Yes, I can see him now,
At that time, just an adolescent kid,
Not wholly dry behind the ears, in fact,
Though he'd a pretty sharp tongue in his head.
Confirmed only that year. (Gerrie, my child,

Fetch me the album!) – Here's a snap of him
And this is one of Bennie; that's the line
That his late mother wrote on the day after . . .
After his er . . . er . . . death. You read it, son,
My glasses don't fit well, and in the smoke
I can't see properly. Yes, read it out:
"Barend Gerhardus Barends" – Right! and then?
"Born on the sixth of May" – That's how it goes!
"Ha –" No, shut up the book, I know it all!
(Take it away, please, sweet. Don't stand there frozen
Just like a frightened rabbit. Pour some coffee!
We should have enough milk, and sugar too,
Seeing it isn't "Martjie Louw" here now!)
Yes, Bennie was a real born gentleman,
My godson, and, though I say it myself,
The sort to be a favourite with the ladies,
With his straight back and smooth, clean-shaven face –
I don't suppose he'd even started shaving.
(Sweetheart, please go and see if Leentjie has
Brought all the wood into the kitchen.)
                              Yes,
My boy, he courted Gerrie here, and I
Was not against the match, because he seemed
Cut out for her, somehow – just the right lad.
You see she's still not quite got over it;
But all of us have crosses we must bear,
Yes, even when it seems our hearts must break.
My darling, too, will, with our dear Lord's blessing,
Surmount her sorrow and forget the pain,
However hard it seems, that's how things go,
Though when we talk about him it seems better
To send her out on some pretext or other.
    Now where was I?

                        Oh, yes, the night they came
To ask for my advice. Ben's plan was this:
Johnnie and he would make for Witkransspruit,
Where, so they understood, Smuts was encamped
With his commando.
                        When they told me this
I nearly fainted. Then I reasoned with them,
But, no!
   Oh, dear, youth is so obstinate!
And Ben was always headstrong: as a child
He often got a whacking just for that!
They had made up their minds and they would go.
I had two horses at my house just then –
The khakis hadn't taken them as yet –
I don't know why, but I can tell you this,
It wasn't my fault that the animals
Just happened to be there, but there they were!
Nonnie, my wife and Gerrie's mother, she
Who died that very year down at Goudini
Of heart disease, but, also, by the war
Broken in soul and body – Nonnie, too,
Added her pleas to mine, but all in vain.
"We can't take any more of this, Oom Gert;
A man must *do* something to aid his nation!"
"Do? Do? Do something! Ach, what can you do?
Or what can any of us do?"
                        In vain.
So Nonnie packed my knapsack full to bursting
With lots of rusks and biltong. As for me
I filled the saddlebags with hard-boiled eggs
And other edibles. For, after all,
He was my godson, and then Johnnie, too,
Was old Saarl's son, and Saarl and I were friends.

So nobody could say I acted wrongly,
Although, it's true, I was a British subject.
Could I stand by and see my own flesh suffer
Whilst I had food? No, I was right, my boy,
And conscience since has never bothered me.
So, in a word, the two were off. Of course,
Next morning the whole mob came swarming round;
The colonel buzzed around us like a horsefly
And swore, and made a fuss, but I stood firm:
It wasn't my fault that the horses were
Still in my garden, and I told him so:
That it was his fault, certainly not mine!
Of course, about the eggs and rusks and biltong,
I thought it better not to mention them!

Don't ask me how we lived through all those months.
A dark cloud seemed continually to hang
Above us, and not just above our town,
But over the whole country, our whole nation.

Then one day came the news . . . (Wait, here she's back –
Please, sweetheart, chase the chickens off the stoep.
Look at that rooster scratching up the flowers!)
Right, one day came the news – and what a shock!
Johnnie and Ben had both been captured and
Ben slapped in gaol. A military court –
You know the rest! And then a further blow:
The sentence was – that both were to be hanged!
And what a dreadful blow, God knows, that was!
We did out best, but all in vain; the rabble
Were shrieking for revenge and they must hang.
That morning the head constable arrived:
"The colonel sends his compliments." My God,

His compliments! – you hear? You understand?
You understand, boy, *compliments*!
                              Oh, no,
Be still, be still, my heart, or you'll break too!
Our crosses we must bear whate'er the cost.

And please would I present myself next morning
To see the treatment meted out to rebels,
Otherwise . . . The head constable was human
And certainly was very ill at ease
At having to deliver such a message.
The khakis, too, I must say, behaved well,
But had to do their duty. I was grateful
They did it without added insolence.
The policeman, Nicholas, yes, that was his name –
He, later, in the Free State, got a dose
Of lead he couldn't stomach – told me, too,
That others had got similar commands
And there'd be quite a crowd of us to witness
The – you know – at the gaol, and also warned me
I'd better come, however sick I felt!

We didn't sleep that night, Nonnie and I.

Yes, I remember well. The day was cool –
You don't forget a day like that so quickly! –
With just a slight east wind – a little cold –
For it brought on Nonnie's rheumatic pains –
She always suffered quite a lot from them
And never could bear cold. Well, as I said,
The day was cool and so I had my jacket
Well buttoned up. You know I always liked
To have my waistcoat show. What is the point

Of wearing waistcoats if nobody sees them?
However, that day it was really fresh,
And so I had my jacket buttoned up.
Down at the bend there, just below the mill,
I met the others in the early morning,
For, as I said, all of us were commanded.
The minister was there, and Albert Louw –
You know old Cock-eye Louw, Klaas? Yes, of course,
And Michiel Nel, and Gys van Zyl, and Piet –
No, you, of course, wouldn't remember Piet;
He was before your time; but that chap was
As strong as Samson – gee! But he was strong!
And just as restive as a scorpion, too.
But droll, my boy, and one who could laugh even
When clouds were dark and stormy and the thunder
Rumbled among the clouds. I know, of course,
We all of us have faults and I don't really
Hold it against Piet Spaanspek that he always
Had to be making jokes, though all the rest
Of us were feeling queer and sick at heart.
"This wind bites shrewdly, Cousin Gert," he said,
"You'd better lend your overcoat to Ben
In case the weather's bad upstairs!" He laughed,
But I was glad the minister was there
To reprimand him on the spot, and, neatly,
He put him in his place.
                        "Is this the time
For jokes, Mr. Van Ryn?" he asked him coldly.
"For shame! For shame! How dare you say such things
Today, when all our hearts are full, our eyes
Half-dimmed with tears for our beloved country?"
(Sweetheart, do chase those chickens out! They make
The yard so dirty. We can help ourselves.)

But Piet Spaanspek was never at a loss
For words and, not put out, he carried on
His little jokes, although the rest of us
Pretended not to hear and took no notice.
I think he felt as sick at heart as I
But didn't want the rest of us to see.

We walked up to the fore court of the gaol
And it was full of khakis. At the gates
They made us come in slowly, two by two.
And there in the back yard the gallows stood,
Beside them Ben and Johnnie, hand in hand,
For they were not in chains. We got permission
To go up close to them and talk to them
But only for five minutes.
       I was speechless
Completely tongue-tied with embarrassment.
But Bennie took me by the hand and said:
"Oom Gert, it's all up now. Goodbye, Oom Gert!
Just tell Aunt Nonnie, and tell Gerrie – no,
Don't tell them anything, they'll understand."
And Johnnie also took my hand and said,
A smile around his lips: "Good morning, Oom.
No, Oompie,[3] don't you cry!" Yes, as I've said,
He always was inclined to be precocious
And cheeky, too. "No, Oompie, don't you cry!
We did our duty, and it's over now."

And then they both talked to the minister,
And I, as Bennie's nearest blood relation,
Accompanied him to the gallows, there . . .
No, boy, it's just the smoke. I'm getting old
And your tobacco is too strong for me.

107

I smoke it mild myself. Because, you see,
It doesn't make my eyes so sore.
                              Where was I?
Oh yes. Then all of us shook hands with them.
We couldn't speak and even Piet was dumb
And just as sick as I, and one of us –
I don't know who it was – began to sob.

They wanted to pull over Bennie's face
A handkerchief or scarf or something, like
A sort of hood. But Bennie bravely asked,
In English too, yes, he could speak it well –
Whether they couldn't hang him, please, without it?
The colonel nodded; then . . .
                              No, boy, let go!
Why do you grab my hand again? Let go!
Confound it! How can I tell you the story
When you will put me off my stroke like that?
And, blow your smoke out on the other side!
My eyes have got too old for your tobacco.
(Sweetheart, fetch me a handkerchief.)
                              Well, now,
There's nothing more to tell. We came on home
And here in this same room we all knelt down.
The minister conducted a short service
For us here on our knees – then – it was finished.

That night, though, Cousin Piet and Cock-eye Louw
Left town and set out for the nearest farm,
And afterwards they joined up with our people.
(Sweetheart, just pass me back the sugar-bowl,
And pour another cup for Cousin Klaas!)

NOTES:

1. Although oom is the ordinary Afrikaans word for uncle, there is really no English equivalent for its use as a familiar yet respectful title for any older man.

2. The Afrikaans colloquial term for martial law.

3. Oompie, a diminutive, is somewhat disrespectful.

Source:
A.P. Grové & C.D. Harvey (eds): *Afrikaans Poems with English Translations*. Cape Town: Oxford University Press: 1962, written c. 1911.
Translated by C.D. Harvey

A Sahib's War

Rudyard Kipling

Pass? Pass? Pass? I have one pass already, allowing me to go by the *rêl* from Kroonstadt to Eshtellenbosch, where the horses are, where I am to be paid off, and whence I return to India. I am a – trooper of the Gurgaon Rissala (cavalry regiment), the One Hundred and Forty-first Punjab Cavalry. Do not herd me with these black Kaffirs. I am a Sikh – a trooper of the State. The Lieutenant-Sahib does not understand my talk? Is there *any* Sahib on his train who will interpret for a trooper of the Gurgaon Rissala going about his business in this devil's devising of a country, where there is no flour, no oil, no spice, no red pepper, and no respect paid to a Sikh? Is there no help? . . . God be thanked, here is such a Sahib! Protector of the Poor! Heaven-born! Tell the young Lieutenant-Sahib that my name is Umr Singh; I am – I was – servant to Kurban Sahib, now dead; and I have a pass to go to Eshtellenbosch, where the horses are. Do not let him herd me with these black Kaffirs! . . . Yes, I will sit by this truck till the Heaven-born has explained the matter to the young Lieutenant-Sahib who does not understand our tongue.

What orders? The young Lieutenant-Sahib will not detain me? Good! I go down to Eshtellenbosch by the next *terain*? Good! I go with the Heaven-born? Good! Then for this day I am the Heaven-born's servant. Will the Heaven-born bring the honour of his presence to a seat. Here is an empty truck; I will spread my blanket over one corner thus – for the sun is hot, though not so hot as our Punjab in May. I will prop it up thus, and I will arrange this hay thus, so the Presence can sit at ease till God sends us a *terain* for Eshtellenbosch . . .

The Presence knows the Punjab? Lahore? Amritzar? Attaree, belike? My village is north over the fields three miles from Attaree, near the big white house which was copied from a certain place of the Great Queen's by – by – I have forgotten the name. Can the Presence recall it? Sirdar Dyal Singh Attareewalla! Yes, that is the very man; but how does the Presence know? Born and bred in Hind, was he? O-o-oh! This is quite a different matter. The Sahib's nurse was a Surtee woman from the Bombay side? That was a pity. She should have been an up-country wench; for those make stout nurses. There is no land like the Punjab. There are no people like the Sikhs. Umr Singh is my name, yes. An old man? Yes. A trooper only after all these years? Ye-es. Look at my uniform, if the Sahib doubts. Nay – nay; the Sahib looks too closely. All marks of rank were picked off it long ago, but – but it is true – mine is not a common cloth such as troopers use for their coats, and – the Sahib has sharp eyes – that black mark is such a mark as a silver chain leaves when long worn on the breast. The Sahib says that troopers do not wear silver chains? No-o. Troopers do not wear the Arder of Beritish India? No. The Sahib should have been in the Police of the Punjab. I am not a trooper, but I have been a Sahib's servant for nearly a year – bearer, butler, sweeper, any and all three. The Sahib says that Sikhs do not take menial service? True; but it was for Kurban Sahib – my Kurban Sahib dead these three months!

Young – of a reddish face – with blue eyes, and he lilted a little on his feet when he was pleased, and cracked his finger-joints. So did his father before him, who was Deputy-Commissioner of Jullundur in my father's time when I rode with the Gurgaon Rissala. *My father?* Jwala Singh. A Sikh of Sikhs – he fought against the English at Sobraon and carried the mark to his death. So we were knit as it were by a blood-tie, I and my Kurban Sahib. Yes, I was a trooper first – nay, I had risen to a Lance-Duffadar, I remember – and my father gave me a dun stallion of his own breeding on that day; and *he* was a little baba, sitting upon a wall by the parade-ground with his ayah – all in white, Sahib – laughing at the end of our drill. And his father and mine talked together, and mine beckoned to me, and I dismounted, and the baba put his hand into mine – eighteen – twenty-five – twenty-seven years gone now – Kurban Sahib – my Kurban Sahib! Oh, we were great friends after that! He cut his teeth on my sword-hilt, as the saying is. He called me Big Umr Singh – Buwwa Umwa Singh, for he could not speak plain. He stood only this high, Sahib, from the bottom of this truck, but he knew all our troopers by name – every one . . . And he went to England, and he became a young man, and back he came, lilting a little in his walk, and cracking his finger-joints – back to his own regiment and to me. He had not forgotten either our speech or our customs. He was a Sikh at heart, Sahib. He was rich, open-handed, just, a friend of poor troopers, keen-eyed, jestful, and careless. *I* could tell tales about him in his first years. There was very little he hid from *me*. I was his Umr Singh, and when we were alone he called me Father, and I called him Sou. Yes, that was how we spoke. We spoke freely together on everything – about war, and women, and money, and advancement, and such all.

We spoke about this war, too, long before it came. There were many box-wallahs, pedlars, with Pathans a few, in this country, notably at the city of Yunasbagh (Johannesburg), and they sent news in every week how the Sahibs lay without weapons under the heel of the Boer-log; and how big guns were hauled up and down the streets to keep Sahibs in order; and how a Sahib called Eger Sahib (Edgar?) was killed for a jest by the Boer-log. The Sahib knows how we of Hind hear all that passes over the earth? There was not a gun cocked in Yunasbagh that the echo did not come into Hind in a month. The Sahibs are very clever, but they forget their own cleverness has created the *dak* (the post), and that for an anna or two all things become known. We of Hind listened and heard and wondered; and when it was a sure thing, as reported by the pedlars and the vegetable-sellers, that the Sahibs of Yunasbagh lay in bondage to the Boer-log, certain among us asked questions and waited for signs. Others of us mistook the meaning of those signs. *Wherefore, Sahib, came the long war in the Tirah!* This Kurban Sahib knew, and we talked together. He said, "There is no haste. Presently we shall fight, and we shall fight for all Hind in that country round Yunasbagh." Here he spoke truth. Does the Sahib not agree? Quite so. It is for Hind that the Sahibs are fighting this war. Ye cannot in one place rule and in another bear service. Either ye must everywhere rule or everywhere obey. God does not make the nations ringstraked. True – true – true!

So did matters ripen – a step at a time. It was nothing to me, except I think – and the Sahib sees this, too? – that it is foolish to make an army and break their hearts in idleness. Why have they not sent for the men of the Tochi – the men of the Tirah – the men of Buner? Folly, a thousand times. *We* could have done it all so gently – so gently.

Then, upon a day, Kurban Sahib sent for me and said, "Ho, Dada, I am sick, and the doctor gives me a certificate for many months." And he winked, and I said, "I will get leave and nurse thee, Child. Shall I bring my uniform?" He said, "Yes, and a sword for a sick man to lean on. We go to Bombay, and thence by sea to the country of the Hubshis (niggers)." Mark his cleverness! He was first of all our men among the native regiments to get leave for sickness and to come here. Now they will not let our officers go away, sick or well, except they sign a bond not to take part in this war-game upon the road. But *he* was clever. There was no whisper of war when he took his sick-leave. I came also? Assuredly. I went to my Colonel, and sitting in the chair (I am – I was – of that rank for which a chair is placed when we speak with the Colonel) I said, "My child goes sick. Give me leave, for I am old and sick also."

And the Colonel, making the word double between English and our tongue, said, "Yes, thou art truly *Sikh*", and he called me an old devil – jestingly, as one soldier may jest with another; and he said my Kurban Sahib was a liar as to his health (that was true, too), and at long last he stood up and shook my hand, and bade me go and bring my Sahib safe again. My Sahib back again – aie me!

So I went to Bombay with Kurban Sahib, but there, at sight of the Black Water, Wajib Ali, his bearer, checked, and said that his mother was dead. Then I said to Kurban Sahib, "What is one Mussulman pig more or less? Give me the keys of the trunks, and I will lay out the white shirts for dinner." Then I beat Wajib Ali at the back of Watson's Hotel, and that night I prepared Kurban Sahib's razors. I say, Sahib, that I, a Sikh of the Khalsa, an unshorn man, prepared the razors. But I did not put on my uniform while I did it. On the other hand, Kurban Sahib took for me, upon the steamer, a room in all respects like to his own, and would have given me a servant. We spoke of many things on the way to this country; and Kurban Sahib told me what he perceived would be the conduct of the war. He said, "They have taken men afoot to fight men ahorse, and they will foolishly show mercy to these Boer-log because it is believed that they are white." He said, "There is but one fault in this war, and that is that the Government have not employed *us,* but have made it altogether a Sahib's war. Very many men will thus be killed, and no vengeance will be taken." True talk – true talk! It fell as Kurban Sahib foretold.

And we came to this country, even to Cape Town over yonder, and Kurban Sahib said, "Bear the baggage to the big dak-bungalow, and I will look for employment fit for a sick man." I put on the uniform of my rank and went to the big dak-bungalow, called Maun Nihâl Seyn, and I caused the heavy baggage to be bestowed in that dark lower place – is it known to the Sahib? – which was already full of the swords and baggage of officers. It is fuller now – dead men's kit all! I was careful to secure a receipt for all three pieces. I have it in my belt. They must go back to the Punjab.

Anon came Kurban Sahib, lilting a little in his step, which sign I knew, and he said, "We are born in a fortunate hour. We go to Eshtellenbosch to oversee the dispatch of horses," Remember, Kurban Sahib was squadron-leader of the Gurgaon Rissala, and *I* was Umr Singh. So I said, speaking as we do – we did – when none was near. "Thou art a groom and I am a grass-cutter, but is this any promotion, Child?" At this he laughed, saying, "It is the way to better things. Have patience, Father." (Aye, he called me father when none were by.) "This war ends not tomorrow nor the next day. I have seen the new Sahibs," he said, "and they are fathers of owls – all – all – all!"

So we went to Eshtellenbosch, where the horses are; Kurban Sahib doing the service of servants in that business. And the whole business was managed without forethought by new Sahibs from God knows where, who had never seen a tent pitched or a peg driven. They were full of zeal, but empty of all knowledge. Then came, little by little from Hind, those Pathans – they are just like vultures up there, Sahib – they always follow slaughter. And there came to Eshtellenbosch some Sikhs – Muzbees, though – and some Madras monkey-men. They came with horses. Puttiala sent horses. Jhind and Nabha sent horses. All the nations of the Khalsa sent horses. All the ends of the earth sent horses. God knows what the army did with them, unless they ate them raw. They used horses as a courtesan uses oil: with both hands. These horses needed many men. Kurban Sahib appointed me to the command (what a command for me!) of certain woolly ones – *Hubshis* – whose touch and shadow are pollution. They were enormous eaters; sleeping on their bellies; laughing without cause; wholly like animals. Some were called Fingoes, and some, I think, Red Kaffirs, but they were all Kaffirs – filth unspeakable. I taught them to water and feed, and sweep and rub down. Yes, I oversaw the work of sweepers – a *jemadar* of *mehtars* (headman of a refuse-gang) was I, and Kurban Sahib little better, for five months. Evil months! The war went as Kurban Sahib had said. Our new men were slain and no vengeance was taken. It was a war of fools armed with the weapons of magicians. Guns that slew at half a day's march, and men who, being new, walked blind into high grass and were driven off like cattle by the Boer-log! As to the city of Eshtellenbosch, I am not a Sahib – only a Sikh. I would have quartered one troop only of the Gurgaon Rissala in that city – one little troop – and I would have schooled that city till its men learned to kiss the shadow of a Government horse upon the ground. There are many *mullahs* (priests) in Eshtellenbosch. They preached the Jehad against us. This is true – all the camp knew it. And most of the houses were thatched. A war of fools indeed!

At the end of five months my Kurban Sahib, who had grown lean, said, "The reward has come. We go up towards the front with horses tomorrow, and, once away, I shall be too sick to return. Make ready the baggage." Thus we got away, with some Kaffirs in charge of new horses for a certain new regiment that had come in a ship. The second day by *terain*, when we were watering at a desolate place without any sort of a bazaar to it, slipped out from the horse-boxes one Sikandar Khan, that had been a *jemadar* of *saises* (head-groom) at Eshtellenbosch, and was by service a trooper in a Border regiment. Kurban Sahib gave him big abuse for his desertion; but the Pathan put up his hands as excusing himself, and Kurban Sahib relented and added him to our service. So there were three of us – Kurban Sahib, I, and Sikandar Khan – Sahib, Sikh, and *Sag* (dog). But the man said truly, "We be far from our homes and both servants of the Raj. Make truce till we see the Indus again." I have eaten from the same dish as Sikandar Khan – beef, too, for aught I know! He said, on the night he stole some swine's flesh in a tin from a mess-tent, that in his Book, the Koran, it is written that whoso engages in a holy war is freed from ceremonial obligations. Wah! He had no more religion than the sword-point picks up of sugar and water at baptism. He stole himself a horse at a place where there lay a new and very raw regiment. I also produced myself a grey gelding there. They let their horses stray too much, those new regiments.

Some shameless regiments would indeed have made away with

our horses on the road! They exhibited indents and requisitions for horses, and once or twice would have uncoupled the trucks; but Kurban Sahib was wise, and I am not altogether a fool. There is not much honesty at the front. Notably, there was one congregation of hard-bitten horse-thieves; tall, light Sahibs, who spoke through their noses for the most part, and upon all occasions they said, "Oah, Hell!" which, in our tongue, signifies *Jehannum ko jao*. They bore each man a vine-leaf upon their uniforms, and they rode like Rajputs. Nay, they rode like Sikhs. They rode like the Ustrelyahs! The Ustrelyahs, whom we met later, also spoke through their noses not little, and they were tall, dark men, with grey, clear eyes, heavily eyelashed like camel's eyes – very proper men – a new brand of Sahib to me. They said on all occasions, "No fee-ah," which in our tongue means *Durro mut* ("Do not be afraid"), so we called them the *Durro Muts*. Dark, tall men, most excellent horsemen, hot and angry, waging war *as* war, and drinking tea as a sandhill drinks water. Thieves? A little, Sahib. Sikandar Khan swore to me – and he comes of a horse-stealing clan for ten generations – he swore a Pathan was a babe beside a *Durro Mut* in regard to horse-lifting. The *Durro Muts* cannot walk on their feet at all. They are like hens on the high road. Therefore they must have horses. Very proper men, with a just lust for the war. Aah – "No fee-ah", say the *Durro Muts*. *They* saw the worth of Kurban Sahib. *They* did not ask him to sweep stables. They would by no means let him go. He did substitute for one of their troop-leaders who had a fever, one long day in a country full of little hills – like the mouth of the Khaibar; and when they returned in the evening, the *Durro Muts* said, "Wallah! This is a man. Steal him!" So they stole my Kurban Sahib as they would have stolen anything else that they needed, and they sent a sick officer back to Eshtellenbosch in his place. Thus Kurban Sahib came to his own again, and I was his bearer, and Sikandar Khan was his cook. The law was strict that this was a Sahibs' war, but there was no order that a bearer and a cook should not ride with their Sahib –

and we had naught to wear but our uniforms. We rode up and down this accursed country, where there is no bazaar, no pulse, no flour, no oil, no spice, no red pepper, no firewood; nothing but raw corn and a little cattle. There were no great battles as I saw it, but a plenty of gun-firing. When we were many, the Boer-log came out with coffee to greet us, and to show us *purwanas* (permits) from foolish English Generals who had gone that way before, certifying they were peaceful and well disposed. When we were few, they hid behind stones and shot us. Now the order was that they were Sahibs, and this was a Sahibs' war. Good! But, as I understand it, when a Sahib goes to war, he puts on the cloth of war, and only those who wear that cloth may take part in the war. Good! That also I understand. But these people were as they were in Burma, or as the Afridis are. They shot at their pleasure, and when pressed hid the gun and exhibited *purwanas* or lay in a house and said they were farmers. Even such farmers as cut up the Madras troops at Hlinedatalone in Burma! Even such farmers as slew Cavagnari Sahib and the Guides at Kabul! We schooled *those* men, to be sure – fifteen, aye, twenty of a morning pushed off the verandah in front of the Bala Hissar. I looked that the Jung-i-lat Sahib (the Commander-in-Chief) would have remembered the old days, but – no. All the people shot at us everywhere, and he issued proclamations saying that he did not fight the people, but a certain army, which army, in truth, was all the Boer-log, who, between them, did not wear enough of uniform to make a loin-cloth. A fools' war from first to last; for it is manifest that he who fights should be hung if he fights with a gun in one hand and a *purwana* in the other, as did all these people. Yet we, when they had had their bellyfull for the time, received them with honour, and gave them permits, and refreshed them and fed their wives and their babes, and severely punished our soldiers who took their fowls. So the work was to be done not once with a few dead, but thrice and four times over. I talked much with Kurban Sahib on this, and he said, "It is a Sahib's war. That is the order"; and one night, when Sikandar Khan would have lain out beyond the pickets with his knife and shown them how it is worked on the Border, he hit Sikandar Khan between the eyes and came near to breaking in his head. Then Sikandar Khan, a bandage over his eyes, so that he looked like a sick camel, talked to him half one march, and he was more bewildered than I, and vowed he would return to Eshtellenbosch. But privately to me Kurban Sahib said we should have loosed the Sikhs and the Gurkhas on these people till they came in with their foreheads in the dust. For the war was not of that sort which they comprehended.

They shot us? Assuredly they shot us from houses adorned with a white flag; but when they came to know our custom, their widows sent word by Kaffir runners, and presently there was not quite so much firing. *No fee-ah!* All the Boer-log with whom we dealt had *purwanas* signed by mad Generals attesting that they were well disposed to the State. They had also rifles not a few, and cartridges, which they hid in the roof. The women wept very greatly when we burned such houses, but they did not approach too near after the flames had taken good hold of the thatch, for fear of the bursting cartridges. The women of the Boer-log are very clever. They are more clever than the men. The Boer-log are clever? Never, never, no! It is the Sahibs who are fools. For their own honour's sake the Sahibs must say that the Boer-log are clever; but it is the Sahibs' wonderful folly that has made the Boer-log. The Sahibs should have sent *us* into the game.

But the *Durro Muts* did well. They dealt faithfully with all that country thereabouts – not in any way as we of Hind should have dealt, but they were not altogether fools. One night when we lay on the top of a ridge in the cold, I saw far away a light in a house that appeared for the sixth part of an hour and was obscured. Anon it appeared again thrice for the twelfth part of an hour. I showed this to Kurban Sahib, for it was a house that had been spared – the people having many permits and swearing fidelity at our stirrup-leathers. I said to Kurban Sahib, "Send half a troop, Child, and finish that house. They signal to their brethren." And he laughed where he lay and said, "If I listened to my bearer Umr Singh, there would not be left ten houses in all this land." I said, "What need to leave one? This is as it was in Burma. They are farmers today and fighters tomorrow. Let us deal justly with them." He laughed and curled himself up in his blanket, and I watched the far light in the house till day. I have been on the Border in eight wars, not counting Burma. The first Afghan War; the second Afghan War; two Mahsud Waziri wars (that is four); two Black Mountain wars, if I remember right; the Malakand and Tirah. I do not count Burma, or some small things. *I* know when house signals to house!

I pushed Sikandar Khan with my foot, and he saw it too. He said, "One of the Boer-log who brought pumpkins for the mess, which I fried last night, lives in yonder house." I said, "How dost thou know?" He said, "Because he rode out of the camp another way, but I marked how his horse fought with him at the turn of the road; and before the light fell I stole out of the camp for evening prayer with Kurban Sahib's glasses, and from a little hill I saw the pied horse of that pumpkin-seller hurrying to that house." I said naught, but took Kurban Sahib's glasses from his greasy hands and cleaned them with a silk handkerchief and returned them to their case. Sikandar Khan told me that he had been the first man in the Zenab valley to use glasses – whereby he finished two blood-feuds cleanly in the course of three months' leave. But he was otherwise a liar.

That day Kurban Sahib, with some ten troopers, was sent on to spy the land for our camp. The *Durro Muts* moved slowly at that time. They were weighted with grain and forage and carts, and they greatly wished to leave these all in some town and go on light to other business which pressed. So Kurban Sahib sought a short cut for them, a little off the line of march. We were twelve miles before the main body, and we came to a house under a high bushed hill, with a nullah, which they call a donga, behind it, and an old sangar of piled stones, which they call a kraal, before it. Two thorn bushes grew on either side of the door, like babul bushes, covered with a golden-coloured bloom, and the roof was all of thatch. Before the house was a valley of stones that rose to another bush-covered hill. There was an old man in the verandah – an old man with a white beard and a wart upon the left side of his neck; and a fat woman with the eyes of a swine and the jowl of a swine; and a tall young man deprived of understanding. His head was hairless, no larger than an orange, and the pits of his nostrils were eaten away by a disease. He laughed and slavered and he sported sportively before Kurban Sahib. The man brought coffee and the woman showed us *purwanas* from three General-Sahibs, certifying that they were people of peace and goodwill. Here are the *purwanas*, Sahib. Does the Sahib know the Generals who signed them?

They swore the land was empty of Boer-log. They held up their hands and swore it. That was about the time of the evening meal. I stood near the verandah with Sikandar Khan, who was nosing like a jackal on a lost scent. At last he took my arm and said, "See yonder! There is the sun on the window of the house that signalled last night. This house can see that house from here," and he looked at the hill behind him all hairy with bushes, and sucked in his breath. Then the idiot with the shrivelled head danced by me and threw back that head, and regarded the roof and laughed like a hyena, and the fat woman talked loudly, as it were, to cover some noise. After this I passed to the back of the house on pretence to get water for tea, and I saw fresh horse-dung on the ground, and that the ground was cut with the new marks of hoofs; and there had dropped in the dirt one cartridge. Then Kurban Sahib called to me in our tongue, saying, "Is this a good place to make tea?" and I replied, knowing what he meant, "There are over many cooks in the cook-house. Mount and go, Child." Then I returned, and he said, smiling to the woman, "Prepare food, and when we have loosened our girths we will come in and eat"; but to his men he said in a whisper, "Ride away!" No. He did not cover the old man or the fat woman with his rifle. That was not his custom. Some fool of the *Durro Muts*, being hungry, raised his voice to dispute the order to flee, and before we were in our saddles many shots came from the roof – from rifles thrust through the thatch. Upon this we rode across the valley of stones, and men fired at us from the nullah behind the house, and from the hill behind the nullah, as well as from the roof of the house – so many shots that it sounded like a drumming in the hills. The Sikandar Khan, riding low, said, "This play is not for us alone, but for the rest of the *Durro Muts*"; and I said, "Be quiet. Keep place!" for his place was behind me, and I rode behind Kurban Sahib. But these new bullets will pass through five men a-row! We were not hit – not one of us – and we reached the hill of rocks and scattered among the stones, and Kurban Sahib turned in his saddle and said, "Look at the old man!" He stood in the verandah firing swiftly with a gun, the woman beside him and the idiot also – both with guns. Kurban Sahib laughed, and I caught him by the wrist, but – his fate was written at that hour. The bullet passed under my arm-pit and struck him in the liver, and I pulled him backward between two great rocks a-tilt – Kurban Sahib, my Kurban Sahib! From the nullah behind the house and from the hills came our Boer-log in number more than a hundred, and Sikandar Khan said, "*Now* we see the meaning of last night's signal. Give me the rifle." He took Kurban Sahib's rifle – in this war of fools only the doctors carry swords – and lay belly-flat to the work, but Kurban Sahib turned where he lay and said, "Be still. It is a Sahibs' war," and Kurban Sahib put up his hand – thus; and then his eyes rolled on me, and I gave him water that he might pass the more quickly. And at the drinking his Spirit received permission . . .

Thus went our fight, Sahib. We *Durro Muts* were on a ridge working from the north to the south, where lay our main body, and the Boer-log lay in a valley working from east to west. There were more than a hundred, and our men were ten, but they held the Boer-log in the valley while they swiftly passed along the ridge to the south. I saw three Boers drop in the open. Then they all hid again and fired heavily at the rocks that hid our men; but our men were clever and did not show, but moved away and away, always south; and the noise of the battle withdrew itself southward, where we could hear the sound of big guns. So it fell stark dark, and Sikandar Khan found a deep old jackal's earth amid rocks, into which we slid the body of Kurban Sahib upright. Sikandar Khan took his glasses, and I took his handkerchief and some letters and a certain thing which I knew hung round his neck, and Sikandar Khan is witness that I wrapped them all in the handkerchief. Then we took an oath together, and lay still and mourned for Kurban Sahib. Sikandar Khan wept till daybreak – even he, a Pathan, a Mohammedan! All that night we heard firing to the southward, and when the dawn broke the valley was full of Boer-log in carts and on horses. They gathered by the house, as we could see through Kurban Sahib's glasses, and the old man, who, I take it, was a priest, blessed them, and preached the holy war, waving his arm; and the fat woman brought coffee and the idiot capered among them and kissed their horses. Presently they went away in haste; they went over the hills and were not; and a black slave came out and washed the door-sills with bright water. Sikander Khan saw through the glasses that the stain was blood, and he laughed, saying, "Wounded men lie there. We shall yet get vengeance."

About noon we saw a thin, high smoke to the southward, such a smoke as a burning house will make in sunshine, and Sikandar Khan, who knows how to take a bearing across a hill, said, "At last we have burned the house of the pumpkin-seller whence they signalled." And I said, "What need now that they have slain my child? Let me mourn." It was a high smoke, and the old man, as I saw, came out into the verandah to behold it, and shook his clenched hands at it. So we lay till the twilight, foodless and without water, for we had vowed a vow neither to eat nor to drink till we had accomplished the matter. I had a little opium left, of which I gave Sikandar Khan the half, because he loved Kurban Sahib. When it was full dark we sharpened our sabres upon a certain softish rock, which, mixed with water, sharpens steel well, and we took off our boots and we went down to the house and looked through the windows very softly. The old man sat reading in a book, and the woman sat by the hearth; and the idiot lay on the floor with his head against her knee, and he counted his fingers and laughed, and she laughed again. So I knew they were mother and son, and I laughed, too, for I had suspected this when I claimed her life and her body from Sikandar Khan, in our discussion of the spoil. Then we entered with bare swords . . . Indeed, these Boer-log do not understand the steel, for the old man ran towards a rifle in a corner; but Sikandar Khan prevented him with a blow of the flat across the hands, and he sat down and held up his hands, and I put my fingers on my lips to signify they should be silent. But the woman cried, and one stirred in an inner room, and a door opened, and a man, bound about the head with rags, stood stupidly fumbling with a gun. His whole head fell inside the door, and none followed him. It was a very pretty stroke – for a Pathan. Then they were silent, staring at the head upon the floor, and I said to Sikandar, "Fetch ropes! Not even for Kurban Sahib's sake will I defile my sword." So he went to seek and returned with three long leather ones, and said, "Four wounded lie within, and doubtless each has a permit from a General," and he stretched the ropes and laughed. Then I bound the old man's hands behind his back, and unwillingly – for he laughed in my face, and would have fingered my beard – the idiot's. At this the woman with the swine's eyes and the jowl of a swine ran forward, and Sikandar Khan said, "Shall I strike or bind? She was thy property on the division." And I said, "Refrain! I have made a chain to hold her. Open the door." I pushed out the two across the verandah into the darker shade of the thorn-trees, and she followed upon her knees and lay along the ground, and pawed at my feet and howled. Then Sikandar

Khan bore out the lamp, saying that he was a butler and would light the table, and I looked for a branch that would bear fruit. But the woman hindered me not a little with her screechings and plungings, and spoke fast in her tongue, and I replied in my tongue, "I am childless tonight because of thy perfidy, and *my* child was praised among men and loved among women. He would have begotten men – not animals. Thou hast more years to live than I, but my grief is the greater."

I stooped to make sure the noose upon the idiot's neck, and flung the end over the branch, and Sikandar Khan held up the lamp that she might well see. Then appeared suddenly, a little beyond the light of the lamp, the spirit of Kurban Sahib. One hand he held to his side, even where the bullet had struck him, and the other he put forward thus, and said, "No. It is a Sahibs' war." And I said, "Wait a while, Child, and thou shalt sleep." But he came nearer, riding, as it were, upon my eyes, and said, "No. It is a Sahibs' war." And Sikandar Khan said, "Is it too heavy?" and set down the lamp and came to me, and as he turned to tally on the rope, the spirit of Kurban Sahib stood up within arm's reach of us, and his face was very angry, and a third time he said, "No. It is a Sahibs' war." And a little wind blew out the lamp, and I heard Sikandar Khan's teeth chatter in his head.

So we stayed side by side, the ropes in our hand, a very long while, for we could not shape any words. Then I heard Sikandar Khan open his water-bottle and drink; and when his mouth was slaked he passed to me and said, "We are absolved from our vow." So I drank, and together we waited for the dawn in that place where we stood – the ropes in our hand. A little after third cockcrow we heard the feet of horses and gun-wheels very far off, and so soon as the light came a shell burst on the threshold of the house, and the roof of the verandah that was thatched fell in and blazed before the windows. And I said, "What of the wounded Boer-log within?" And Sikandar Khan said, "We have heard the order. It is a Sahibs' war. Stand still." Then came a second shell – good line, but short – and scattered dust upon us where we stood; and then came ten of the little quick shells from the gun that speaks like a stammerer – yes, pompom the Sahibs call it – and the face of the house folded down like the nose and the chin of an old man mumbling, and the forefront of the house lay down. Then Sikandar Khan said, "If it be the fate of the wounded to die in the fire, *I* shall not prevent it." And he passed to the back of the house and presently came back, and four wounded Boer-log came after him, of whom two could not walk upright. And I said, "What hast thou done?" And he said, "I have neither spoken to them nor laid a hand on them. They follow in hope of mercy." And I said, "It is a Sahibs' war. Let them wait the Sahibs' mercy." So they lay still, the four men and the idiot, and the fat woman under the thorn-tree, and the house burned furiously. Then began the known sound of cartouches in the roof – one or two at first; then a trill, and last of all one loud noise and the thatch blew here and there, and the captives would have crawled aside on account of the heat that was withering the thorn-trees, and on account of the wood and bricks flying at random. But I said, "Abide! Abide! Ye be Sahibs, and this is a Sahibs' war, O Sahibs. There is no order that ye should depart from this war." They did not understand my word. Yet they abode and they lived.

Presently rode down five troopers of Kurban Sahib's command, and one I knew spoke my tongue, having sailed to Calcutta often with horses. So I told him all my tale, using bazaar-talk, such as his kidney of Sahib would understand; and at the end I said, "An order has reached us here from the dead that this is a Sahibs' war. I take the soul of my Kurban Sahib to witness that I give over to the justice of the Sahibs these Sahibs who have made me childless." Then I gave him the ropes and fell down senseless, my heart being very full, but my belly was empty, except for the little opium.

They put me into a cart with one of their wounded, and after a while I understood that they had fought against the Boer-log for two days and two nights. It was all one big trap, Sahib, of which we, with Kurban Sahib, saw no more than the outer edge. They were very angry, the *Durro Muts* – very angry indeed. I have never seen Sahibs so angry. They buried my Kurban Sahib with the rites of his faith upon the top of the ridge overlooking the house, and I said the proper prayers of the faith, and Sikandar Khan prayed in his fashion and stole five signalling-candles, which have each three wicks, and lighted the grave as if it had been the grave of a saint on a Friday. He wept very bitterly all that night, and I wept with him, and he took hold of my feet and besought me to give him a remembrance from Kurban Sahib. So I divided equally with him one of Kurban Sahib's handkerchiefs – not the silk ones, for those were given him by a certain woman; and I also gave him a button from a coat, and a little steel ring of no value that Kurban Sahib used for his keys, and he kissed them and put them into his bosom. The rest I have here in that little bundle, and I must get the baggage from the hotel in Cape Town – some four shirts we sent to be washed, for which we could not wait when we went up-country – and I must give them all to my Colonel-Sahib at Sialkote in the Punjab. For my child is dead – my baba is dead ! . . .

I would have come away before; there was no need to stay, the child being dead; but we were far from the rail, and the *Durro Muts* were as brothers to me, and I had come to look upon Sikandar Khan as in some sort a friend, and he got me a horse and I rode up and down with them; but the life had departed. God knows what they called me – orderly, *chaprassi* (messenger), cook, sweeper. I did not know or care. But once I had pleasure. We came back in a month after wide circles to that very valley. I knew it every stone, and I went up to the grave, and a clever Sahib of the *Durro Muts* (we left a troop there for a week to school those people with *purwanas*) had cut an inscription upon a great rock; and they interpreted it to me, and it was a jest such as Kurban Sahib himself would have loved. Oh! I have the inscription well copied here. Read it aloud, Sahib, and I will explain the jests. There are two very good ones. Begin, Sahib:

In Memory of
WALTER DECIES CORBYN
Late Captain 141st Punjab Cavalry

The Gurgaon Rissala, that is. Go on, Sahib.

Treacherously shot near this place by
The connivance of the late
HENDRIK DIRK UYS
A Minister of God
Who thrice took the oath of neutrality
And Piet his son,
This little work

Aha! This is the first jest. The Sahib should see this little work!

Was accomplished in partial
And inadequate recognition of their loss
By some men who loved him

Si monumentum requiris circumspice

That is the second jest. It signifies that those who would desire to behold a proper memorial to Kurban Sahib must look out at the house. And, Sahib, the house is not there, nor the well, nor the big tank which they call dams, nor the little fruit-trees, nor the cattle. There is nothing at all, Sahib, except the two trees withered by the fire. The rest is like the desert here – or my hand – or my heart. Empty, Sahib – all empty!

Source:
Rudyard Kipling: *Traffics and Discoveries*. London: Macmillan: 1904.

Bridge-Guard in the Karroo

Rudyard Kipling

". . . and will supply details to guard the Blood River Bridge."
District Orders – Lines of Communication. South African War.

Sudden the desert changes,
   The raw glare softens and clings,
Till the aching Oudtshoorn ranges
   Stand up like the thrones of Kings –

Ramparts of slaughter and peril –
   Blazing, amazing, aglow –
'Twixt the sky-line's belting beryl
   And the wine-dark flats below.

Royal the pageant closes,
   Lit by the last of the sun –
Opal and ash-of-roses,
   Cinnamon, umber, and dun.

The twilight swallows the thicket,
   The starlight reveals the ridge.
The whistle shrills to the picket –
   We are changing guard on the bridge.

(Few, forgotten and lonely,
   Where the empty metals shine –
No, not combatants – only
   Details guarding the line.)

We slip through the broken panel
   Of fence by the ganger's shed;
We drop to the waterless channel
   And the lean track overhead;

We stumble on refuse of rations,
   The beef and the biscuit-tins;
We take our appointed stations,
   And the endless night begins.

We hear the Hottentot herders
   As the sheep click past to the fold –
And the click of the restless girders
   As the steel contracts in the cold –

Voices of jackals calling
   And, loud in the hush between,
A morsel of dry earth falling
   From the flanks of the scarred ravine.

And the solemn firmament marches,
   And the hosts of heaven rise
Framed through the iron arches –
   Banded and barred by the ties,

Till we feel the far track humming,
   And we see her headlight plain,
And we gather and wait her coming –
   The wonderful north-bound train.

(Few, forgotten and lonely,
   Where the white car-windows shine –
No, not combatants – only

Details guarding the line.)

Quick, ere the gift escape us!
   Out of the darkness we reach
For a handful of week-old papers
   And a mouthful of human speech.

And the monstrous heaven rejoices,
   And the earth allows again,
Meetings, greetings, and voices
   Of women talking with men.

So we return to our places,
   As out on the bridge she rolls;
And the darkness covers our faces,
   And the darkness re-enters our souls.

More than a little lonely
   Where the lessening tail-lights shine.
No, not combatants – only
   Details guarding the line!

Source:
Rudyard Kipling: *The Five Nations.* London: Methuen: 1904.

Gods of the Jingo

F.W. Reitz
(In reaction to Kipling's poem "Recessional".)

A "progressional" dedicated to "Mudyard Pipling".

Gods of the Jingo – Brass and Gold,
   Lords of the world by "right divine"
Beneath whose baneful sway they hold
   The motto "All that's thine is Mine",
Such Lords as these have made men rotten
   They have forgotten – they *have* forgotten.

The nigger, as is fitting, dies
   The Gladstones and the Pitts depart
But "Bigger Englanders" arise
   To teach the world the Raiders' art
Such Lords as these have made men rotten
   They have forgotten – they *have* forgotten.

They've got the gold, the ships, the men,
   And are the masters of tomorrow —
And so mankind shall see again
   The days of Sodom and Gomorrah,
These are their Lords, and they are rotten
   They have forgotten – they *have* forgotten.

Drunken with lust of power and pelf
   They hold nor man nor God in awe
And care for nought but only Self

   And cent-per-cent's their only law
These are their Lords, and they are rotten
   They have forgotten – they *have* forgotten.

Their braggart hearts have put their trust
   In Maxim guns and Metford rifles
They'd crush their foes into the dust
   And treat what's Right as idle trifles.
For boastful brag and foolish "fake"
   Th' "Imperialist" must take the cake!
                             Amen?

Source:
F.W. Reitz: *Oorlogs en andere gedichten*. Potchefstroom: Het Westen Drukkerij: 1910.

Outnumbered

Gustav Preller

The grass was high and heavy with seed on the Highveld so that the hills looked plump and rounded when it was dry, like sheep just before shearing.

But it was raining, a steady widespread rain over the Highveld, for weeks and the dense *steekgras* bent over into bushy shapes, so that the sheen on the stalks looked yellower than usual, when in the hollows there were deep purple and saffron splashes painted on the flowering clumps of seed.

On the Highveld there was a stifling silence.

From Vaalkop the world lay wide and endless in all directions – one rolling sea of hills which sank down from the heights, creating the impression that in prehistoric times the billows could have been that of a mighty ocean when it became earth, rolling waves and all.

But except for the ripening grass and the yellow flowers in the hollows on tall bright green stems which bent fluidly from side to side, there was no life on the Highveld. The blessing of creation was gone and with it the wild animals and the cattle of the earth, according to their species. Because the perfect creation, made in God's image, was waging war there!

To the naked eye the world was void and still from an intense desolation.

On top of Vaalkop lay the recent remains of an English camp, a wide circle of small turf forts and inside it, the bare, trampled, messy camp which showed where tents had stood, wagon tracks and the fodder streaks of horses. At sunrise, when the hill was suddenly visible dipping down to the hollow, the beaten tracks could be seen against the hill, eight wagon paths next to one another, parallel, and leaving deep ruts in the soaked earth except where an antbear hole or an ant hill was in the way and broke the broad curve with other ones.

The track was fresh, the soft drizzle had barely formed pools in the wagon tracks which lay deeply embedded in the heavily drenched earth.

Far below, at sunset, a single horseman came riding cautiously over the hills, then up the gentle slope of the hill. The grass was so high and thickly overgrown that it almost seemed as if he was walking but then the head of his horse reappeared.

He rode at a careful trot. On the first hill, he reined in and looked around in all directions. There he went to the highest point again at an uneasy dogtrot, looking around regularly until he was high enough to see the fresh tracks on the other side. He rode higher so that he could see down into the hollow and after he had gazed at the area for a while, he dismounted, loosened the girth and lifted the saddle away from the steaming back of the horse. Then he tightened the girth again, hooked the reins over his arm and sat down on one of the turf walls to look at the countryside through his binoculars.

He started there where the tracks of the camp wound over the nearest hill and slowly scanned the entire horizon, moving the binoculars from left to right and back again, checking every hill and hollow through the lenses.

He was still busy with the binoculars when another horseman appeared from the back of the hill. When he arrived on the summit and saw the other spy, he made a detour to the camp, dismounted and collected some things here and there – a few English newspapers, a few bits of wood and a small log. The tattered newspapers he folded carefully and tucked them into a pocket and balanced the log on the pommel before riding up to the other man.

"There's no point in bringing wood, Piet," said the other with a smile both friendly and rueful – "or you must be prepared to take it with you across the railway line tonight."

"What do think, Field-Cornet?" asked the other as he threw the log down in front of the horse and dismounted rather stiffly. "Won't the Rooineks allow us to make a small fire?"

"No, not here," came the reply. "They're all around us and it seems to me the plan is to come and catch some of us tonight."

"They shouldn't be so irresponsible. One can't only live off green peaches for four days!"

The first man who was addressed as Field-Cornet, was still busy examining a few points through his binoculars especially a high hill right ahead and replied somewhat absently while he wiped a few drops of rain from the glasses.

"And nothing more than that, Double-barrel! Because it seems to me that we can only do one of two things: if the others see their way clear to spending another two days in this kraal, we must attack the English; or we must get past the blockhouse tonight and across the railway line."

"Attack? When they're everywhere?"

"Yes," the Field-Cornet replied, "and just the two of us, Piet! I have a plan; we can do it alone and the rest can simply follow, taking prisoners and loot."

Piet didn't reply. He unslung the short little Mauser, pushed in the rainplug more tightly and waited for the unfolding of the plan. He was a small, pale little man with a natural goatee and a pair of piercing bright eyes, set so closely on either side of his nose that it had given him the nickname of "Double-barrel". Over his clothes he wore a brand-new raincoat with English military buttons and his hat was one with a stiff brim and a leather band around the crown which had three dents, Rhodesian style.

The Field-Cornet was also fairly small but with a stronger build and also slightly taller. He couldn't have been older than twenty-eight with friendly but sharply-drawn features which were enhanced by a pair of lively eyes. He wore a full beard and also wore a raincoat but his wasn't as good as the other one's; his sweat-stained old greyish felt hat was turned up on one side and pinned with the Republican badge.

While they were talking he took out a tobacco pouch and offered it to the other with the remark that "it's leaves mixed with tamarind".

"I thought about a plan this morning, Piet, and I think we can carry it out on our own if the others' horses are only strong enough to keep up for half a day and to help in the rear. Look," and he put the binoculars into the other man's hands, "there are only two separate camps in the area and they're busy making the blockhouse kraals smaller with two lines laid across from Wilger River's line to the Olifants River. They're on their way to the Olifants River now – there's one, do you see on the curve of the nearest high hill? And there's the other, just this side against the third grey hill there . . ."

"The third grey hill," Piet repeated while he moved the binoculars back and forth across the hills. "O, there it is and a blasted large camp it is too! They're on the move now."

"Exactly," said the Field-Cornet, "the third camp left here this morning and is apparently moving in the direction of Ermelo although they're aware of our small group, of course, and might send a cavalry commando back here tonight. But if they can't find us, they'll certainly be on their way. My plan is that tonight when it's fully dark, we must pass them and tomorrow we must lie in one of the hollows as closely as possible to that blockhouse camp. It's not far from the place where you and I blew up a train last week. Tonight you and I are going as far as the railway line and fetching one of the armour plates of the dynamited train. Tomorrow we'll find a way of fixing it to the old spider we saw on Doppies's farm and the day after tomorrow you and I attack the Wilger River blockhouses one after another with a case of dynamite behind the armour plate! What do you think? The other . . ."

It was a movement from Piet with the binoculars which caused the Field-Cornet to be silent. He had taken the binoculars from his eyes and gazed fixedly in the direction of the tracks of the new camp.

"A Kaffir spy," he decided eventually.

"Oh, well," said the Field-Cornet, "that suits us; they'll be back here by daybreak tomorrow and we know what to do. But what do you think of my plan? Do you see, the rest of our group simply follow us, down the line, to capture the soldiers in the forts and disarm them?"

"No," Piet said as he considered the plan, "the only problem it seems to me is the armour plate, if we can still get it . . . If we can get close enough, one milk tin will be enough for a blockhouse. The old Rooineks will complain about the dynamite but what do they expect us to do if they obstruct us from importing less violent weapons?"

"And then trap us in a kraal as well!"

Both men smiled at the lively picture they were drawing: down the line one after the other until they had enough of it or were stopped! Even so their was no gaiety or lightheartedness in the laughter; it was rather the laughter of men who had no other option, who were desperate, who felt things closing in on them and looked for air to breathe on the wide Highveld.

"If only we had one old French Creusot here, with enough ammunition, I see my way clear to do the same thing just using the cannon. But the English know full well we can't shoot with cannon any longer; that's why they're fencing us off in this way, like blesbuck, and making the world far too small for a man, simply because there are so many of them."

The Field-Cornet would remain there to spy while Piet had to go to the farm beyond the hill to halt the little commando of no more than twenty men and make them rest until nightfall.

And when dusk fell and the horses had been caught and saddled again, the Field-Cornet also came back and they all moved slowly up the hollow in the direction of the railway line. By ten o' clock they could unsaddle and catch some sleep in a dip a few miles from the blockhouse camp. After the Field-Cornet and Piet had also allowed their horses to rest for a while, the two were on their way again, around the camp, to the railway line. There was a slight glow in the east when the two reappeared in the small laager with a heavy steel plate on a yoke which they were dragging on ox-riem behind the horses across the wet grass.

The entire little commando was saddled up, each man next to his horse. In the dusk of the early morning they were hardly distinguishable from the dull black spot which was the ruin of an old farmhouse on the hill opposite. A fine drizzle made the figures even more difficult to distinguish than the early dusk allowed. Some still sat in the warm spot where they had slept, a ragged blanket over their shoulders, heavy with rain. The horses were standing motionless, half-asleep, their heads down, feet together, ears drooping. Virtually no one spoke.

As it became lighter towards daybreak, a single horserider could be seen clearly against the hill, descending, and then taking to the veld.

The arrival of the Field-Cornet and Piet with their armour plate resulted in a general movement in the small commando in the hollow. One after another the horses sleepily lifted their heads and pricked their ears when one of the approaching horses neighed softly. Among the men there was a mumble of recognition and when the two came nearer, there was an inquisitiveness about the object which they were dragging. Most of them got up, stretched their tired and stiff limbs and made abortive efforts to ignite a tinderbox to light a little ash in the bowl of a pipe.

"Men," said the Field-Cornet, when he had dismounted, cheerful and without a sign of exhaustion, "this afternoon we're going to have a good meal for a change at the expense of the Tommies."

"And loot a suit and a new raincoat for each one of us!" Piet added, slowly dismounting, hanging in a stirrup for a moment before landing on the grass with a satisfied "Aa!"

Now the Field-Cornet explained his plan to the boys. Most of them were young men with the exception of two or three older burghers, only one of whom had a long grey beard. At the old farm across the stream, was the old spider undercarriage and there was also a mound of charcoal from burnt-out wagons. They would, if the enemy allowed, immediately devise a bellows, make a fire and bend the armour plate on either side before fixing it to the spider's undercarriage.

By now it was daylight and the spy came back with the information that there wasn't an enemy in sight except at the blockhouse behind them.

An hour later, while Piet and the Field-Cornet were sleeping to recover from the previous night's arduous ride, everything was in full swing under the peach trees on the opposite side to execute the plan for the armoured cart. One of the men was working with an iron pipe, a few planks and other objects to devise some type of bellows with which to increase the heat of the charcoal already burning on the plate, so that the latter could bend more readily.

Hobbled, the horses were grazing peacefully in the hollow at the stream. As long as the bellows weren't ready, the fire on the plate was kept burning with the aid of various hands; a kettle could be boiled for mealie coffee or a piece of biltong roasted.

Despite the slow drizzle which kept falling although there were short moments of bright sunshine, a happy mood prevailed among the small group. One read aloud from the English newspapers which Piet had brought with him, reports of brilliant victories in which they themselves had taken part and which were no more than skirmishes between patrols. They laughed and joked loudly at that until he read about the women's camps and the deaths.

Some had made a shelter from corrugated iron sheets and sat in there almost totally naked, to check their gear and where possible to repair it. Most stood around the big fire wearing their coats, or a blanket or a piece of canvas or an old carpet over their shoulders, happily talking, especially about the Field-Cornet's plan with the armoured cart and the dynamite bombs. Jokes did the rounds, causing hearty laughter. Sometimes crude, like those from men who had spent more than a year in the saddle; they spoke of the desire for new Bedford cord riding breeches, coats and blankets, real coffee and sugar with the possible chance of bread or army biscuits. Or the conversation turned to their last encounter with the English and the derailing of a train in which one of the slowest of the small commando was captured because he wanted to loot too much. Often they spoke about the terrible plague of lice which in the past few months had made everyone's life difficult and the feeling of shame, the desperate attempts at cleanliness until they discovered that even the General was given no peace!

"Look at Koos, under the corrugated iron!"

A general laugh at Koos's expense, then the tormenter addressed Koos directly.

"I told you, brother, to leave the English rags alone, now you see the result!"

The commando's teasing and joking carried on until the food – one single piece of biltong, with mealiepap, black mealie coffee and yellow peaches for dessert – was eaten, and when the bellows had also assumed a usable appearance. And after the meagre breakfast, the armour plate got their undivided attention again. The plate had to be bent at both sides so that it could be mounted with long bolts on the front axle of the undercarriage thereby protecting the men behind it from a Lee-Metford bullet. All the available charcoal was gathered together and with huge exertion the plate was heated to such an extent that it was possible to bend it. The place where it had to be bent, lay ready between two rows of stones. Then the coals were removed and a heavy iron stave was placed on the white-hot plate, its length along the line on which the stave rested and the uppermost points of the iron inserted into a piece of wood, parallel to the bottom part of the stave. The plate was held down on both sides with heavy stones and using a log of wood, the upper part was hit as hard as possible. The first blow seemed to make no impression at all but after the strongest man had brought the log down on the upper piece of wood with all possible strength, the stones on either side slid slightly to the inside and after the third blow they could lay the plate on one of its sides and using the log, could bend it to the required shape with no further heating.

Then the other side of the plate, using the same technique but with much greater difficulty because a few iron bands had been laid across it, the bellows no longer worked and the charcoal was finished.

Two long bolts had to hold the plate in position with double screws in the front and the back of the undercarriage. But before that could happen holes had to be drilled through the plate.

With this aim the plate was placed on stones over the fire again and a fire made on top of it, the bellows mended somehow or another and a sharp-pointed stone found to knock the holes into the plate. All this while Piet roasted mealies and a piece of beef on the plate – when a few of the men crouched low and ran hurriedly to the horses without making any noise or uttering cries of alarm.

"The English are here!" cried one of the men busy at the fire, dismayed and afraid of being captured but certainly more annoyed than alarmed. He and the others grabbed their saddles and bridles.

"Slowly, men," the Field-Cornet ordered, short and to the point, "don't scare the horses! Piet, you and Koos must remain here."

Within twenty seconds they were all on their way to the horses except the Field-Cornet and the other two. They jumped behind the garden wall and prepared to shoot.

"Wait until they've collected the horses," the leader ordered his men who had already taken up their positions and were ready to have some fun.

The English who realised how exhausted the horses of most of the commandoes were by that time, started shooting from afar to get them to scatter. The first two men were already there, however, and started catching horses while the others arrived soon after.

The enemy had appeared above the old camp on the curve of the hill, a few hundred men strong and raced around one side intending to cut off the horses.

Then the three behind the garden wall started shooting, aiming at the leaders. Two horses fell and the one that was behind them fell over the others. This checked the pace for a moment and most of the soldiers dismounted to shoot. The three decided to aim at the men who were still mounted: if they dismounted the curve of the hill was enough to offer protection to the others who were now coming up from the hollow in a hurry.

Within a minute an incessant rain of Metford bullets whizzed across the garden wall but most of them just a fraction too high and as the other Boers were halfway up the hill with the horses, it was just as well. So incessantly and quickly did the English shoot, that the first sound of the double "koe-ka" crack of the Metford disappeared in the one following, and became one continual sound. The occasional thump! of the Mausers could be heard above the general din. The English had overestimated the brisk resistance and all had dismounted.

In the worst of the uneven duel the first men arrived, hastily saddling their horses and racing down the hill to the hollow. The horses of the three behind the garden wall were saddled by a few friends and when it was done the last one sank almost unnoticed down into the hollow while the others, two thousand yards lower down were already climbing the opposite hill.

There was no pursuit. With a few sighting shots over the Metford bead, the English let them go, in the direction of Vaalkop again.

When they moved over the hill, Piet and the Field-Cornet got together.

"Now we can bring the dynamite and a few milk tins with us tonight, Piet," he remarked laughing.

"They saw the fire of our smithy," said Piet laconically.

At about ten o' clock that same evening, four men rode back across the hill, where they had disappeared from the sight of the English, in the direction of the farmyard.

The rain which had ceased for a while that afternoon, was falling softly again and made the moonless night darker than it would otherwise have been. Occasionally thunder rolled in the distance and lightning flashed behind the hills, a rayless ball of light. Then the figures of the four men were brightly lit for one blinding moment. Piet ahead, then another, at the back another two men next to one another, eyes fixed to the front, on the opposite hill to see if anything untoward was happening. Their hats had sunk deep over their eyes, heavy with rain and their clothes gleamed with dampness. The horses instinctively evaded ant hills and antbear holes and moved at a slow canter, heads low.

No one said a word. If a horse wanted to snort, it was instantly cut off with the heel of a shoe in its ribs.

When they were below the old camp in the hollow, where the horses had grazed the previous day, Piet reined in, looked around and dismounted. The others arrived and did the same. They unfastened a few halter reins and three of them walked warily up the hill to the ruin while one remained with the horses.

It could be that the English had left a sentry on duty. They crept carefully up to the old farmyard and the trees, step by step, and made good use of the flashes of lightning to establish whether there was anything unusual to be seen. If there were any English there would be no chance of a fight but each one automatically held his rifle at the ready.

A halt was called at the bottom garden wall to make a thorough reconaissance from a spot among the trees from where they couldn't be seen. The gable of the burnt-out old house frowned threateningly at them above the horizon, every time there was lightning in the background. The shadows of the ruin and the trees were sharply etched against the grey grass on the other side so that an object there could be seen in the dark because sometimes in a pitch-black moment it seemed as if there were a translucence in the air which makes some objects clearer than others. The barn was straight ahead with a few oak trees in front of it and to their right was the kraal wall.

After they had studied the position carefully and seen nothing suspicious, they advanced to the place where the spider's undercarriage and the armour plate had to be. The first – with only the two front wheels and the axle – still stood there but the plate had gone.

"Well," Piet said morosely, "it can't be too far but they must've seen from the shininess on one side that we'd fetched it from far away and planned something with it. They've probably hidden it somewhere."

The three men waited for another flash of lightning to catch sight of where the fire had been made and eventually they could see the tracks of the plate on the ground. And when they saw that it went in the direction of the little dam, and nearer to the horses, they decided to take the undercarriage with them. Koos and another who would move it, walked to the barn with this in mind when Koos suddenly gave a terrible yell in the sombre graveyard loneliness of the deserted yard and the stormy night.

"Hey! you Khakies," he shouted, "hands up!"

And in the next lightning flash he was aiming his rifle on the barn wall, one leg still ahead of the other in walking stance, his body bent over, ready to shoot. The other two brought up their Mausers and did their best to see in the darkness.

It took a second or two without Koos shooting or any reaction from the other side. The next moment the explanation came from Koos himself but in a hoarse whisper:

"No! They're dead!"

In the dark of the barn wall lay three objects which at a distance, looked like sleeping men: two on their backs, close to one another, the other sitting against the wall, his head on his chest, the hands lying uselessly on the ground.

"Hm," said Piet when he had arrived, "our skirmish here wasn't totally useless!"

"We've got to move," said another, "the one who's sitting there wasn't dead when they left and they'll fetch him shortly."

"We can't take their stuff, poor beggars, but this man won't need that tobacco pouch that's lying over there and we still have a use for it."

Piet picked it up and was just about to turn and leave when he suddenly put his hand to his ear in a listening position.

"Shh! Be quiet, men, I can hear something moving!"

They listened for a while to ascertain from which direction the sound was coming but it wasn't until one lay with his ear to the ground that they could establish that a cart or a wagon was approaching from the camp. Because it was in all probability an ambulance, with an advance patrol, they decided to return immediately.

They dragged the undercarriage carefully down the hill to the dam and could establish where the armour plate had been thrown in by following the tracks. One man had to take off his shoes and roll up his trousers and after searching for quite a while, and the ambulance wagon could be heard quite clearly, they found the plate, dragged it out and took it downhill with the undercarriage. There a length of rawhide was tied around every piece and at the end of it a wooden yoke so that two horsemen would be able to drag it, each holding a rawhide strip.

The wheels were so light that they made no noise in the wet grass and the plate glided soundlessly behind the last two men.

When they rode up the hill on the other side, they could see the hostile ambulance opposite, with lights and lanterns, on the curve of the hill where the English had been that morning, searching for their dead.

When daylight came they were back with the plate and the undercarriage in the hollow to the right of Vaalkop where the little commando would spend the day and after they had assured themselves that there were no English in the immediate area and that the ambulance had also returned, they unsaddled under the trees of a ruined old farmyard to further prepare for the Field-Cornet's plan.

At least two more holes had to be drilled through the plate for the bolts which had to be fixed to the undercarriage. The only tool they had was a steel punch which they had picked up somewhere and the plate had to be re-heated and softened. Before that could happen they had to dig up a nearby layer of coal, the seam of which showed in the banks of the stream and had already been partly uncovered by the owner. So it wasn't until late that afternoon that they could continue the forging. The smoke had probably betrayed them the previous day but there was nothing they could do about it. They had to work as quickly as possible and then push off to another hollow for the following day. And as there were no bellows to help them now, the heating of the plate was very difficult and an undertaking that tried their patience to the utmost. It took hours before the plate began losing its natural colour in the coal fire; after a while it was red-hot and eventually there was a white-hot line between the two rows of stones on which the plate rested and below where the men continually blew and stoked.

Only then could the punch come into play. They had found a sledgehammer in a razed barn, which was again provided with a handle and with this they attempted to pierce a few holes in the plate, large enough to take the bolts. The plate remained lying on the fire, the stones underneath and the coal fire removed from the top only.

It was a job which cost far more effort and endurance than the bending of the plate. Every time the plate had to be covered with coals again and the work halted to reheat it but eventually both holes were large enough to take the bolts when the plate had cooled again. On the axle of the undercarriage two strong staples were attached, the bolts bent to fit into them and the height could be established by judging the distance between axle and ground. And when it was nearly time to change their quarters for the night, the armour plate had been firmly fixed to the undercarriage.

At their stop the following day, they put some sort of chest on the axle for "bombs" of which a few dozen had already been prepared. The preparation was very simple. In an empty milk or jam tin one or more pieces of dynamite were placed and tamped down with earth while the percussion cap with a length of fuse was stuck into the dynamite before the lid was tightly replaced.

Now everything was ready for the attack, the plate was tested at various distances with Metford bullets and after Piet and the Field-Cornet had thoroughly examined the region along the Wilger River's blockhouse line, at dusk the whole commando moved in the direction of the blockhouses.

The plan was to start at daybreak with one of the little forts which stood in a hollow and wouldn't be in a position to get assistance from the two others on either side. Then the twenty men would divide into two sections, one moving behind the armoured cart to help with the apprehension and capture of the soldiers while the other section had to serve as a rearguard in case of an attack from the blockhouses at the back.

That day they weren't far from the blockhouses because on both sides the lines were only a few hours apart on horseback. And before midnight they could call a halt and have a little sleep. At three o' clock they were on the move again. Piet and the Field-Cornet in the lead with the little cart, dragging it as close to the blockhouse as possible without attracting the attention of the sentry but near enough to the fort to reach it with a thrown object – a bombthrow as Piet described it. Then the little cart was softly turned around so that the armour plate faced the fort and everything was brought into readiness. The other men covered the two at the cart. The horses remained behind the nearest hill. Everything was now waiting for daybreak.

The two behind the plate would be in full sight of the fort and the terrain was such that if they didn't succeed in overpowering the fort, they wouldn't get away before the following evening.

Both sat flat on the ground behind the armour plate waiting for the first morning light. The incredible tension of such a wait affected the most hardened nerves but neither of the two uttered a word. Occasionally one turned slightly to see whether there was any sign of dawn. Or they stared fixedly ahead across the armour plate into the darkness where the faint outlines of a corrugated iron fort stood against the horizon.

The roof – this they could make out – was a high-pitched one which could cause problems with the bombs. Because if one wasn't thrown at a precise moment, it could roll down the roof and explode on the ground without the desired effect. Or the fuse could be extinguished by the water on the ground. And if the garrison wasn't overwhelmed quickly, their shots would bring the soldiers in the other forts down on them. Apart from that, a telegraph wire ran past the blockhouse which wasn't the case with all the lines. The one at Wilger River had to be a main line and there was no chance at all that some of the blockhouses were merely blinds with an imitation soldier as sentry as they had sometimes seen elsewhere. They heard a horse snorting and asked themselves whether there was perhaps an entire cavalry commando in the area which they hadn't spotted! The telegraph wire was unimportant; it could be cut as soon as the fort was occupied and then Koos – a field telegraphist of the old Artillery – could send misleading telegrams to either side: that a group of Boers had been captured and that they were being sent the other way. But should there be, besides the garrison, a separate commando somewhere in the immediate area, things were not going to be easy for the two behind the armour plate!

The darkness of the night and the slow drizzle multiplied these thoughts. For a while the meditation dealt with the immediate danger without the prospect of alternative plans or escape, so great seemed the odds stacked against them. Then it flashed to the effect of the dynamite and an image of winning and success appeared. In between there were the sad figures of women clad in black, and wasting away in concentration camps; of girls whose hands they had squeezed two years ago and had promised to do their duty towards the fatherland. Image upon image changed like a kaleidoscope of a childhood long gone; one by one of a happy youth in school and the small worries of carefree schooldays: was it three or four hundred lines Piet had to write out on his own and various other borrowed slates because he had played a forbidden joke on someone or another? And who was it? The same day that he had played truant . . .

The Field-Cornet dug him in the ribs to indicate that it was only just starting to dawn in the east and Piet was suddenly aware again of the soaked earth, the soft rain and dynamite bombs right next to him, on the axle of the undercarriage.

A few more minutes passed, day was breaking and one could recognise things quite far off. He wanted to peer through the grass to check whether there was no life in the blockhouse when the English sentry caught sight of the strange object so near them against the hill, and demanded surrender.

The reply to his call was a firm order from the Field-Cornet to surrender immediately! Swearing, the sentry jumped behind the retaining wall and disappeared inside to wake the garrison.

Then the Field-Cornet spoke once more. They were so close that he didn't even have to raise his voice. He warned them in English that he would let a dynamite bomb explode on their roof within twenty seconds if they didn't surrender immediately and that he had a whole commando surrounding them.

The reply was a challenging shout, and simultaneously, a couple of rifle shots, the bullets striking the armour plate with an intimate "zip-zip" sound. Then the Field-Cornet struck a match and lit one of the fuses. He balanced the milk tin in his right hand for a few terrible moments until the fuse had virtually burnt down to the tin.

Then with a forceful swing of his arm, he threw it onto the roof of the blockhouse.

Without waiting for the result, he lit a second fuse because the rifle fire was increasing and soon one wouldn't be able to lift your hand above the armour plate to throw, without having it shot off! They were also shooting underneath the armour plate into the ground which had an extremely unpleasant effect. To tell the truth, the armoured cart was drawn just a little too closely to the blockhouse and if it went on like this, they would pierce the armour plate especially if they had steel-pointed bullets! And then . . . on the dynamite bombs!

Before he threw the second milk tin, the result of the first could be seen in a tremendous explosion, like a lyddite bomb on rocky terrain. Even the little cart shook. But he could lose no time because the fuse in his hand had burnt down virtually to the tin. Using a brief moment when the rifle fire had abated, he threw the tin straight ahead but with so much power that within seconds it jumped into the air just beyond the blockhouse with a bang which made one's ears sing and echoed far and wide in the dusky hollows.

One single shot sounded in the blockhouse when they heard an order to halt the fire and a moment later someone called that the garrison was surrendering.

Then it was time for the others to approach so that the Field-Cornet could accept the surrender and the laying-down of weapons, without fear of being overwhelmed.

About six of the boys heard his whistle and rushed a little closer, while he peered speedily around the armour plate to assess the effect of the first bomb. It was only for a second because he didn't know if there were still twenty Lee-Metfords positioned in the double row of loopholes but it was long enough to convince him that the enemy couldn't have borne it any longer. One entire side of the blockhouse had been torn away as if one wanted to knock out a huge door from the inside and since it was on the side of the attack, the garrison was completely exposed.

The Field-Cornet ordered the enemy to come out and lay down their weapons. It took a few seconds until the noncommissioned officer appeared in the opening, followed by three others. They threw down their rifles and were ordered to remove themselves in the direction of the other burghers who were now jumping up and approaching.

There were no more; they were eight altogether but two didn't belong to the garrison, they were there to repair the telegraph wires and three of the troops had been killed by the explosion.

Without waiting for a moment, except to give the necessary orders to his corporals to cut the telegraph wires, send the telegrams and to examine the fort, Piet and his Field-Cornet moved on.

In the light of early morning they followed the telegraph wires but knew that the other fort wouldn't be such an easy target. To begin with they dragged the little cart with the armour plate behind them but when they had advanced a few thousand yards, and the shape of the next fort was clearly visible, they turned the cart with the plate to the fore and pushed it ahead of them as fast as the roughness of the terrain would allow. They had to be so close that they could reach the fort in one throw and the garrison would perhaps start shooting while they were still too far away with the result that a bullet might put one of them out of action. To their surprise the garrison allowed them to come quite close, so close that they didn't want to go any nearer and only then was the demand for surrender given.

The Field-cornet cautioned the soldiers in the same manner as at the previous fort and with the same result. He had scarcely finished speaking when the Metford bullets rained against the armour plate. The ground here was stony and so the shots into the ground were more dangerous than at the previous fort. While he was speaking Piet had already lit the fuse and he had to throw it before the enemy had completed their second round.

And the result was even faster than at the first fort. They were about to light the second tin when the officer loudly announced their intention to surrender because the first bomb had exploded against the wall and destroyed the whole business with an ear-splitting noise. The other men were in the area by then and nine soldiers and a corporal surrendered.

It was now broad daylight. The men in the rear arrived with the horses and the prisoners of war. Without hesitation the little armed cart pushed forward to the next blockhouse. To reach it, they had to traverse a fairly high hill and just as they reached the curve, the enemy attacked from a completely unexpected quarter with heavy artillery fire.

It appeared that there was a large loose-standing fort with an encampment to the right of the blockhouse line in a curve of the river which they hadn't known about. The river lay so deeply embedded here that no one could guess what could be found below the high banks.

The first few cannon shots were much too high and if that was all it wouldn't have mattered very much. But while the two hesitated for a moment with their little armoured car to assess the position, they saw the English advancing with a large cavalry commando.

There was nothing to be done. For the umpteenth time they were outnumbered.

Still, they wouldn't allow themselves to be caught. The two swung round, ran down the incline to the others with the horses, the loot and the prisoners-of-war. Here the cart was hooked onto two horses, the way in which they had dragged the plate along before. That same night, after hiding the cart, they went across the railway line in constant rain and wet.

Source:
Gustav Preller: *Oorlogsoormag en ander sketse en verhale.* Cape Town: Nasionale Pers: 1923.
Translated by Madeleine van Biljon

I Killed a Man at Graspan

M. Grover

(The tale of a returned Australian Contingenter done into verse)

I killed a man at Graspan,
   I killed him fair in a fight;
And the Empire's poets and the Empire's priests
   Swear blind I acted right.
The Empire's poets and Empire's priests
   Make out my deed was fine,
But they can't stop the eyes of the man I killed
   From starin' into mine.

I killed a man at Graspan,
   Maybe I killed a score;
But this one wasn't a chance-shot home,
   From a thousand yards or more.
I fired at him when he'd got no show;
   We were only a pace apart,
With the cordite scorchin' his old worn coat
   As the bullet drilled his heart.

I killed a man at Graspan,
   I killed him fightin' fair;
We came on each other face to face,
   An' we went at it then and there.
Mine was the trigger that shifted first,
   His was the life that sped.
An' a man I'd never a quarrel with
   Was spread on the boulders dead.

I killed a man at Graspan;
   I watched him squirmin' till
He raised his eyes, an' they met with mine;
   An' there they're starin' still.
Cut of my brother Tom, he looked,
   Hardly more 'n a kid;
An', Christ! He was stiffenin' at my feet
   Because of the thing I did.

I killed a man at Graspan;
   I told the camp that night;
An' of all the lies that ever I told
   That was the poorest skite.
I swore I was proud of my hand-to-hand,
   An' the Boer I'd chanced to pot,
An' all the time I'd ha' gave my eyes
   To never ha' fired that shot.

I killed a man at Graspan;
   An hour ago about,
For there he lies with his starin' eyes,
   An' his blood still tricklin' out.
I know it was either him or me,
   I know that I killed him fair,
But, all the same, wherever I look,
   The man that I killed is there.

I killed a man at Graspan;
   My first and, God! my last;
Harder to dodge than my bullet is
   The look that his dead eyes cast.
If the Empire asks for me later on
   It'll ask for me in vain,

Before I reach to my bandolier
 To fire on a man again.

Source:
Michael Chapman (ed): *A Century of South African Poetry.* Johannesburg: Ad. Donker: 1981.

Drummer Hodge

Thomas Hardy

They throw in Drummer Hodge, to rest
   Uncoffined – just as found:
His landmark is a kopje-crest
   That breaks the veldt around;
And foreign constellations west
   Each night above his mound.

Young Hodge the Drummer never knew –
   Fresh from his Wessex home –
The meaning of the broad Karoo,
   The Bush, the dusty loam,
And why uprose to nightly view
   Strange stars amid the gloam.

Yet portion of that unknown plain
   Will Hodge for ever be;
His homely Northern breast and brain
   Grow up a Southern tree,
And strange-eyed constellations reign
   His stars eternally.

Source:
Thomas Hardy: *Poems of the Past and the Present.* London: Macmillan: 1901.

The Camp Sister

Jan F.E. Celliers

Sister Anna, I feel death calling:
fold the tent flap open, outwards please
so my eyes can freely roam the hills –
Sister Anna, I hear a church bell tolling.

That I alone should be the one to stay;
I hear my children calling me.
Dear Sister, you who were so good to us,
Take my hand in yours, I pray –

Where the Tugela flows, my husband lies,
no-one knows where he slumbers in his grave;
Oh Sister, and now God will take me too,
Only Pieter stays behind, while Mother dies.

I know he stands there, rifle in his hand –
grant it please that God protect him too,
I beg you Sister, say his mother greets him,
faithful unto death, his people and his land;

And say that even on the brink of death
you felt no fear nor trembling in her hand;
knowing her Pieter would never
abandon his God, his land, his troth.

My children, Breggie and Japie and Faan,
you saw them, Sister, leaving one by one;
you say there's still a place for me,

waiting next to Fanie, my littlest one.

Our old farmhouse, that once stood there
– everyone gathered at Mother's knee –
is just a ruin now, bare and scorched.
They all are scattered far, yet in God's care

Across the fields the evening comes rolling;
But, Sister, I still see blue sky above –
Thunder sounds from beyond the hills –
Sister Anna, I hear a church bell tolling . . .

Source:
Jan F.E. Celliers: *Die vlakte en ander gedigte.* Pretoria: Volkstem: 1908.
Translated by Herman Fourie

Forgive and Forget

Totius (J.D. du Toit)

"... lest thou forget the things that thine eyes have seen ..." Deut. 4: 9

Hard by a country road
a tiny thorn tree grew,
where teams of plodding oxen
their heavy wagons drew.

One wagon with big, heavy wheels
Was passing by one day
And right across that little tree
It rolled while on its way.

"You pricked me, little shrub,
as I passed along that day;
which is why my wheels have crushed
your thorny crown this way."

And on the heavy wagon went,
cresting the next rise,
while the sapling slowly raised
its stem up to the skies.

Its beauty sorely marred,
its bark torn right to the wood,
its spindly stem half through
still the little thorn tree stood.

But time has passed and gently healed

that broken little tree:
its wounds were soothed by many tears
of balsam, flowing free.

The passing of so many years
has eased away its pain –
but one spot still shows a mark
that will never fade again.

Its wounds must surely heal
as years draw nigh and go,
but that one mark won't fade away –
time just makes it grow.

Source:
Totius: *By die monument.* Potchefstroom: Koopmans:1917.
Translated by Herman Fourie

The Boer War

William Plomer

The whip-crack of a Union Jack
In a stiff breeze (the ship will roll),
Deft abracadabra drums
Enchant the patriotic soul –

A grandsire in St James's Street
Sat at the window of his club,
His second son, shot through the throat,
Slid backwards down a slope of scrub,

Gargled his last breaths, one by one by one,
In too much blood, too young to spill,
Died difficultly, drop by drop by drop –
"By your son's courage, sir, we took the hill."

They took the hill (Whose hill? What for?)
But what a climb they left to do!
Out of that bungled, unwise war
An alp of unforgiveness grew.

Source:
William Plomer: *The Fivefold Screen*. London: The Hogarth Press: 1932.

Afrikander Cattle

Eugène N. Marais

This was the tenth day that Gool Winterbach had been cut off from his commando and now, on the tenth day, he was overpowered by a feeling of black depression which occasionally turned to despair. He had fully realised during every hour of the bitter ten days, that he was constantly in deadly danger but until now total despair had not been able to get a grip on his strong mind.

Gool Winterbach was the most famous scout in our northern commandoes during the last war. He was a Waterberger by birth and knew the northern Bushveld like the palm of his hand. He was a child of the veld in every sense of the word.

Apart from the exceptional knowledge and experience which his incidental surroundings had contributed to his mental growth, he had certain inborn gifts which, from his boyhood, had made him an outstanding scout. He could see and hear and smell like a wild animal and even more, he could instantly arrange the information gathered by his almost supernatural senses and act accordingly. In the north, nobody matched him as a scout. Anything strange in his natural surroundings – every small dust cloud, every sign of smoke, every broken twig – sent him a signal which his unusual brain could automatically convert into a message.

Almost as famous as Gool Winterbach was his horse, Kousband, who served him throughout the war. He had raised Kousband as a pet foal and had taught the horse an astonishing range of tricks which were of enormous advantage later, during his days as a scout. With a single whistle he could summon Kousband. At another signal, he could send him off in full flight, with or without a saddle and bridle. At his command the horse would lie down immediately, and no other command, except from his master, could make him move again. By tying a thong around one of his ears, he could forbid him to neigh as long as the knot remained in position. At his command he could let him force his way into overgrown guarri bush until he was completely invisible and there he would stay without moving or making a sound until his master called him.

For years Gool had been famous in the north as a horse trainer. And here, in the middle of the most deadly danger which threatened him from all sides, fate had willed it that he would meet another child of the veld whose familiarity with animals would make him unworthy to tie the velskoens on his feet – a man who could associate with animals as equals, who could speak their language and become part of their mental processes. He would meet one, the memories of whom would fill him with admiration until the end of his life. It was the admiration of one genius for the gifts of a greater one.

It is understandable why the dangerous work of scouting was assigned to Gool. Ten days ago he had been sent to investigate certain rumours which had reached the commando – rumours regarding a colossal concentration of enemy forces, a rumour to which the Boer officers attached little importance but that had to be checked out nonetheless. And for the first time in his scouting service, Gool found himself in a wasps' nest of enemy columns and scouting divisions. He saved his life at the last minute by riding Kousband to the verge of collapse to the great maze of the Banks. Here in the heart of deep, trackless ravines, overgrown bush and impenetrable stretches of black-thorn, he had found temporary safety.

Now, on the tenth day of his fatal scouting expedition, he left his horse in a bush and climbed to the top of the mountain, Uitkyk, on a route hidden by overhanging rocks. From there he had a view of the horizon on all sides and from there he could ascertain without the least doubt that he was surrounded in a way that made escape, with or without Kousband, an impossibility. That whole day he viewed the arrival of new columns which transformed the cordon around the Banks into an impenetrable wall of rifles.

He knew well enough that only death awaited him if he could find no opening in the cordon.

With a feeling of deep depression he saw the sun go down. The melancholy silence of the dusk of evening sank quickly over mountain and ravine and as far as he could see in the dark, the fires of the enemy cordon appeared, flickering all round the Banks. Immediately below him the mighty maze of the Banks stretched for miles and in three directions – a cloak of unyielding darkness.

This was the hour of the deepest silence in the Bushveld. Very soon, the inhabitants of the night would go about their business and from all sides he would hear the joy of the night birds, mixed with the rejoicing and crying of murderous lust and terror which the night always mercifully covered with its dark veil. It was at night when the carnivore left its hiding place to stalk its defenceless prey.

Despite his despair, his mind was devising a plan. Tonight would be his last chance. Tomorrow the enemy would invade the Banks in their hundreds and from all sides. He could see that they were preparing for that. His plan was to unsaddle Kousband and to let him go and he would try to creep up to a post of two sentries. If such a sentry post were to be found – and it was highly unlikely! – then he could stab one to death with his jack-knife and beat the other to death with his gunstock before either of them could make a noise! Shooting was obviously impossible. Then, if he succeeded, he would attempt to flee on foot. The chances were slender but that was all that was left. He would, in any case, fight to the last.

He knew precisely why the enemy had invaded the Banks. They had traitors as guides with them who had heard rumours that a great herd of cattle had for months been hiding in the ravines among the hook-thorn. He had also heard of the herd and during the past ten days had often crossed their tracks. But they were all old tracks and he was sure that the herdsmen had long since fled with them to the endless forests of the northern mountains.

If the herd were still in the Banks, he would have noticed them ages ago. He would have seen the dust rising above the trees and heard their lowing; and although he had listened constantly and carefully, he hadn't once heard the sound of a single ox in the Banks.

In all probability the traitorous guides had also found Kousband's fresh tracks. But whatever the reason for the movements, one thing was certain: they were planning to search the Banks with a fine-tooth comb on the morrow. They would find his tracks very soon and then the end was a question of a few hours.

Before it was completely dark, he climbed down again. A soft whistle brought Kousband cantering towards him. Here, underneath the huge candlewood trees and between overgrown bush, he had to find a pathway step by step and with the greatest effort, followed by his horse.

So suddenly had darkness fallen that within half-an-hour he could no longer see more than a few steps ahead of him. With arms outstretched he had to find a way between the vicious thorn bushes.

Occasionally he stopped to listen but everything was still quiet except for the sad "whoo-whoo" of a single owl already out hunting.

It was so dark that it was only his veld instinct that made it possible for him to keep on course up to the point where he had decided to force his way through the column using violence.

Sight was of very little use and he virtually had to feel his way with his bare hands until his feet convinced him that he was on more or less level ground.

And here he decided to leave Kousband until he could ascertain the precise conditions ahead of him. He first wanted to find out how the enemy was stationed. If it seemed preferable, he would unsaddle Kousband and leave him to find his own way. Otherwise he would try to gallop past the sentries and trust to luck.

All these thoughts passed swiftly through Gool's mind while he was carefully concealing Kousband in a dense guarri bush. He knew that the faithful animal would stay there until he gave him the signal to follow him.

He had made a definite decision that he would not be taken alive. It was difficult to accept that Gool Winterbach was scared that evening but that he was alert, that every muscle in his body was tensed, that his feelings were those of a brave man expecting death at any moment – that could not be disputed.

The biggest danger facing him was that in all probability there were traitorous scouts with the enemy. In that case it was also highly probable that the scouts had penetrated the undergrowth under cover of the dark – scouts who would light no fires, who had probably followed his tracks before dark and now awaited him at several places. In the surrounding darkness, he could expect a bullet at any moment and be killed before even catching a glimpse of his enemies.

He had barely walked ten yards after he had left Kousband behind, when all his suspicions, all his preparations became undone, caused by an event which struck him like lightning out of a clear blue sky.

He had walked very softly, both hands on the barrel and the breech of the rifle, the muzzle facing forward while with the eyes of a born son of the veld, he carefully checked each opening ahead or to the side of him. And suddenly, when perhaps his guard had dropped slightly, his right wrist was caught by an invisible hand coming out of a dark shadow! His first movement, of course, was to jerk away. Gool was known in the north for his gigantic strength but he realised immediately that he had been caught by something which would need the exertion of both hands to free himself. A momentary feeling that it was something supernatural, did more than mere fright to confound him and to weaken his resistance. But it didn't take him long to ready himself for counter-attack. His left hand was still loose and holding the barrel of his gun. Devil or human, he would not let himself be overpowered without doing anything. He had already lifted the stock of his rifle to demolish his invisible enemy, when a human voice in the dark calmed him as quickly as he had been frightened.

"Stand dead quiet, Master Gool – it's me, old Hendrik."

Gool had known the old Bushman well before the war, as herdsman of the Boshoff family. During the war, the northern commandoes had also regularly heard of him and occasionally shot slaughter stock from his herd. Slowly old Hendrik became famous and to this day the most wondrous tales are told about him and his herd of Afrikander cattle. Then, on his own, he had more than a thousand head of cattle under his care and although columns of thousands of enemy soldiers cut across the Bushveld and mountains in all directions, with the single purpose of stealing cattle from friend or foe and letting them "disappear without trace" not one of old Hendrik's cattle had ever fallen into enemy hands. His Afrikanders speedily became wild – so wild that no stranger could come near them. Only for old Hendrik were they tame, and not only tame, they had accepted him as their leader. He lived with them as if he were one of them. He taught them all kinds of wonderful tricks. Old Hendrik could whistle surprisingly well. He could imitate the voice of any animal or bird so accurately that no person could ever discover the imitation, and it was with whistles that he communicated with his cattle. He had altered the usual manner of "herding". Instead of driving his herd, he was always at the forefront. They followed him the way dogs follow their master and if he were separated from them for half a day (he occasionally had to visit the commando to confer with the general), their lowing could be heard for miles and the dust they raised, rushing about, rolled above the trees like storm clouds. They couldn't rest until they had old Hendrik back.

During the course of the war, the stories about old Hendrik and his cattle became more and more remarkable. Gool, who had also grown up with cattle and knew the Afrikander breed well, regarded most of these stories as fabrication. Everybody knew the red cattle of the Du Toit family, next to the Hangklip Mountains. They were "wild" in all respects and had to be shot in the veld like big game. The red Afrikanders which old Hendrik herded, were descendants of the same breed. His master, the old gentleman Freek Boshoff, was married to a daughter of the old gentleman Du Toit. As a child Gool had often come into contact with these wild cattle and he found it simply impossible to believe that any person on earth could control a herd of wild Afrikander cattle the way it was said old Hendrik did. But his disillusion was at hand.

"Stand still, Master Gool. First I must calm my cattle. They noticed you a long time ago, although the wind is coming from their way. They heard you coming down the mountain."

"Your cattle?" Gool asked, astonished. "Where are your cattle?"

"Here, near us, Master." And Gool could distinguish that the dark little figure next to him was pointing ahead. He could see that the bushes in front of them were thinning out and that they stood on the edge of an opening beyond which lay a large, level area, shadowed by giant candlewood and tamboti trees but without any shrubs. He had often crossed the place while he was wandering about the Banks and seen the cattle tracks, also that they had spent the night there on several occasions.

With his hand still gripping Gool's arm, the old Bushman led him in the direction of the opening. Suddenly – to his surprise – they came to a small depression where a little fire was burning.

"What stupidity is this, old Hendrik?" he asked. "Don't you

know that we're surrounded by the enemy and that your fire can bring them down on us at any moment?"

Old Hendrik gave a dry little laugh. "I know all about them, Master. I've watched them for a long time, just as I've been watching you, Master Gool, for three days. I could give you no sign before tonight because my cattle were very restless when they saw they were hemmed in. They caught the smell of the enemy from all sides and it took me a great deal of trouble to keep them quiet during the day. If they had stampeded during the day the enemy would've shot many of them. If I had suddenly brought you and your horse down on them they would've done one of two things: they would've charged and killed you or they would've spread out and stampeded. You don't have to be worried about the fire. It's only visible from one direction and that direction is guarded by the cattle. It's only a short distance and no stranger or Tommy has been born who – day or night – can come near them."

Under the big trees Gool noticed a stretch of black shadow which seemed to be in perpetual motion. In the dim light of the small fire he could occasionally see eyes shining, like many searchlights aimed in his direction, and then he also noticed for the first time the pleasant odour of a great herd of cattle, breathing.

For the first time he could also focus his attention on the little old Bushman. It was a strange figure who became visible in the light of the fire. From top to bottom, his clothes were made of tanned skins sewn together with sinew. Even his hat and his velskoens had obviously been made by himself of the skins of small buck. He had no firearm and snared duiker, steenbuck and dassies to keep himself alive. A long jack-knife on his belt was his only visible weapon. On his back he carried a small, rolled kaross – his only bedding. His food and all his other veld gear he carried in a small knapsack. The colour of his clothing harmonised so well with the ordinary colours of the veld that he was completely invisible at a distance of a few yards unless he betrayed himself by moving.

"I know you haven't had hot food for three days. You were scared of making a fire. And your dried meat was finished the day before yesterday. I was at two of the places where you slept at the fountains and could see that rusks and water was your only food. Here's a fresh duiker rib and some hot mealie porridge. Eat, Master Gool, we have a big task ahead of us tonight." He passed the spit-roasted meat to his guest and took another piece for himself which was also spit-roasting over the fire.

They took turns to quench their thirst from a large military water bottle.

"I crept up to one of their sentries at Bospoort one night and stole the water bottle. I could've robbed them of the lot but this was all I needed and I didn't want to let them know that I was so near," old Hendrik explained.

Seldom in his life had the famished young scout enjoyed a meal more. But his hunger was barely appeased or the danger, the hopelessness of their situation, again came to the fore in the darkest of colours.

"And now, old Hendrik, we're finished. I've taken a good look at the area and we won't get out of here. You'll have to give up your animals and I my life. It's my own fault that I let myself be trapped like a stupid wether in the corner of a kraal."

The old Bushman again gave his dry little laugh. "Fault you can't call it. I, who have my herd as guard dogs, also allowed myself to be trapped. No one could've known about the three sets of troops who approached the mountain from behind. They knew about us and we knew nothing about them. That's why they only moved in the dark of night and never lit any fires. It was Boers – Waterberg Boers – who led and advised them. All they're looking for are my cattle. It's our tracks which brought them down on the Banks. But listen, Master Gool, I also watched them very carefully. Be assured, Master, we'll get out of here tonight. The only thing I'm worried about is that they might shoot a few of my cattle – and then there's your horse. You have to come with me on foot and we'll have to leave your horse to fend for himself. He could flee with my cattle but long ago I had taught them to hate and fear horses. They'll run away from him as if he's death itself, and if he suddenly appears, they'll gore him from all sides. Last month a patrol of six saw a few of my cattle near Geelhoutbos when they were coming through the ravine and they decided to drive them to the camp."

The memory caused a cheerful little laugh. "If they had only known – they might just as well have tried to drive a herd of wild buffalo to the butcher in the village. They came through the bushes above the wind and when the animals saw them they were less than three hundred yards from one another. It so happened that the animals were trapped in a narrow ravine with the six riders in front of them. There was an old sterile cow who headed the group but there were also four young red bulls in the herd. Old Strepie only lowed once when she saw them and then the herd charged. You know how they roar and carry on when they're really angry. The soldiers were so terrified and bewildered that not one of them fired a shot. Of course they had never expected anything like it. I sat watching the commotion from the mountain. When they realised the danger, they only had one purpose – and that was to flee. But they were stupid enough to gallop through the hook-thorn. Old Strepie chose one and trapped him in the thorns so thoroughly that it took his comrades an hour to free him. The bulls gored two horses, and the men had to crawl into the hook-thorn on hands and knees. They were a terrible spectacle when they got together later to get their horses unsnagged and to examine the dead. Among the six of them there weren't enough rags left to make a decent shirt.

"Now come along, Master, the first thing we have to do is to make the cattle accustomed to you. Just hold my arm and never make a sudden movement and never lift your other arm. Leave your gun here."

And in this manner old Hendrik and Gool slowly neared the herd.

The old Bushman immediately started talking and whistling. "Never mind, my children, it's me. Don't move. Lie still, Roman, old Kandas – you're nice and fat, aren't you?"

Most of the herd were lying down but everywhere there were small groups which were still standing and, blowing restlessly, turned their heads towards the two disturbing their peace. Old Hendrik walked back and forth and in circles through the herd as if he wanted to introduce the stranger to each and every animal. Their reception was diverse. Most of them raised their heads and tested the stranger's smell with distended nostrils. Here and there groups of younger cattle showed signs of fright and some were in the process of jumping up when the two came nearer but a word from Hendrik was always enough to calm them immediately. Several times an enraged young bull, with a muffled roar and lowered head, came past his mates towards them, challenging in a cloud of dust.

In such cases old Hendrik pushed the scout behind him, faced the enraged animal head-on, grabbed it by one horn and turned its head aside. Only a few words from the old Bushman were always enough to restore immediate silence and to let the threatening bull's temper evaporate. Never before had Gool seen anything like it. With growing amazement he followed the old Bushman. It really seemed to him as if there were a mental affinity between the animals and their herdsman, as if they could understand him, if not his actual words then the tone of his whistle and the modulations of his voice.

Eventually he halted in the farthest corner of the herd and peered into the darkness. "There is one more – the General – who has to look at us closely. He must lead the herd out tonight." With two fingers in his mouth he imitated the melodious call of the peculiar pygmy owl of the northern Bushveld. At a distance between the trees, Gool could make out a single animal which got up slowly from the place where he had been lying in isolation. Like a great black shadow he moved through the lighter shadows of the giant trees. He came straight towards them and when he was near, Gool saw that he was a superb Red Afrikander bull, one of the most beautiful he had ever seen in his life. Even in the dark he could see that the skin was like velvet with the sheen of satin. He was "a Bushveld calf", old Hendrik told him. He had arrived here just before the war as a wild animal and he had never been in a kraal. This was his first meeting with a white man. Gool could barely believe that the giant animal was only in his fourth year. His unusual way of life had enhanced the "wild" attributes of the build of his breed. In each movement of the superb animal, Gool could see speed and nimbleness, despite the mighty muscles and the enormous weight. "Truly," he whispered to his guide, "the Afrikander is the most beautiful animal in the world!" The bull greeted his herdsman with soft blowing. Here there were no signs of fright or excitement. With all kinds of endearments the old Bushman stroked the smooth head and taking a rough stone out of his knapsack, he groomed the bull's back, something which obviously afforded the animal the greatest pleasure. When it was done he moved towards Gool and blowing deeply, smelt his clothes.

"Now he knows you," said Hendrik in a confidential tone when they walked away.

The bull lowed once or twice as if he wanted to halt their departure but made no effort to follow them.

"How many cattle do you have?" Gool asked when they reached the fire again.

The old Bushman took out a tally-stick of hardwood which he carried on a sinew around his neck. After he had smoothed it with his fingers a few times, he replied: "There are one thousand and twenty-six. But there are six cows who have hidden their calves. Later on I'll send them to fetch their children. I can't be bothered with them now."

The events that followed – as Gool would always state later – seemed to him like an adventure in a dream.

Ordered by the old Bushman, Gool unsaddled his horse and left him. The saddle and bridle old Hendrik hid in a thick shrub with the promise: "I'll fetch it later and bring it back to the commando."

When they stood next to the fire again, old Hendrik carefully inspected the scout from head to toe. Any unnecessary weight had to be left behind and anything that could shake or make a sound, was tied tightly around his body with strips of rawhide. One of Gool's two bandoliers he fastened around his own body. To his regret he also had to hide his water bottle. "I won't need it for a long time. I'm going to a land now where there is plenty of water . . . Come, Master, come, the morning star is shining above the trees. Within two hours it'll be daybreak, and we have to be out of here long before there's any sign of light."

Then he told Gool quickly but in great detail what he was planning to do and what was expected of the scout. There were only two places where the cattle could get through and the old Bushman had chosen one where there was a fairly wide ravine between a dry sloot and the rocks stacked below the cliffs. Gool had also examined this way out very carefully, from the mountain that afternoon, and speedily come to the conclusion that it was impassable for a man on horseback. It was less than four hundred yards wide, overgrown with hook-thorn through which a myriad of game paths ran. Before sundown this passageway had been guarded by no less than eight enemy sentry posts. There were at least eight tents in a row across the whole width and so many troops, that hand in hand, they could bar the entire exit. High above, between the rocks under the cliffs, were two mountain guns which could pelt both the Banks and the passageway. And this was the bastion through which old Hendrik wanted to take his herd of a thousand cattle! An attack on a blockhouse by a boy with a sling Gool regarded as a more feasible undertaking but his mental state was such at that moment that he was prepared to accept, without the least resistance, everything old Hendrik proposed.

The last precaution of the Bushman was to tie a long twine of sinew to Gool's wrist and to tie the other end to his own belt. "Just follow in my tracks, master. Don't speak at all and do just what I tell you. You'll never have to use the gun. Leave it on your back."

And so the great adventure began.

Old Hendrik took him through the herd of ruminant animals for the second time but this time his behaviour and the result were wholly different. On a small calabash flute he imitated never-ending the high-pitched drone of the cicado. The effect on the animals was like a war cry. There was an immediate movement throughout the entire herd as if a great muscle had suddenly been brought into action.

"But they won't low," old Hendrik whispered.

In a deathly hush the herd immediately rose and moved soundlessly through the soft dust of their sleeping quarters to bunch together at one central point.

When Gool and old Hendrik were through the undergrowth, they could still see the movement and the only sound was the occasional clatter of horns when the animals probably accidentally touched one another. The old Bushman had stopped his whistling when they were about fifty yards from the herd and immediately everything was completely quiet again.

"Are they coming?" Gool whispered, inquisitive and excited.

"No, they'll do nothing until they receive my order," the old herdsman bragged.

It was evident that neither night nor day made any difference to the old Bushman's ability to see. Gool followed him with bated breath, with the sinew twine always taut. He never accidentally touched either a twig or a log despite the fact that they often had to find a way through thick black-thorn. It seemed to Gool that they had been going for nearly an hour, measured by riding time, when the Bushman suddenly stopped and with a gesture, pushed him down flat behind a bush. Right in front of them, barely three hundred yards away, he now saw the sentry fires of the encircling enemy.

"Stupid of them to make fires," the old Bushman whispered. "But of course they know that only one herdsman and the cattle are trapped."

About twenty yards from the row of tents, the sentries walked up and down between the bushes, so that each one met his compatriot on the other side. They were determined that this time, the herd of cattle wouldn't escape! Around every fire there were three or four soldiers with rifles in their hands. The relief sentries were probably asleep in the tents.

In silence and with great precision, old Hendrik studied the situation. He counted the visible troops, guessed at the number inside the tents, and also the number of horses, and estimated the time it would take a trooper to reach the horselines and saddle his horse. Then he touched Gool's arm and said: "Come, Master."

Within a few yards they were on the edge of the donga which was thickly overgrown with yellowwood trees. With a shudder, Gool looked at the black depths when he discovered that the old Bushman was planning to cross the ravine. Down the side, he helped Gool foot by foot and hand by hand. Invisible tree trunks and undergrowth was the ladder by which the two climbed fifty feet down and fifty feet up on the other side, not without effort and danger. When they reached level ground again, old Hendrik, without resting, led the scout at a jog trot along a footpath through thick hook-thorn. Eventually, when Gool was so exhausted that he could barely lift his feet, the old Bushman lay down on a ledge of rock under the branches of a wild plum tree. To his surprise, Gool noticed that they had passed the enemy lines! They, at least, were safe! They could now walk away and the enemy would never know how and where they had passed through. But the cattle were still victims! It soon appeared that the old Bushman had plans other than only to ensure his own safety. Far behind them he showed Gool the crown of a baobab tree, clearly visible against the end of the Milky Way.

"Keep your eye on that tree, master Gool. When I give the word, you must move in that direction. I'll try to stay with you but we may be separated. I'll meet you there."

Old Hendrik took his calabash flute out of his knapsack and softly at first and then more and more loudly, imitated the "whoo-whoo-whoo" of the tufted Bushveld owl. The imitation was so perfect, and so used was the enemy to the sound, that Gool could see they paid no attention to it.

"But old Hendrik, the cattle can never hear it, whatever your plan with them might have been, they're miles away from us."

"They're much nearer than you think, Master. We walked in a huge circle to get behind the enemy. Listen!"

Far away, in the direction from which they had come, Gool heard an extraordinary sound. It was like the far-off rumbling of storm water over a rock-strewn river. The sound was immediately picked up by the enemy sentries. They could clearly hear a bewildered "Halt, who goes there?" from one frightened soldier. Then there was the clatter of rifles, and bayonets gleaming in the light of the fires. All along the line small groups of officers gathered, obviously discussing the mysterious noise.

The rumbling from the Banks became louder and louder and when it was so near that Gool could distinguish the muted sound of lowing, old Hendrik gave a few loud "whoo-whoo's" on his flute and within minutes the first cattle appeared through the hookthorn. They were divided into four parallel columns. There was a flash of eyes in the light of the fire, the clash of horns and a cruel bellowing. Gool could easily empathise with the state of mind of a raw outlander who unexpectedly had to put up a resistance against such a hullabaloo in the darkness.

At the forefront of the first columns Gool could clearly see, in the light of the fire, an enormous shape running at full speed. It was the General who, head lowered, was leading the charge. The actual shock of the meeting was less visible. It was covered in a dense cloud of dust but Gool could see burning logs scattering in all directions and people, blankets and bits of cloth along the line flung into the air with frightening violence. The noise was terrifying. The thunder of hooves and the enraged lowing of cattle were not enough to muffle the screaming, swearing and moaning of badly injured humans.

At the start wild shots were heard here and there in the tumult but the surprise was obviously so complete that to all extents and purposes there was no armed resistance. One could count the gun shots.

Above all the confusion and uproar Gool could hear a terrible sound to which this war had long accustomed him. It was probably the worst sound that could be heard on earth – the bloodcurdling screams of tormented horses which couldn't free themselves.

The morning dusk had swiftly disappeared but as far as Gool was concerned, the brighter light only served to heighten the nightmarish quality of the drama. Thickening, the dust rose heavenward like a black column but it was never thick enough to cover completely what was happening below it. Towards the end it seemed to Gool that a tornado had passed, flinging a great many objects into the air.

Just as suddenly as the storm had begun, it abated. It had all passed like an awful dream. When Gool heard the voice of the Bushman next to him, there was a comparative silence in the enemy lines – except for the constant screaming of the wounded horses and the soldiers who had landed in the black-thorn. When the dust slowly drifted away from the scene, they could see the terrible destruction which had been caused in the line in such a brief time. All the tents were flattened; there were pieces of sailcloth everywhere in the hook-thorn, bits of blanket, overcoats and clothes, and out of the bushes they could see soldiers emerging getting up or crawling. Of the horses who had stood tethered behind the tents, there was no sign. Those who could succeed in breaking loose had fled into the bush and those who hadn't, were flattened.

As far as the cattle were concerned, Gool could see, according to the dust that rose above the trees, that they were already spreading far and wide but still at a thundering speed.

"Come, Master," the Bushman ordered, "we have to be at the baobab tree before daybreak."

"It'll take a month for you to get your herd together again," Gool said in a depressed tone.

But the old Bushman gave his dry little laugh again.

"Master doesn't know my veld chickens. They're just like small children and I'm their old nurse. They won't rest, day or night, until they've found me again. All I have to do is to stay in one place until they all gather there and it'll take three days at most. I'm going to wait for them in the Middleveld and if the enemy can trap us there, he'll have to be very clever. Master has seen that their whole commando isn't capable of driving on my children. The only damage they can inflict is to shoot some – and for that they'll have to pay."

With that Gool agreed unreservedly.

The last event of the great battle which Gool would remember to the day of his death, happened just as they got up to leave. Suddenly they became aware of a great noise in the bush in their immediate vicinity. It was as if a column of cavalry was trying to force its way through the thickest of hook-thorn bush. For a moment it put old Hendrik on his guard again. With a hand he pushed Gool under the branches of the wild plum while his bright beaded eyes carefully surveyed the area. Through the branches Gool could see a huge shape bearing directly down on them. And when the colossus appeared below their pile of rocks, old Hendrik greeted it with a peal of laughter.

It was the General, the beautiful young Afrikander bull which Gool had admired in the dark the previous evening. Around one horn a coat was so closely wrapped that he had tried in vain to rub if off on tree trunks and between branches. Both horns, his hump and one muscled shoulder was heavily smeared with blood. With distended nostrils and a soft lowing, he greeted his friend on top of the rocks. Old Hendrik had to use his jack-knife to release the bull from his irritating burden.

"My officer captured their battle flag," old Hendrik remarked.

Everything happened just the way old Hendrik promised. The next day he and Gool were safely in the Middleveld. Here and there they saw patrols on the tracks of the cattle. But it was child's play to get rid of them. Within six days the herd was together again without any necessity of searching for one of them. He checked them carefully and his report was: six absent, of which four were cows with hidden calves who would join the herd later, ten heavily wounded and about thirty with light injuries. Ten days after the "battle" Gool found his horse, Kousband, again. Almost a month later he reached his commando after his friends had mourned him as "killed" or "murdered". He came riding up on Kousband, bare-backed with not even a rope for a halter.

Source:
Eugène N. Marais: *Die leeus van Magoeba*. Pretoria: Van Schaik: 1934.
Translated by Madeleine van Biljon

A Transvaal Ulysses

C.R. Prance

OOM SAMSON VAN DONDER'S ODYSSEY

The changes and chances of our transitory mortal life are incalculable, and even a quite minor war is apt to cause life-long reactions and reverberations in the lives of honest civilians caught up as the raw material of cannon-fodder by the wheels of the war-machine.

That difference of political outlook between Paul Kruger and Joseph Chamberlain at the end of last century, led to a sort of war which today would hardly have been front-page news, though its reactions on subsequent history, including the World War of 1914-1918, will be a problem yet for historians of the 21st century – unless in the meantime civilisation with all its records goes up in a cloud of mingled smoke and poison-gas, leaving cabalistic fragments to intrigue the best brains of a new human species "Homo Sapientior", to puzzle scholars of A.D. 6000 in the same way that present-day pundits pore over fragments of inscribed brick records from Nineveh and Babylon.

To some 200,000 civilians of the world-wide Empire, life after 1902 never again resumed the even tenor of its way, and thousands of them remained as war's jetsam on the far-flung frontiers, only occasionally disturbing the orderly routine of Downing Street by suggestion of their grievances.

But to our friends the temporary "enemy" the war was not a mere disturbance of the peace to ten per cent of the population. It was a national earthquake which tore open a new channel for the normal current of their lives; and though most of them settled down to the new conditions with the aplomb inherited from Voortrekker ancestors, there was a five per cent minority amongst them who preferred to kick against the pricks like any Army mule caught in the toils of a dismantled barb-wire trench entanglement; a minority whose conscientious sufferings for the patriotic cause must have provided a fund of amusement to the Ironic Spirit of the Universe.

For instance, there was Oom Gideon van Oswegen, war-prisoner in Ceylon, who refused the offer of freedom to enjoy life at large in the island on condition that he would give his word not to risk being mutilated by a shark in the hopeless effort to escape. An obdurate patriot, when the day came that the Boer leaders had made peace, he refused again to take the oath of allegiance which would enable him to return home to his wife and family. And the time came when he was the last and only prisoner left in the Camp, with a Colonel, two Majors, some Captains, a litter of Lieutenants, and some hundred of N.C.O.'s, Privates, Medical Officers, and Nursing Sisters to look after him.

The officials all had "a cushy job" and were quite satisfied to continue to guard Oom Gideon in the intervals of race-meetings and polo matches, so long as the Empire should remain at peace. But a time came when some peevish economist in the Treasury posed the question whether Oom Gideon's safe-keeping was worth its cost to the British taxpayer; and the Colonel was instructed confidentially to ascertain what Oom Gideon's price would be to pocket his patriotic pride, to "cut the crackle" and go home to his farm in a blaze of glory as the last Free State "bitter-ender" to stand out against Pax Britannica.

Exactly what terms were struck is a State secret even yet; but they certainly included a new outfit from Army Ordnance Stores, and clad in Bedford-cord breeches, puttee-leggings, a cork helmet, and a khaki drill tunic with plain buttons, Oom Gideon was solemnly "piped aboard" with all honour by the bo'sun of a ship carrying "Army details" to Cape Town.

A guest of the Mess, Oom Gideon was on velvet for the voyage, and at Cape Town he received a free railway-pass to Bloemfontein, including the meals served at wayside halts in those days before the need for Dining Cars had dawned on the General Manager of Railways. But there his triumphal progress was cut short, because he had given his postal address as Bloemfontein, forgetting to state that his farm lay in the district of Bloemfontein, it was twenty weary red dusty miles from the town.

Had he gone into detail in the Ceylon orderly-room, no doubt some Adjutant at Tempe would have been told off to see him delivered in triumph at Vlakvarksholte by a mule-lorry with a mounted orderly. As it was, he had to trudge out on his flat feet, a form of exercise to which the horse-loving Afrikander has never taken kindly and never will, especially when still suffering from "sea legs". And when, with his tongue hanging out, he called in at Skuilhoek, the halfway-house, expecting super-hospitality in recognition of his super-patriotism, Tante Katrina van Ammenies (known as Tante "Rooikat" from her temper and the colour of her hair) chased him with insult and contumely, threatening to loose the dogs on him because, by his breeches and leggings he must be a khaki-Englander; and when he remonstrated in Afrikaans she denounced him as a renegade and "hands-upper" which is even worse. So easy is it for man's highest hopes to gang a-gley? It was a hard case indeed; but that of Oom Samson Golias van Donder of Sjambokfontein in Skranderberg was harder still.

When Oom Paul's gallopers called up the commandos in October 1899, Samson Golias would have up-saddled and ridden in to Doodstildorp, if he had a horse able to carry a rifleman who went 300 lb. in a "birthday suit", or nearly 400 lb. including clothes, saddle, blanket, rifle and ammunition, and a store of biltong and biscuit calculated to see him through a war which would last at least a month. As it was, he had to report for duty by ox-wagon; and the Commandant, plagued to death with military detail, wired to Pretoria to suggest that Herr Nagel's famous Circus should be commandeered to provide Oom Samson with an elephant.

The suggestion was turned down, but General Joubert found a place for Samson on the limber of a 1 lb. quick-firer, known as a "pom-pom" from its noise; his special duty being to sit on the "trail" when the gun was in action, to keep it true on the target. So as "anchor" to the pom-pom Oom Samson did good work, and covered himself with temporary glory during the British assault on Slabbert's Neck near Bethlehem in July 1901.

He had got his gun cunningly into position to rake the geometrical straight line of the British batteries, and was doing fearful damage when Brabant's Horse retaliated by getting on to his flank at 800 yards with a 9 lb. galloping Hotchkiss under cover of a Kafir kraal, with murderous rifle-fire in support.

In a moment the pom-pom carriage was a wreck, and so were half its crew; but Brabant's Horse ceased fire and cheered Oom Samson when he collected himself from the debris, picked up the ruined pom-pom, and staggered off with it.

They cheered him generously again a week later, when at the great surrender of the Free State army he came in riding on another gun; but after that, as a war-prisoner in Bermuda, he disappeared from history and almost from the memory of all save his attorney for many years; till in 1932 he stepped into the limelight once again; when tidings spread in Skranderberg that Oom Samson, already a mere legend to the new generation and a history memory to the old, was coming home at last; and that his attorney had engaged a new girl-clerk, this time a truly pretty one at last, to attend to all the extra correspondence which the re-settlement of Samson on his ancestral acres would involve.

In a way Oom Samson had grown almost to relish his "imprisonment", which was made easy for him because it was so obvious that he had no intention to escape. And though of course he felt home-sick at times, cooped up in an island no bigger than some Afrikander farms, he felt that he had the London Government "by the short hairs" as the Settlers say; because if they got tired of paying for his keep and let him go back without taking any oath, all those who had taken the oath of allegiance in order to get home, would "ask for their money back"; while if he was paid to take it quietly, the others would all sue the English Government for payment too.

Nor could the Government try to deport him, except to some other English Colony where he would cost them just as much, because he was still legally a war-prisoner and an ex-burgher of a State which did not now exist, so that it would be impossible for him to get naturalised anywhere in the world. And by every mail he used to write long letters all about it to his attorney and to Sjambokfontein, just to compel the English Government to pay double postage because he had no money to buy stamps; so that all the time Downing Street had to keep a special clerk to do nothing but attend to the file of "Van Donder, Samson Golias, war-prisoner; V.B. 01/17603", all of which petty detail was pure joy to Oom Samson's patriotic soul.

Yet in truth he had at last got tired of having no one in all Bermuda with whom he could talk Afrikander politics, and weary of having nothing on earth to do day-long except to "go for a walk" round and round the island every day like any Londoner, to keep himself from getting too stout even to ride on a pom-pom or an elephant. So he had learned enough English to be able to join a Circus in America, and made the English Government pay twopence on a letter to his attorney in Nergensdorp to make a plan to get him permission to enter the United States.

That proved beyond the powers even of an LL.B. of Stellenbosch, because the Americans had got almost as frightened of foreigners as Paul Kruger had ever been, and had followed General Hertzog's lead in adding a Quota system to their Immigration Law; and when the LL.B. wrote to the American Consul in Bermuda for a permit for Oom Samson to enter on the quota of the Suid-Afrikaanse Republiek, the answer was that (at least for the moment) there was no such country now; and if Samson could not wait till the Republiek was set up again, he could only get into America by taking the oath of allegiance to the English King, which would make him legally "one of God's Englishmen" like the other "Boers"; because until he took the oath he was not, by international law, "a legal entity". And it cost the London Government another twopence on Samson's reply to his attorney that a person who is not a legal entity cannot be made to pay a lawyer's fees.

So it seemed clear that there was no place in the world where Oom Samson had any higher status than that of an English war-prisoner, which is not very high and has no colour-bar to keep "black stuff" in its place; and the American Consul urged him to be a man and swallow the oath like castor-oil, because he could cough it up again in a few weeks when he made application for American burgher-right.

But Samson was adamant, saying he had taken an oath already that he would never take the English oath, and no Van Donder had ever yet been caught out in a lie; so he must stay in Bermuda till the Lord should soften England's heart to let the Transvaal have its Republiek again, with compensation to an upright Afrikander for keeping him in pawn as a legal non-entity for so many years.

So there he stayed in Bermuda, all through the Great War and the years of so-called peace, while Governors and garrisons came and went, till at last there was nobody left in Bermuda who had any interest in him at all; and even the seventh successive clerk in Whitehall who attended his "file" was getting sick of it. But at last news filtered to Bermuda that South Africa was now a Sovereign Independent State under its own King, who was only by coincidence the King of England too, and might any day have to call himself President instead if his South African Ministers advised him that it was best.

That helped to ease Oom Samson's ticklish conscience; and it is possible too that, at the Imperial Conference, someone in Whitehall had persuaded General Hertzog to persuade Oom Samson to go home to Sjambokfontein and so enable Downing Street to close its file and save the clerk's salary. But there were legal obstacles even yet; because it appeared that, although he still claimed to be a Burgher of the dead Republic, he was still an English war-prisoner and not a British Subject or a Union "national" – though he was naturally ultra-Nationalist in politics; and so it was only the King of England who could get the King of South Africa to consent to let Samson go back to his farm. But if the King of South Africa were to allow him to return, he would not be able to deport him, even for "riotous assembly" on his farm, except to another of his farms. And if he refused to take the oath of allegiance to the King of South Africa, it would be the King of England's job to protect this "war-prisoner" if he were charged with privy conspiracy and rebellion against the Union Government – just as Queen Victoria had to protect her "uitlanders" against Oom Paul.

It was all very difficult; but the Publicity Expert of Skranderberg saw "money in it" if Oom Samson could be brought back with thanksgiving and procession on Dingaan's Day or even a Special Public Holiday in 1932 as the very last "bitter-ender" who had refused to accept the Peace Terms of 1902; and Samson consented to return on the footing of a legal non-entity and a national hero, until he should see which had most money in it, entity or non-entity.

Of course the LL.B. was hoping to persuade him to take the oath of allegiance to the King of South Africa (at least "without prejudice" and "pendente lite", which are lawyers'-Latin words and quite often cost a farmer a pound each), because as a legal entity he could be compelled to pay his lawyers' bills. But Tante Rebella van Donder, being his half-second-cousin-in-law, urged him to make a brave example to the young by insisting on remaining a legal non-entity until the Super-Republicans of Skranderberg can work out their plan, which would give him the glory of waking up to his early coffee one morning as a Burgher of the Suid Afrikaanse Republiek still – or once again. And she said it would come cheaper too in the meantime, because not even Mnr. Havenga or Mnr. Pirow could make a legal non-entity take out a motor-license or pay Income Tax.

So he came back at last in a blaze of glory, "pendente lite" and with everything unsettled yet. But as the Settlers say, it "took the gilt off the gingerbread" of the Civic Reception, headed by the Mayor of Nergensdorp with his Civic Trumpeter and his Great Seal, when it appeared that, after so long in foreign parts, Oom Samson could only speak kombuis-Engels and some High Dutch and the old Cape Dutch, because he had never had a chance to learn the up-to-date Afrikaans which the Afrikaans Akademie had been working up and polishing, while Oom Samson walked twice round Bermuda every day to keep up his appetite and keep down his weight. But the LL.B and his pretty girl clerk even now cannot sleep at night, thinking of the fearful legal mess if Oom Samson were to die before he has taken the oath or the Republic has been set up again; because if he died as a legal non-entity nobody would ever be able to make a proper settlement of his deceased estate.

Source:
C.R. Prance: *Tante Rebella's Saga: A Backvelder's Scrapbook.* London: H.F. & G. Witherby: 1937.

REVENGE (EXTRACT)

J. VAN MELLE

What follows, is the dramatic end of Van Melle's story "Wraak". The "bywoner" Strydom, who was a joiner during the war, killed the son of Berend Viviers, the farmer on whose farm he stays. After the war, Strydom admits his guilt and pleads for forgiveness. Berend tries to forgive him, as he believes a true Christian should – but he finds it impossible. The story starts with Berend hallucinating that the war is still on.

Half an hour after Martiens had left, Uncle Berend went into the living room again.

He sat down in the chair in a corner of the room, his body bent forward. Then he looked through the window. He moved as though he meant to get up but then remained seated, leaning back. A first an evil, and then slowly an absent expression crossed his face. "Yes?"

He got up and went to stand at the table, then moved to the wall where the rifle hung. His behaviour was strange. One could see that he was not fully aware of what he was doing. His movements were slow and hesitant. Suddenly he raised his head and listened intently. He spoke hastily: "What was that? It is cannon fire. The English are here. I must saddle up quickly." He walked to the window, put his head outside and called loudly: "Wildebees, Wildebees, fetch the horses and saddle up quickly. The English will be here any moment." He withdrew his head and stood staring outside for a few moments. A shock went through him. He gestured at something outside and mumbled, put his head through the window again and shouted: "Wildebees, wait, I want to settle something first." He stood as if thinking. "What do I have to settle first? Oh, I remember." He went to the wall and took down the gun. He kneeled at the window and aimed. Now his movements were hurried, almost wild. The shot rang out.

He got up and hung the rifle in its place. For a few moments he stood unmoving again as though thinking. He spoke in an undertone: "Is everything all right now? Yes, everything is all right." He went out and immediately Susarie came into the room. She was astonished when she saw that there was no one in the room. She looked at the gun. Aunt Hannie came in, startled, pale as death and shaking. She also looked at the gun and spoke in a relieved voice: "Oh – Who shot? Do you know?" she asked Susarie.

"I don't know, Ma; I thought it was Pa who had shot."

"Your father has gone to bed."

"I heard Pa getting up. Perhaps Pa simply shot at something through the window."

"What would your pa shoot at?"

"Perhaps at a hawk, Ma." At that moment Martiens also came into the room.

"Who shot here a while ago?"

"We thought it was in this room," Aunt Hannie said.

"Here in the room, Ma?"

"Yes, it sounded like that but there was no one here. I had a dreadful fright. Susarie, do go and see where your father is."

Martiens went to the window and looked outside. "What is going on there?" he asked, concerned.

Tant Hannie came and stood next to him. "What are they doing there?" They stood looking for a short while. "I want to see what's going on," said Martiens. Aunt Hannie wanted to accompany him but changed her mind and stood at the window again.

Susarie came in hurriedly and startled:"Oh, Ma, Strydom has been shot."

Aunt Hannie became as pale as a sheet, she almost fell but then sat down. "What do you mean?" she asked.

"Strydom has been killed, Ma. He's lying next to the fence," said Susarie more softly.

"Who shot him?"

"I don't know, Ma, but he's lying under the big blue gum, in the same place where Boetie was killed. Geelbooi found him there. He says the bullet pierced his heart. Who could have shot him, Ma? How could such an accident have happened? Ma, you're so pale! Shall I fetch you some water?"

Susarie hurried to the kitchen as Aunt Hannie walked to the wall, took down the rifle and looked at the bolt. The rifle wasn't on safety. She opened the bolt and a spent cartridge fell to the ground. She let the rifle slide out of her hands and clutched her hands despairingly against her forehead. "Berend shot him. It's Berend! It's Berend!" she cried desperately. She fell into a chair with her head in her hands and rocked to and fro in despair.

Susarie came in with a cup of water. "O, Mummy, Mummy," she cried in a panic and kneeled next to her mother.

"Susarie, it's your father. I knew it; I knew it would happen like this. We waited too long to do something. If Martiens had had time to talk to Strydom then everything might still have turned out fine. I was only one day too late. Oh, Berend, oh! oh!" Swaying, she got up and walked outside anxiously followed by Susarie. Martiens came back into the room. He picked up the rifle and the cartridge case; looked through the window. He hung the gun in its place and put the cartridge case in his pocket. His movements were hurried like someone who wanted to hide something. Then he suddenly stood still. He balled his fist, his face distorted by hate and sorrow. "The bastard," he said furiously. He stood thinking for a few moments, anger and despair in his attitude.

Uncle Jannie, of Vyefontein, went to Aunt Hannie. It had just become known that Uncle Berend had been found not guilty and he was on his way to congratulate her. She might be away and then his journey was in vain but he was willing to take the chance. He had his youngest child with him, a boy of about twelve, because Uncle Jannie had married for the second time and his wife was younger than him. The child had learnt not to speak when his father was in a brown study. He would get no reply in any case or replies which made no sense. Uncle Jannie was thinking about the case of Uncle Berend. It was something one couldn't stop thinking about in a hurry. Not the court case but the event itself. That Uncle Berend would have been found innocent was, as far as he was concerned, always obvious. It would be a strange jury, indeed, who would have found him guilty. Anyone could see that he committed the deed in a moment of insanity. But the deed itself? What had driven him to commit the deed against his will? It was clear. The hate had always been there, suppressed, but not overcome. It had to erupt one way or another and it had happened like this. This was the result when man wanted to do something beyond his capabilities. Then something broke. It was like the story of Saul and David. That was just such a case. Hate, suppressed, hate which bubbled up against your will. A suppressed longing but too strong to be repressed. So he contended, the same viewpoint he had so often explained to himself and to others. Saul wanted to kill David but his sense of duty prevented him. But the longing to do so was too strong and at times drove him demented and incapable of controlling himself; it made him like one possessed of the devil.

When they reached Uncle Berend's house, Susarie invited them in. "I'll tell Ma that you're here, Uncle," she said. "Please sit down." Meanwhile Uncle Jannie and the boy looked around the room. They moved their heads to look at everything but they didn't speak.

"The rifle hung there," Oom Jannie whispered and pointed at the wall where the gun no longer was.

"Yes, Pa."

"He shot him through that window."

"Yes, Pa," the boy whispered. At that moment Aunt Hannie came in.

"I came to express my pleasure that Cousin Barend has been declared innocent," said Uncle Jannie.

"Thank you, Uncle."

"When do you expect him back?"

"We expect him on this afternoon's half past four train. Martiens has gone to fetch his father in Pretoria."

"Yes."

"Please see if the horses are still all right, my son." The boy went out and Uncle Jannie said: "We're all truly happy that the verdict was so favourable but then no one expected anything else."

"So am I, Uncle. From the start I was convinced that the Lord wouldn't try us more heavily. I didn't doubt the outcome for a second." There was a silence. Then Aunt Hannie said: "The statements of the two kaffirs, Geelbooi and Kameel, made a great contribution. You see, Uncle, they heard Berend shouting that the English were coming and that he called Wildebees who was his groom during the war and who had been dead for years. With all the other evidence the judge and the jury decided that at that moment he wasn't entirely sane."

"Yes."

"The biggest help, of course, was the doctor's statement. He said that it sometimes happens that someone who has always been normal, loses his mind for a brief moment." She looked at the door and spoke more softly: "He said that it might have been so. If someone has a great desire with which his mind is always busy and he suppresses that desire, it is possible that it temporarily unhinges his mind. According to him that was the case with Berend."

Oom Jannie became talkative. "I understand. I think it is very like the case of Saul. Saul had the same struggle between his conscience and his longing to be rid of David."

Aunt Hannie nodded.

"I find the cases remarkably similar. Saul hated and feared David like poison but he couldn't bring himself to have David killed, at least not at first. His feeling for justice prevailed. But then he had moments when he was filled with the spirit of evil and at such moments, desire was paramount and twice he considered stabbing David to death."

"Yes, Uncle."

"You see, Cousin Hannie, that was the way it happened with Cousin Berend. He wanted to forgive Strydom but he couldn't. It was too hard. He wanted to do what none of us could do. It was superhuman. But he wanted to because he thought that he should. There was, so to speak, a constant struggle between the two desires and it affected him and in the end, broke him. He had moments when he was out of his mind. He thought: had I met this man during the war, I would have shot him. And then a moment arrived when he thought it really was war and at that moment he saw Strydom. And he had to shoot. It could not have been any other way. I've considered the matter a great deal."

"Yes, Uncle," said a depressed Aunt Hannie. "That's just about what the doctor said."

"It was God's will," said Uncle Jannie.

Aunt Hannie didn't reply to this.

"We have been really worried about you, Cousin Hannie. Berend and I have always been friends. He was my old comrade in arms. I'm truly grateful that he has been acquitted."

"Yes, Uncle."

"Everything will be fine again," said Uncle Jannie. "You have to keep up your courage. No one will reproach Berend. We actually admire him. He tried to do which none of us would attempt."

"Yes, Uncle."

"You say Martiens has gone to fetch him?"

"Yes, Uncle, I also wanted to go but Berend sent a message to say that I musn't come."

"I think that's right. It will be better if you meet him here in the house."

"Then I'll leave now," said Uncle Jannie. "I would rather visit Berend at another time."

"Yes, Uncle, perhaps that would be better." Uncle Jannie stood up and said his farewells. "Goodbye, Cousin Hannie. May the Lord be with you." He left. Aunt Hannie accompanied him to the stoep. She came inside again and sat at the table in a depressed mood, both nervous and restless. She looked at the clock which showed a quarter to five. "They'll be here soon," she said to herself. Susarie came in and sat down. They didn't speak.

"Ma, I'm scared," said Susarie.

"Don't be scared, my child. Your father is himself again. He was only out of his senses for that very short time. You don't have to be worried at all. Now your father is exactly as he always was. And, Susarie, don't let on to your father about any of your thoughts, do you hear?"

"No, Ma, of course not," Susarie said firmly and somewhat hurt. They sat in silence for a few more minutes and then Susarie left again. Aunt Hannie went to stand at the window and looked outside. She felt nervous and restless. Suddenly she pressed her hand to her breast. "Here they are." She gazed fixedly through the window, then after a few moments, went outside. A little later Uncle Berend came inside followed by Aunt Hannie, Martiens and Susarie. Uncle Berend walked slowly, less upright. He had become greyer. His face was sombre and serious. He went to sit in his chair. He looked round as his eyes remained fixed on the window through which he had shot and then to the place where the gun had been. He sighed deeply. He spoke in a somewhat dull and despondent voice but with a great deal of the old power still present. "And how are things here, Hannie?"

"Well, Berend. How are you feeling now?"

"So-so. Not too bad."

"Pour some coffee for your father," she said to Susarie. Aunt

Hannie sent a message with her eyes to Martiens who got up and went outside. She rose and pulled up a chair next to Uncle Berend. She stroked his hand which lay on the arm. "I'm so grateful that you're back, Berend," she said. "God helped us wonderfully."

"God helped me wonderfully but the Lord also let me go through deep waters, through great terrors." Aunt Hannie put her head against his shoulder. She constantly stroked his big, strong hand. Occasionally she wiped away her tears. "The Lord made me see how small and insignificant man is," he went on, "that he is worth nothing . . . I thought I was a good Christian, that I could do a great deal, that I could forgive the way the Lord wanted it. But I couldn't. My heart rebelled."

"It was too difficult, Berend. It would have been too difficult for any human being. No one with human feelings could have borne something like that. Don't worry about it any longer. It's over. It was the Lord's will. You couldn't help it."

Uncle Berend leant his head on his hand and gestured with the other: "I could help it. My sinful heart was the cause. But how far I have fallen! I said: vengeance is the Lord's. And yet, I still wanted to take revenge. Until God said to me: Well then, if you want to take back what you have given me, take it. And I took back the sacrifice I had given God. I robbed his altar." He groaned.

"You couldn't help it," said Aunt Hannie pleadingly. "You didn't know what you were doing."

"Not at that moment. But the longing was always there. I lusted after the man's blood until the desire overcame me. I know it so well, better than the doctor knows it." There was a silence.

Susarie came in with coffee and a plateful of rusks. She gave her father the coffee and he accepted it wordlessly. She put the rusks on the table. Then she went outside. "Don't you want to eat something with it?" Aunt Hannie asked.

"No." He drank. Aunt Hannie took the empty cup out of his hands and put it down on the table. She sat next to him on the arm of the chair and put her cheek against his hair. "The Lord has forgiven you, Berend," she said. "You must be courageous again, my husband. The Lord will help you again. He has forgiven you everything. Look how merciful the Lord has been to bring you home again."

"Yes, the Lord is merciful – but I? What am I ? . . ."

Aunt Hannie put her arm tightly around his head and her face contorted with the effort of not starting to weep.

Source:
J. van Melle: *Begeestering*. Cape Town: Nasionale Pers: 1943.
Translated by Madeleine van Biljon

The Shield of Old Sem

Toon van den Heever

Fear, Jannie found, crept up on one at its worst when dusk fell, even if one sat pressed up against the fireplace in the kitchen and were scorched on one side just like a roasted mealie. The house, too, was so dark and empty and in an empty house the rafters creaked all the time. His father and his brothers were on commando and he had remained in the care of Aia Koema, an old Griqua woman, and her husband, Outa Sem.

Life was like a bridge which one saw in perspective: the first few arches spanned enormous distances, and then they became shorter and shorter. In his loneliness Jannie thought about his late mother whom he had lost a long time ago while he was still in short frocks. He still remembered the clatter of horses' hooves in the long cortege up to the family graveyard of the farmstead where the tall, dark cypress trees stood like sentinels; he remembered how bitterly he had cried and how the aunts wanted to invade his grief to find out whether he had a sense of loss, how in self-protection, he told his first lie by complaining that he had a headache and was thirsty.

Yes, and it was lonely here in the kitchen; Outa Sem was at the kraal and Aia Koema was fetching wood. Anxiously Jannie listened to every sound in- and outside the house and drew nearer to the hearth at every rustle and creak.

Suddenly he shrank back, felt the beating of his heart and his scalp crawled because he heard a shuffling noise at the back door, like something or someone who was stealthily approaching. The crown of a dilapidated hat appeared over the lower half of the door, followed by the floppy rim and then the wrinkled face of Outa Sem with the shiny ape-like eyes which stared fixedly at Jannie for a long time.

When Jannie felt that the tension was becoming unbearable, Outa Sem whispered in a deep, conspiratorial tone: "*Stephanus, Johannes, Jacobus, Kastrol! En weet jy wat?*" ("Stephen, John, Jacob, Cooking Pot! And my boy, do you know what?")

When he was christened Jannie hadn't been given any of these names but Outa Sem's whole attitude was enough to make Jannie shake in his shoes. "No, Outa Sem, what?"

"Guess who's coming?"

"No, I don't know, Outa Sem. Who?"

"God Roberts!"

Jannie knew everything about God Roberts – Outa Sem had seen to that. He often heard the far-off whine and the lengthy sigh of heavy artillery fire; then the Highveld was shocked into silence – a silence so deep that one's ears popped. Then Outa Sem would always raise his crippled finger and say with a meaningful gesture: "God Roberts!"

Outa Sem was not a man of many words but he was a master of suggestion and in Jannie's imagination he had conjured up a terrifying picture, more terrible than the Three-toed Monster and the Old Hairy Man together, followed by hordes of a wild cavalry who with long swords put everything and everyone into the cookpot.

That night Jannie couldn't sleep. As soon as his eyes closed, God Roberts was at his heels; across the water furrow, through the fields and the poplar grove; over the kraal wall and up the creepers against the gable. Added to this was the fact that Jannie couldn't run. He felt like a wet hare in front of a greyhound and his legs were paralysed with fear. Whenever his attackers grabbed his leg, he jumped up with such a shriek that Aia Koema came running, breathless and puffing hard.

"Oh, oh, jissis, people," Aia Koema complained when she ran to the bedroom for the umpteenth time, "but the devil is worrying the child tonight!" She was so sick of the whole performance that she asked Jannie which berries he had eaten – she nagged and badgered him until she eventually discovered what was bothering him. By that time Jannie was wide awake. Aia Koema left the room with that come hell or high water expression of hers. In the kitchen she grabbed the heavy iron skimmer and with that she set off down to the barn where old Sem slept. Through the ceiling Jannie could hear every expression of married bliss, also the heavy-handed way in which Outa Sem was woken.

"You darn yellow dog! And with what kind of fearsome stuff and terrible murder stories have you filled the child's mind today?"

"Jissis, woman, but what kind of carry-on is this? The old thing attacks me in the dark like a wild cat!"

"Wild cat! I'll wild cat you on your crown, you wrinkled wretch! Did you frighten the child today?"

"Never upon your life, old thing! I don't play with children!"

"Don't lie there lying to me, Sem! I can see you're stingy with the truth! Your eyes look like holes in a skin blanket. What did you tell the child today?"

"H . . . m, h . . . m," Sem pretended to think. "By my soul, perhaps it was God Roberts . . . I told him a little bit about God Roberts!"

"God Roberts! I'll give you God Roberts, you shrivelled old swine! You always want to talk about such scary things and you fill the child's head with all kinds of ideas! If it happens once more, old man, I'll scalp you and pull the skin over your ears! Go on, it's your doing that I have to stay awake the whole blessed night – now you can feel what it's like! I'm going to bed now and you can stay with the young master. If I hear one more peep from that room God Roberts will get you!"

There was a rustling in the barn and later Jannie heard old Sem shuffling down the passage, softly singing

"Japie Olyn, sy snaar is so fyn,
Maar hy sit in the moddergat vas!"

("Jacob Olyn, his gut is so fine,

But he's stuck in a pool of mud!'")

Eventually old Sem came creeping in, a tallow candle on a bottle in one hand and a belly bag under the other arm.

"Oh, jissis! And why is the white man's child not sleeping?"

"I don't know, Outa Sem. As soon as I fall asleep God Roberts wants to catch me."

"God Roberts? And who is perhaps scared of that Rednek dog? But wait, my young Master, here I have the thing that comforts – it comforts almost as much as those round enamel jugs with ears which the white railway people have."

Outa Sem took a red violin out of the belly bag, a bow and a piece of resin. Jannie was elated with pleasure.

"Oh, please, Outa Sem, please play for me!"

"Wait a bit, my old Master's child, I don't want any molestations with Aia Koema, she's very handy with the skimmer tonight!"

He held his head at an angle to listen, just like the old dog, Boel, so that Jannie spluttered with suppressed laughter. Through the ceiling came the sawing noise of Aia Koema's triumphant snoring. Outa Sem winked mischievously and softly tuned his violin. He pushed the bow over the resin a few times and began playing very softly; it was a cheerful reel which giggled and babbled like water running over the sluice and which danced just as heartily as Outa Sem's stiff fingers . . . he couldn't bend or press on the strings; he was crippled and had to play as well as he could, the crippled finger upright, the others pressing the notes. His shadow on the wall made the most silly bounds.

When this modern David paused for the first time, Jannie said with shining eyes: "Outa Sem, I would also like such a red violin. Where can I find one?"

"Buy, little Master!"

"But I have no money, Outa Sem. Where does one get money?"

"From the bank."

"And where do the people at the bank get it from?"

"They get change from the blind man, little Master."

"Go on, Outa Sem, please teach me to play your violin!"

"Play the violin? No, little Master, playing the violin is not something that can be learnt!"

"But Outa Sem, you play the violin, you must have learnt."

"White man's child, if you want to strum on this red ramkie, you'll need a big beard and porcupine quills on your chest."

"But Outa Sem, you don't even have a beard – only fluff – and you play the violin so beautifully. How is that?"

Old Sem threw his head to one side again and listened attentively but Aia Koema was still snoring away.

"Little Master, I'll tell you how it can be done but then you musn't tell Aia Koema anything. It's not every boy who can play this thing and one who stands back for a bugaboo, a *hottentotsgod* like that praying mantis, God Roberts, that one will never learn to play the violin. One must stand firm. You see these hairs on the bow? They were pulled out of Three-toes's tail. Then when the blind man changed your money, you buy a violin. Then you creep up to Three-toes when he's heavy with drinking children's blood and is sleeping in the moonlight. Zip! you pull out a handful of hair from his tail and run like a hare to stay ahead. Then you steal an egg from the nest of a basilisk and dry the yellow; that's this resin. And when you've collected all these things, you wait until one evening you feel as brave as a bull. Then at midnight you go to the crossroads and put the violin, the bow and the resin on an ant hill and you wait and you wait. Then you hear something coming down the road: 'shuffle-shiffle; shuffle-shiffle'. If you haven't run away by then, then you'll see, faintly in the starlight, the Old Hairy Man coming along: 'shuffle-shiffle, shuffle-shiffle', so that his coat tails make little dust clouds, knock-knock, puff-puff in the road. Then your hair stand on end, your knees knock, your stomach starts rumbling like someone who's hungry and your tongue wants to stick to your palate. If you're a man and haven't run away yet, then you say:

'Hoo-ha!' and whistle a little between your teeth to gather your courage. Then the Old Hairy Man will say:

> *'Stephanus, Johannes, Jacobus, Kastrol!*
> *As jy bul is kan jy bly, maar ek raai jou om te hol!*
> *Dis 'n swaar saak wat jy soek en 'n duur saak om te durf,*
> *As jy bly, sal ek jou herrie; as jy hardloop, sit jou turf!'*

> ('Stephen, John, Jacob, Cooking Pot!
> If you're brave you can stay, but you'd much better not.
> It's a heavy task to carry out, an expensive one to dare
> If you stay I'll give you what for, if you run, a beating rare!')

"When he's said that then he'll put out his hand like someone who wants to shake your hand but oh, jissis, please, please, little Master, never ever touch his hand! Quickly put the violin and the bow and the resin in his hand. Don't be clumsy. Look, Outa Sem touched the Old Hairy Man's hand with only the top of his finger when he handed the resin over and look at that finger today! Then the Old Hairy Man will show you how to tuck the violin under your chin and how to tickle its belly with the bow until it wants to shout with laughter, while you choke his throat with your fingers so that the laughter can only escape the way you want it. That's the art, my little Master: the choke and the tickle. So that the red ramkie will weep with the need to laugh and has to laugh because of the need to cry.

"If you just remember to leave the Old Hairy Man a roll of strong chewing tobacco on the ant hill, then you'll be master of the red ramkie. Then you can also make people sob or laugh, make them dance or make them grieve, just as your heart tells you that day. Now, goodnight, my little Master, now we're going to sleep."

Jannie flew out of bed and grabbed Outa Sem's legs. "I'm scared,

Outa Sem, I'm scared, you can't leave me here alone!"

"Scared? My dear jissis and who is little Master pretending to be afraid of?"

"I'm afraid of the Old Hairy Man, Outa Sem."

"But my goodness! The Old Hairy Man doesn't simply visit every youngster! The only crossroads are across the stream and he doesn't walk over water. Or is it still God Roberts perhaps? Who in the world can be scared of that Rooinek when Outa Sem is here? If Outa Sem could have made him look down his nose at the Tugela when he was so vengeful on the Master, will the white man's child be scared of a nobody when the whole yard is full of broken wagon hoops?"

"I don't know what you mean, Outa Sem, what about the old Master and wagon hoops?"

"Little Master, I'll tell you about a fine spectacle now. Down at the Tugela, when I was the Master's groom and it's just as well that this yellow dog was there. One day when the commando rode out to look for Rooineks, God Roberts sat on a hill between his cannons and looked through his binoculars. He saw the Master riding and said: 'Me goodness, thet is a pretty Boer dere' (that's how they speak the red language, my little Master), 'shoot him for me!' One, two three the English put out a whole lot of their lyddites – that's their best ones – aimed at the Master and let go.

"'Ghwar-a-a,' the cannon roared and I could see them spitting fire.

"'Too-loo-loo-loo!' I heard the cannon bullets coming just like horses neighing.

"'Duck, Master,' I shouted. But the Master remained upright on his horse.

"At first I thought: No, truly, tonight my Master will be deader than dead. Just then I saw a piece of wagon hoop lying there – it was part of an English cannon wheel – and I thought, here I must make a plan. And where was the white man's child to see? In a second Outa Sem grabbed the piece of wagon hoop and ran ahead of the Master! Wham! Wham! Wham! One after another he slammed away the stinkbombs of the English so that they flew back to the English camp like stray dogs with turpentine under their tails. Bang! Bang! they burst in front of God Roberts so that his moustache was burnt! Scared of God Roberts? Who's scared?

"After that, when God Roberts spied at the commando through his binoculars and saw that Outa Sem was present, he always said to his artillery: 'Nothing shooting with the cannon today! De shooting is oraait; the troubles is the shooting back!'"

The candle was almost guttering in the flask. Crouched on the rug in front of the bed, Outa Sem played softly: a gentle tune, full of sadness which he had learnt when he was still a young boy, a song he sang when he herded sheep in the lee of the mountain when the sun moved its head away; a tune which blended with the far-off bleating of lambs, the beating of a red-winged starling's wings, the laughter of children playing down in the valley; the rustling of the grazing sheep – all blended with the echoes of all those sounds to a hymn of gratitude for the day which had ended but also a grieving song, a farewell song to wonderful moments never to be repeated.

Whether it was the homeopathic influence of the Old Hairy Man on God Roberts is difficult to say; or whether it was old Sem's song – why are lullabies always so sad – or was it perhaps Outa Sem's untrained psychology? In any case, for the rest of that night and during the following nights, Jannie sank into the depths of sleep and his overstretched nerves calmed down.

One quiet Sunday morning, time hung heavily on Jannie's hands until he eventually made a lovely discovery: in a kist in the spare room, he found amongst all kinds of clothing and accessories, six ladies' shoes. He didn't know it but they were the shoes of his late mother. In a second they were inspanned in front of the work basket and Jannie spoke to them as only Outa Sem could speak to a team of oxen. Something else of which Jannie was unaware, was that a battery of field artillery had positioned itself opposite them, against the hill; that the company for some days had had a great many setbacks in this area and that a few farms in the district had shown so much opposition that the commanding officer was a trifle annoyed.

Across the plains of the spare room floor Jannie was driving his shining black team with the spreading horns at a swinging pace, so that the stanchions rattled and the axle pins clattered against the drums.

"Vaalty-y-y-y-n, you fine leader! Left there, left, Rooil-a-a-and! Witvoet, darn you, dash it! Blinkbla-a-a-r, you rascal! Pull, you forage feeders, pull! Pull the-e-e-re!"

The next moment heaven and earth were muddled and Jannie felt as if all the thunderstorms in the world, all the whirlwinds and all the earthquakes had come over him – and him alone. Half-dazed, he wiped the dust out of his eyes and looked up – half of the roof and the gable had disappeared and the rest was at an angle like a bonnet in a high wind. Nonplussed Jannie went to the front door to see what had happened to the world.

"Crr-u-ump!" a bomb fell just this side of the stable and threw a tree into the air.

"God Roberts," it suddenly occurred to Jannie and he ran to the kraal so fast that his little back was virtually hollow.

"Outa Sem! Wagon hoop! Outa Sem! Wagon hoop!"

"Crr-u-ump!" another bomb fell a little way ahead of him. Dumbfounded he stood still and looked round in the din. Everywhere in the yard huge clumps of earth were erupting. "Ghwar-a-s-a-a!" The roof of the barn went. He looked to the left: there, far past the poplar grove, Outa Sem was running. He was moving so fast that he became small in the distance and seemed barely to move in the passing wind.

Jannie dived head over heels into a heap of mealie leaves and there he sobbed and shivered until the attack had subsided. There he discovered that one could feel more deserted than lonely. When he crept out again the world was less bright than before: something of its splendour had gone. The ruins of a house and the shards of a great trust lay scattered but in later life, it saved Jannie many disillusions, great grief and heartache. It was unnecessary and superfluous for him to go through the rites of passage of the young: on this earth he never again sought or expected perfection.

Source:
Toon van den Heever: *Gerwe uit die erfpag van Skoppensboer.* Johannesburg: Afrikaanse Pers-Boekhandel: 1948.
Translated by Madeleine van Biljon

Always Light

Stuart Cloete

Boetie Theron sat leaning against a rock. His hat was tilted over his eyes. His head and body were in the shade of the rock, but the sun was on his feet. He could feel the warmth of the sun on his bare ankles, his feet and toes. His toes and the soles of his feet told him where he was. They knew the feel of the sand, and the stone, and the different kinds of grass.

To his right a *fink* twittered. It seemed to him that he knew what it was saying. It was talking about the new nest it was going to make. It was saying, "Boetie, it will be a beautiful nest, softly woven of grass and torn reeds. It will hang with the others, like a great pear, from the swinging willow by the drift."

It seemed to him that he knew what all the birds and beasts said to one another. Because he was blind, they let him into their world, made him, because he was helpless, a party to it. He never spoke of this except to his brother Dirk and his grandfather Servaas. They never laughed at him for his fancies. But it puzzled him that the great hunters and killers of beasts should also love them. Perhaps you had to have great sight – Oom Servaas could see a buck at a thousand paces and kill one at six hundred – or no sight at all to be at one with the wild. Dirk, too, was a great hunter, but Dirk was wonderful and above all other men.

Boetie knew that people were sorry for him. It made him draw back from them into his own world. If only they could guess how beautiful it was, it was in his heart that they would envy him. Everybody was kind to him, nothing distracted him. He had all time to himself. Time in which to think and wait, listen and feel.

Most people heard nothing. They did not know about the little rustlings in the grass, or the sound of wings in the evening as the doves flew down to water. They did not know the warm feeling of a tarentaal's nest filled with eggs. They missed so much. They did not know the feel of things – round things like eggs, and water-worn stones; rough things like the surface of hot rocks beneath their fingers, or of leather, or of skins. They did not know anything about smells. They went through life with blind noses. They might be sorry for him, but he was happy because he had so much.

He spent his life herding his father's two hundred big Boer goats. He knew them by the sound of their cloven hoofs on the stones, by the feel of their horns and hair, by their smell. The rank smell of the billy, the sweet smell of the ewes, and the milky smell and the soft hides of the unweaned kids. Their colours he did not know. How could he, since "colour" was only a word to him? He could see no colour. Yet he had a feeling for it. Sometimes it seemed to him that a thing felt red or blue or white beneath his hands – which was strange, since he did not know red, blue or white.

The leader of his father's goats was Witboi – a big white goat, they said. But he knew Witboi by his height, by the rasp of his long hair under his hand, by his smell and the nicks in the rings of his horns.

Sometimes as he lay in the sun, a goat would come up and nuzzle him. Their noses were not wet and smooth-cold like a cow's, they were not feather-soft like a horse's, they were not hard like a donkey's. A goat's nose was smooth like leather, with little stiff hairs and lips immune to thorns. A kid nibbled at him and then butted him, rearing and charging with little leaps. He put out his hand to it and felt for the scurfy bulbs where its horns were growing.

It was easy to herd goats. When he called to them, they came. When he piped, they followed. He had made himself a pipe out of soft wood. An old bushman had helped him. Together they had burned the little holes that made the notes and had hollowed it. He knew many tunes. His brother took him to the dances, leading his horse beside his own. He would sit there till it was over, listening to the dancing feet and making every melody his own. There were other tunes, also, ones he had heard here and there; and there were still others that he had made up.

These last were very beautiful to him. They were like grasshoppers climbing in the grass stems, like chameleons on a tree, walking slowly, with one eye turned forward and one turned back. They were like running water, like rain falling on a canopy of leaves; and some were like things you could feel with your hands, like the silk of a tasselled mealie, like the warm udder of a cow, or a dog's nose – wet and pushing. No one cared for this kind of music. Only he and the goats liked it. The goats followed it. Men said let Boetie play, since the goats follow him. So he played and the goats followed him over his father's veld and the mountain beyond the house – a long stream that pattered, on small hoofs, behind him.

There was less heat in the sun now. It was only reaching his toes. The shadows were lengthening. It was time to go. He got out his pipe. He smoothed it with his hand. He would play a minute. In a minute he would go down the mountain playing, the goats spilling down all round him, jumping from rock to rock and playing as they came. The mountainside was steep, but he knew it. His feet knew the path. He raised the pipe to his lips. He blew a note softly. He could feel a movement about him. The goats had raised their heads and were looking towards him. He blew again. The same note, but louder; and louder still, till his cheeks were blown out like fruit and his eyes were closed. The goats were running. They were all about him. He put down his hand to feel them. He sought head after head, horned heads and hornless. He felt the cuts in their ears by which they were marked, till he found the head he sought. Witboi was there. Now they could go. He turned and began to play. He would play them down the mountain. He would lead them into the kraal, and to-morrow, when his mother had given him breakfast and food for the day, he would lead them out again. It was a happy life.

The only thing that worried him was this talk of the war with the

English. He did not like to listen to it. He was too busy with other thoughts, but when he did think of it, it made him sad. It meant killing. Killing was wrong. To kill was to take something away that you could not give back. Besides, he liked the English. He had met an Englishman once. He had spent the night at his father's house, and on going, had given him a knife. It had several blades, a pair of scissors, a hook for removing stones from the feet of horses, and tweezers to pull thorns from your hands. No one in those parts had seen such a knife before. He had been a nice man, who had spoken softly, and his horse had had a neck like warm silk. It was said that they brushed their horses daily. It had felt red; and when he had asked, they had told him that it was a red horse, and asked how he knew. "I do not know how I know," he had said. "It felt red, that is all." But he did not know what red was.

He stopped playing to smile and shake the water from his pipe.

There were some who said he was simple. His brother Dirk had struck a man who had said he was simple. "If all the world was as simple as our Boetie," his brother had said, "it would be a better place." Then there had been a great scuffle and a chair had got broken. He had run away to the kraal and hidden under the bellies of his goats. They had covered him like a cloak.

He began to play again. He did not want to think of fighting or war. But when he got back the war had come. His father and Dirk were saddling their horses. They kissed him good-bye, pressing their bandoliers into his chest as they held him. Their rifles were slung over their shoulders. While he had been on the mountain, the war had come.

He stood very still as they mounted. He listened to their movements, the scuffle of the horses' unshod hoofs on the ground, the creak of the leather, the rattle of bits and stirrups as the horses swung together, turning. He must remember this sound of his father's and brother's going.

"*Tot siens,*" they shouted. "*Tot siens, Ma . . . Tot siens, Boetie.*"

He could feel the horses buckle under their riders as they raised their reins and put their heels into them. They broke from the stand into a canter. Though they ran together he could distinguish them apart. Dirk's horse was lighter and faster than his father's. Its feet struck the ground harder, with quick little beats as if it was eager to get on, as if it hated to have its hoofs upon the ground. Dirk's horse was a hot little horse, very urgent and strong. His father's was more solid and slower. He knew Dirk would be having to hold his horse. He knew how they would ride side by side, his father leading only when they came to a narrow path with Dirk's horse snatching at its bit and pulling to get up as soon as the ground opened again. He stood mouse-still, listening as the sound of the hoofs faded into the distance.

He stood frozen by the silence and the emptiness of their going. Now there was nothing for him but to strain his ears for their return. Among a thousand hoofbeats he would know those horses. He felt his mother beside him. She put her arm about him.

"What shall we do, Ma," he asked, "now that they are gone?"

"We are going to trek, Boetie. We are going to Oom Servaas."

"We are going from here? We are going to trek? Because of the war?"

"It will be better there."

"Yes, Ma, it will be better there," he said. Perhaps it would be better there – but what would they do without his father and Dirk? Without them it would be no world.

"You love your grandmother," his mother said.

"I love *Tante* Lisa. But it will be dark for me there. I do not know that veld, and how shall I graze my father's goats in strange place where it is dark?" For the first time he knew what it was to be blind. If they moved him to a strange place, he would be lost.

All that day he sat waiting while things were prepared. He sat listening to his mother's voice as she gave orders about the beasts. Old July was to stay on the farm. He was a good Kaffir, very faithful, who would not move far from the house.

In the morning the horses were inspanned. The wagon box was lashed on the back. The loose horses, cattle and goats were collected. They were to be driven behind the cart.

"Come, Boetie," his mother said. "Come, we are ready."

He felt under him for the long parcel. It was wrapped in sacking and tied with a riem.

"What is that, Boetie?" his mother said. "What are you bringing?"

"I am bringing my brother's other rifle," he said. "Be careful, Ma, I have loaded it."

His mother began to say something and then stopped. He knew what had been on her tongue. She had been going to ask what a blind boy would do with a rifle. But she had not said it. Often he knew what people were going to say and knew that they bit off their words before they hurt him.

"Take it, Ma." He held it up, waving it a little till he felt her hand on it. "Listen," he said, "it is my brother's rifle. He may want it or I may. Those who look at me do not know that I am blind. They say my eyes are clear and blue. Therefore, it is in my heart that if anything happened to us, you could stand me right with the gun in my hand, and no one would know. All that they would know was that a boy was in front of them with a gun in his hands. All they would wonder would be why he was there and not with the others." He got up beside her. His feet were against the dashboard. He put out a hand to touch the reins his mother held in her hand. "That is Meisie on the near side," he said, "and Bles on the off. Is it not so?" he asked. Now he must be more alert than ever.

"Yes, I have got Meisie and Bles as wheelers," his mother said. "How did you know?" They were not generally used as wheelers in the Cape cart.

"I do not know, Ma, how I know," he said, "but I know; and for leaders you have the two new horses my father bought from the

Free State. I know that also. But I am nothing, Ma," he said suddenly. "Now I am going to a strange place that my feet do not know and I am nothing." As the wheels turned he knew this more than ever. But he strained all that was in him to feel and listen. "We are going uphill," he said. "The ground is more stony here."

Somehow he must know the changes of the ground. He could tell much by the sound of the iron tyres. Then came a bank of oaklip – he could feel how easily they ran; then to some other kind of ground – it was covered with small loose stones, hard ones that slipped away from the wheels or that the wheels passed over without crushing. The hoofs of the horses sounded different too.

"Tell me what you can see, Ma," he asked. "Can you still see the mountain?"

"Which mountain?"

"Our mountain where I graze my goats?"

He felt his mother turn. "*Ja*, I can see it, and you can still see it from Oom Servaas's place."

They did not outspan. It was only ten miles, but when they got there he found his grandfather had gone. Old Servaas was over seventy, but he had gone with the others. Servaas Theron was not one to stay at home when the others rode. Everyone had gone, all the old men and the boys as well. He alone was left. He was almost a man. He was fourteen but useless. Blind and useless. There was nothing for him to do but wait, and he was afraid here.

The days that followed did not make him less afraid. It was new and he was lost. The feel of it was new to his feet. The smells and sounds were new. His goats in the kraal were mixed with his grandfather's goats, and he did nothing but listen for the coming of a mounted man. Sometimes strange men passed, sometimes someone he knew. Then he would call to them for news. If it was a friend, he could tell who it was when he was far off.

Only once he was wrong. He called to Martinus du Plessis.

"I am not Martinus, I am Barend Fourie."

"You are on Martinus's horse," he said.

"Ja, he has lent me his horse. Mine has been shot under me."

There was no mistaking horses. But Barend had no news of his father or Dirk.

Each day he went out with the goats, allowing himself to be led like a dog at the end of a line by the picannin who herded them. But some days he would go out alone with Witboi, holding him by his collar, the goat's bell beating beneath his hand. He had put a bell on the big billy so that he could tell where he was. When they were together like this, if the wind was right, it seemed to him that he could smell his mountain. Then he would stand smiling into the wind with his hat off and his hair blowing. At those times he was happy.

There were no days and nights for him. There was a time when it was cold – that was what they called night; and there was a time when it was warm – then it was day. But often he slept in the warmth of the sun and walked by night. By now he had learned his way about the home place. He knew the kraals. Sometimes in the moonlight, they told him it was moonlight. He felt different and restless and would go out and play his pipe softly so as not to wake his mother, but loud enough for his goats to hear; so that when he came to the kraal, his father's goats had separated themselves from the others and were waiting for him, ready to greet him with nibbling lips. Ready to stand with their feet on his shoulders and lick the salt sweat from his face.

Day after day was the same. There was no news. There was never any news. Before, Boetie had never wanted news. Before, there had been no outer world. He had lived in his home with his father's goats, his mountain and accustomed things about him. He had never thought that things could be different. He had been like a plant that had grown, and was rooted in one place. It was his place. He was part of it, as much as the trees and the rocks, as much as the river that he used to listen to, as much as the birds and beasts of that particular part. He was finding his way about better now. He was almost accustomed to his grandfather's farm, but it was not home. He was always alert, always on edge and ready to leap away from something. It was a strange place. It would stay strange. He, Boetie Theron, did not belong here.

Once a commando passed – tired men on tired horses. He stood listening to them. The shuffling steps of the horses, the smell of men, sweat-sour, told him all he need to know.

"Have you seen my father or my brother?" he asked.

"Who are you?" they said.

"I am Boetie Theron. I am blind," he said. "My father is Groot Dirk Theron," he said. "He is with Joubert's commando."

"We are joining Joubert. We will tell him we have seen you," they said.

For a time he followed them, smelling the dust that lay on the veld behind them. They were joining his father's commando. They had been fighting. With his feet he felt for the spoor of their horses. They were going and he must return. He was useless. People were gentle to him, but he was useless, a charge upon his family. It was very hot and he turned back.

More horses were coming. But these were different. They were not the horses of his people. They were heavier and were handled differently. They were not being ridden loose-reined. He stood leaning on his long stick and waited. They came nearer. He could hear the jingling of chains, the strike of metal on metal. These were English. He turned his eyes towards them. The horses were very near. For a moment he thought they would ride him down, but they pulled up right at his feet; he could feel the breath of the leading horse upon him. He was splattered by the foam from its mouth as it shook its head. The horses were excited. They plunged and reared. There was a small wind, and the dust blew on to him as he stood. They must be pursuing the tired men who had passed him earlier.

"Have you seen any men, boy? Have you seen a commando pass?"

It was the man on the horse nearest to him. It was passaging in front of him and he turned his eyes to follow it, looking upwards towards the rider. No doubt it was the officer in command. He seemed young and was breathing hard.

"I have seen nothing," Boetie said. "I have been out all day and I have seen nothing."

"You'll get nothing out of that boy," a man said, "but they came this way all right and have gone towards the hills. They can't be far away. Their horses are tired."

Their horses were tired, Boetie thought, but it was strange that these men could not see where they had gone when he could read their spoor with his feet; when the dung of their horses was still warm and dustless.

"Come on, then," the officer said: "they can't be far."

The troop swirled past him. He sat down. He was trembling. The English were fresh, their horses were full fed – corn fed. They were well armed. He had heard the rattle of their sabres and the sound of their carbines creaking in their saddle buckets. There were, as far as he had been able to make out, some thirty of them but there might have been some led horses or pack horses with machine or mountain guns. He could only count horses. He could not tell what they carried. It was very hot, but he felt cold with fear. He wanted to go back, but was unable to move. He strained his ears. He knew what he was waiting for. It would come soon.

It came. A single shot. Two more, singly – those were his people. The English did not shoot like that. Those were aimed Boer shots. Those shots would empty saddles. Tears came into his eyes. If only I were with them! *If only I were not useless!* Now came the answering fire, much faster, a rattle of shots from the carbines. The English would have dismounted. They had to have horse holders. That meant that one man out of three or four was occupied holding the horses of the others, whereas all the Boers could shoot. Their horses would stand alone. He breathed a sigh of relief. He had been afraid of the English charging with sabres. If his folk had made them dismount, they were safe. They would be able to fight them off as they retreated towards Joubert. His father and Dirk were there. They would come and help them. Perhaps they would be able to lead the English into a trap. If they stood and ran as was their custom, they might lead them into an ambush. He was happier now and got up.

But the war which had been distant was now near. If there was one troop of English cavalry, there would be more. They did not fight like his folk, in small bodies. He began to be afraid for Dirk and his father. The shots were fainter now. They were fighting a running action. That was the way the Boers fought. They were fighting their way back from kopje to kopje towards the mountains. But it was not that troop that worried him; it was the fact that it might be only one of many.

He did not know how many men Joubert had. Or how fresh their horses were, or if they had food, ammunition and water. He thought of his father and brother, tired with fighting, faced by fresh troops. The English could do nothing against his folk if they had room to manoeuvre, for the country was theirs. They were fighting on their own farms, and in every commando, no matter where they were, there were men who knew the country. Men who owned it, or who had been there hunting or going to visit relatives and friends.

He made his way back slowly.

"Did you see the English?" his mother asked.

"*Ja*, I saw them, Ma," he said. "They spoke to me. They were following a commando." His Ma knew what he meant when he said "saw". For him it was seeing, only he saw in other ways. "There was firing," he said. "My father and Dirk are there, they say. I spoke to the commando. They are with Joubert over there." He pointed to the west.

"I wish we had news," his mother said. "It is hard to live without news."

"*Ja*, Ma it is hard to live without news. It is hard also to be a man and to be here. *Magtig*, to-day I was ashamed. First to face our folk and then to face the English. I told our people, but I did not tell the English. They did not know that I could not see. Oh, Ma," he said, "I am ashamed." He clung to her. He was a man. He was fourteen and too old to cry. But his father and brother were fighting and he was doing nothing to help them. "Is there nothing I can do? Is there nothing, Ma?"

"There is nothing, Boetie. It is not your fault."

"It is not my fault, but it twists my heart inside me. Everyone has gone," he said. "Boys younger than I and old men like Oupa. I alone in all the land am left like a woman or a Kaffir, and I am no use here. I cannot even herd the goats, for they are mixed with the others that will not follow me."

That night Boetie did not go out. He lay down and tried to sleep, but could not for thinking of those others. It seemed as if by not sleeping, by suffering, by thinking, he could help them. He tried to build up a battle in his head. Tried to think what it would be like. But it would not come. He could only feel and smell things. It came to him that he did not even know what a man or a horse was really like. So he built up his battle by the feel of the sweating necks or horses, by the smell of men like those who had passed him to-day, acrid and bitter from coated sweat and dust, from spilt food hurriedly eaten, and strong tobacco; by the sensation of rifles hot with firing, by the sound of bolts opening and closing, by the soft click of the cartridges as they rose from the magazine into the breech; by the reek of exploding cordite and the crackle of shots – the whip crack of a high bullet and the bee sting of the low. In this way he could think of a battle, by bringing all the noises and scents and feelings that he knew together – the sound of hoofs, the rattle of chains, accoutrements. Suddenly he sprang up. Had he been sleeping? Was he dreaming? Sometimes you dreamed a dream within a dream. It was not a dream.

"Ma, Ma," he shouted. 'It is my brother. It is my brother on Swartkie. He is riding hard." He ran to his mother. He felt her sitting up in bed. "The gun," he said. "Get me the gun."

"I can hear nothing, Boetie my heart," his mother said.

"It is my brother. I can hear him. Give me the gun."

She jumped up. "I can hear it now," she said. "It is a horse galloping."

"It is Swartkie. He is riding hard. It is my brother; he is pursued."

His mother pushed the rifle into his hand. He opened the bolt and closed it. The cartridge slid into the breech; he half opened the bolt to feel it and closed it again. How cold the gun felt in his hand. Even the walnut butt was cold. He found the door and opened it. The horse had not slowed down.

Tante Lisa was up. "It is as black as pitch," she said. "What a night to ride like that."

"Light up the lamp, Ma," Boetie said. "Light it quick, so that I can be seen against it."

He heard her strike a match. She was slow. Her hand was trembling as she fitted on the glass.

"Is it alight?" he asked. "Is it on the table behind me?"

"It is on the table, Boetie."

"Then get a horse, Ma. There is a good one in the kraal. His tail is rubbed a little near the root."

"What colour is it?" his mother asked.

"Colour?" Boetie said. "I do not know. It is a big horse, a stallion. You can't mistake him. He is the only one with a rubbed tail."

"It is a bay horse with a star," *Tante* Lisa said.

By raising his right elbow, Boetie could feel the door frame. He was in the middle of the doorway. His bare feet gripped the stone floor. His gun was held across him ready to raise. The horse was on him; above the sound of the hoofs he could hear it gasping for breath. Swartkie was done. But the horse he had sent his mother for was a good one. Once his brother was off, he would go outside and let them shoot towards the light. Then he could shoot back towards the sound. If he shot fast and kept moving, they would not know he was alone.

"Stop or I shoot," he shouted. It was Dirk's horse, but it might not be Dirk.

"Boetie – Boetie, what are you doing?" It was Dirk.

"The horse is coming, Dirk. Ma is bringing you a fresh horse," Boetie said. "Take off your saddle and go on."

The horse was dragged on to its haunches. Its hoofs were sliding along the ground.

"What is it, Boetie?" Dirk said.

"Are you all right, Dirk? I thought you were being chased. I have never known you to ride like that. It was in my heart that you were being pursued, and that Swartkie could do no more."

"I am not being followed. I have come for you. I want you to come with me."

Boetie could hear his brother off-saddling. He heard the saddle clap on the back of the horse his mother had brought.

"Why so fast? What is it, Dirk?" his mother asked. "You take a chance riding so hard on such an night."

"*Ja*, Ma, we take chances. I have no time to explain. I must have Boetie. I have come to fetch him. Joubert needs him."

"Joubert? You are taking Boetie to the war. What can Boetie do?"

"*Ja*, what can I do?" Boetie said.

"I'll tell you on the way. Come here."

Boetie went towards the horse and felt for his brother's leg. His hand went down behind it for the leather. It would be hanging loose. He held the stirrup with one hand and put his foot into it. His brother had his left hand. He was up.

"Hold fast, Boetie, we are going to ride."

He had hardly got hold of his brother's waist when the horse was off. Dirk had turned his head and they were galloping. It began to rain. Dirk's back sheltered him from it, but he felt it on his hands. Under them the big horse moved easily. He was fast and strong. Where were they going? What was he to do? What use could he be to Joubert? He was going to the war with his brother. He would see his father. He tried to ask Dirk, but his brother did not answer him. He was bent over the horse's neck. The ground grew rougher. There were loose stones. He remembered the stones slipping away from the cart wheels. Suddenly he sat up straighter. He could smell the mountain. They were getting nearer and nearer. He wondered where the camp was. Were they laagered? Had they wagons with them? Dirk was turning; he felt the horse swing under him.

"We are nearly there," Dirk said. "There are the fires." He pulled up. "I am back," Dirk shouted. He dismounted, throwing his leg over his horse's neck.

Boetie felt his brother's arms round him. He lifted him down.

"Have you got him?" someone said.

"Is Boetie there?" It was his father's voice.

"I am here, Pa. Dirk has brought me."

"Can he do it, Dirk?" his father said.

"I have not asked him, but I know he can if you do not hurry him . . . Get back," Dirk said to the men who had crowded him . . . "Get back. You will bewilder him. Where is Joubert? Where is the commandant? Are the men ready? He said that he would hold them ready for we have little time."

"*Magtig*, it is dark," a man said.

"Dark like the inside of a beast."

"Where's the boy?" It was Joubert. "Where is Dirk Theron? Has he got him?"

"We are here," Dirk said. "Explain what you want of him. I have said nothing."

What was going to happen? Boetie felt crowded. There were men all round him, very near. Sometimes their rifles touched him. His father's hand was on his shoulder. Dirk was near him. He could smell him. He felt safe again and reassured. Someone took his hand.

"I am Joubert and you are young Boetie Theron."

"*Ja*." The hand he held felt good. It was the hand of an old man, hard with work, but warm and confident.

"Listen, Boetie," Joubert said, "to what I tell you. We are here with a hundred men. We have got the drift. The English are to the north and a big commando is driving them back. Our plan is to hold them here and not allow them to cross. You understand? They do not know we are here and are retreating towards the drift we are holding."

"I understand," Boetie said. "you hold it and they will not be able to cross, then the commando will have them – they will be caught between two fires."

"*Ja*," Joubert said, "that is it. But something has gone wrong. A force of English has got to the top of the mountain. We command the drift, but they command us. They got there before we did. We were going to get them out to-night. We were going to attack them, but there is only one path from this side. It is very small, a goat track, and the night is so dark that we can do nothing. If we do not get them out, we cannot hold the drift and it will all have been for nothing." Joubert stopped talking. "It was your brother's idea," he said.

"What was his idea?" Boetie asked.

"He said you could lead us."

"Me lead you? Me lead Joubert's commando?"

"Yes, you, Boetie," his brother said. "You know the path."

'*Ja*, I know the path." Of course he knew the path. Had he not been up it almost every day of his life?

"I can find it if you take me to the drift, Oom Joubert. It is never dark for me."

They set his feet on the path where it began, by the drift. His father was behind him; then came Dirk, and then the others, many others, a long file of men on his goat path, all following him, all holding the riem he held. Each man had taken a spare riem from his saddle and they had tied them together to make a long snake of hide. It was his mountain. He was leading the commando. His feet found the path easily; they knew each stone and root, each bend, each rock. He recognised the scents of the mountain herbs. He recognised the little breezes, the small eddies of air that came from the kloofs or swept upwards from the steep kranses. Here it was warmer; there it was colder. It was always colder here. He knew them all. The rain had been hard. He could hear the water running off the mountain. It was pouring down the cliffs in cascades that roared into the void beneath them.

"This is a path for goats and baboons," his father said. "I never knew you came up here. I would never have let you come. If you slipped –"

"I do not slip. It is my mountain."

He laughed to himself. He knew what it was, for often he dropped stones from the path and listened to them bounding down. Perhaps it was as well it was dark. Perhaps had there been more light the burghers would not have climbed. But now they could not see. Among them all, because he was blind, only Boetie Theron could see. And they would be ashamed not to follow where a blind boy led.

"We are nearly there, Pa," he said, stopping as he came to the face of a cliff. A baboon barked above them. Boetie waited. "Here you must climb," he said, "but it is the last krans; after that you are on the top."

He felt for a fingerhold in the wet rock. He could feel his father behind him. They were up. Man after man passed him, breathing heavily. There had been no challenge. The English were sleeping, or miserable with wet and cold, were paying no attention to what went on. Joubert was whispering instructions. The men were spreading out.

His father pushed him down behind a big stone. "Stay there, Boetie. Wait, we will come back for you."

He must wait now. They were done with him. He felt cold and very alone. He could feel the men leaving him – feel them creeping forward. He knew how they would be crouching. Joubert had told them not to show themselves against the skyline. They had gone. They were creeping on towards a camp of sleeping men. There was a shout and a shot. Then everyone was shouting and shooting. There were cries from the wounded. Shots and more shots, a hoarse cheer from the Boers and the shout "They are running."

For a moment he thought he was dreaming. He had been dreaming of battle. It was only to-night that he had been dreaming before Dirk had come. In his dream there had been shouts, cries, shots and calls. He was trembling like a dog that is held from a buck. He wanted to run forward. There was a terrific burst of fire. He could smell the burning cordite. A single shot and then nothing till he heard his father call him.

"Boetie, Boetie, are you there?"

"I am here." He went towards his father.

"He is here," his father said.

Someone took his hand. It was Joubert. He knew that hand, but it was wet with hot blood.

"You are hit, Oom Joubert," he said.

"It is nothing, just a cut. I want to thank you, *jong*. Without you this could not have been done; and had it been a fair night, I do not think it could have been done. I do not think we would have faced that climb had we been able to see. We are burghers, not baboons. The English came up another way, from the back of the berg," he said.

"I know that way, too, but it is far."

They were all round him now, pressing against him and taking his hand. Boetie could not understand it. As they came to congratulate him, they had tears in their throats. "If it had not been for you," they said.

Yes, if it had not been for him, there would have been many dead and homes left fatherless. This they knew. The English would have got through. But why this talk? He had done what it was in him to do. What each one of them would have done; and now that it was over, it seemed to him that he had never done it. That it was not he; that these folks were talking past him, talking of a stranger, *I did it*, he thought. *Yes, I did it, but it was not me.* All the time as he did it, it had been in his mind that it was another who did it. *I could not be doing this,* he had thought as he did it. He was exhausted. He had walked far in the morning, following in the spoor of the commando. He felt as if he was a long way off from them. He had known when he began that this thing he had set out to do could not be done. Yet it had been done and he had done it. More men kept coming; the whole hundred must be shaking his hand; ever more people who said, "If it had not been for you, Boetie –"

"They will make songs of this," an old man said. "Songs of Boetie Theron's climb. It was the will of God that he should lead us."

Ja, it must have been the will of God that had guided his feet in unaccustomed places, for he had never been up to the top of the mountain before. His goats had been, and he knew that, for he could feel their footholds in the rocks. But he had never been. He had never dared. Not to the very top.

Source:
Stuart Cloete: *The Silver Trumpet and Other Stories.* London: Collins: 1961.

Concentration Camp

Sampie de Wet

My mother and I were driving along the tarred road to Middelbult. We had been visiting my elder sister, who is married and lives on a farm. My brothers are also married and my father was killed at Monte Sole in Italy. So there are only the two of us, and we do a lot of things together. I love my mother best in the world, and mean never to leave her. But I wish she weren't so quiet, and that I could more often get her to talk.

It was a beautiful day in early winter, cold and clear and sunny. All round us stretched the tawny undulating grasslands of the highveld. Here and there, in the wide-stretching plains of grass, there were ploughed lands, windbreaks of black wattle trees, or clumps of bluegums. Suddenly my mother pointed to one of these clumps, some distance to the right of the road. There was a monument among the trees. "Go slowly, darling," she said, "I'd like to have a look at that. There ought to be a road somewhere, which will take us to it."

There was no road, only a rough, rutted track, and the long dusty grass which grew on both sides of it brushed against the car, as we drove the short distance off the road. The long grass was everywhere. It crowded against the barbed-wire fence, pushed through the cracks in the broken brickwork, and waved its yellow seeded heads above the rows of graves, in what I now realised was a cemetery. Only round the four-sided granite monument in the centre a patch of red veld has been cleared. We went up to it and read the inscription on the nearest face, "To the memory of 53 men, 182 women, and 1,357 children who died in the concentration camp at Middelbult, and were buried here between May 1901 and October 1902."

It was very peaceful. The bluegum trees grew round the fence, tall and straight, with the beautiful white trunks that are only attained in maturity. From their foliage sounded the coo-COO-roo, coo-COO-roo, coo-COO-roo of Cape turtle doves. The inscriptions on the monument were faded. Many of the letters had lost their gilt. We stood silently before the fourth face, with its brief inscription.

Hoevele dierbare
Rust in de aarde
Uit liefde voor Vaderland en Geslacht.

I looked at my quiet, aloof mother, and her eyes were full of tears. She said. "It has changed a great deal. You never knew, did you, that when I was a little girl I was in the concentration camp near here, and that two of my brothers are buried in this cemetery."

It made me feel that I, too, had a share in that peace and beauty. "No," I said, "I never knew. Why have you never told me? I tell you all about myself, everything that happens to me, yet there is so much I don't know about you, so much you never tell me. You have often spoken about the more recent wars and never about this one, which belongs to us."

"Your father did not like me to talk about it," said my mother. "He was always grieved when anybody spoke bitterly about the khakis, and about those others, the 'hensoppers' and the joiners, our own people who helped the enemy. Your father was a Smuts man, as you know, and he always preached tolerance. Since his death I often think about the past. Let me walk about a little, without talking, and when we are back in the car I will tell you the story."

"You have often heard," she said, as once more the car moved easily along the tarred road, "that your Oupa Van Rensburg, my father, was a burgher of the South African Republic, that he was caught early in the war and was a prisoner of war at Simonstown. But my two elder brothers, Oom Jan and Oom Klaas, though they were both under sixteen, joined my uncle, and fought through the war in General De la Rey's Commando. Later your Ouma Van

Rensburg, my mother, and the rest of us were sent to the concentration camp. I was nearly ten and your Aunt Lena was twelve. There were three brothers younger than I, the youngest a baby of a few months. One of them is your Oom Dirk.

"In the early days of the war things went well, but later food was scarce and I remember how hungry I was. I remember even the clothes I wore, the sunbonnet and the pinafore with a square yoke of hand-crocheted lace, as I stood and watched the khakis burning mealies in our market place. I vividly remember the feel of the warm sand under the soles of my bare feet, as I smelt the coffee and sugar they were burning.

"Yes, they burnt large quantities of coffee and sugar, and we were starving. We had to make coffee out of bran. The mealies were put out to dry on the flat roofs of the sheds, and the khakis scraped them off, poured oil over them and set light to the oil. When they had gone the women used to rake what they could out of the fire. They had to feed their children, and I remember days when I was so hungry that coarse burnt mealie-meal tasted better than the best dinner does today. My mother was alone in her house with us five children. We were always hungry. The khakis said that our men came home at night, and that if they left us food we would feed them and give them provisions to take on Commando. That was true enough. What else could we do? My father was then already a prisoner, but sometimes my uncle came, or one of my brothers, with his friends. We gave them what we could, even though we went hungrier than ever. I was glad that we gave them our food, because they were fighting for our country.

"Then we were sent to the concentration camp. We were sent by oxwagon, with a lot of other women and children. I remember my mother, before we left, standing on a kitchen chair and shaking pepper into her sitting-room curtains. They were of red velvet and she was very proud of them. 'The khaki who takes these down,' she said, 'will get a surprise.' My mother was a strong-minded woman.

I don't know who took the curtains. When we got back everything was gone.

"I liked the journey by oxwagon. There was more to eat than at home. We used to walk or run ahead of our wagon and talk to the khaki officers. One of them, Captain Smithson, carved me a doll out of wood. He used to give us children sweets and other food, and when they killed a sheep he saw to it that the women and children got an extra ration of meat. In the evenings he encouraged us to come to his camp fire and told us stories. When I spoke bitterly about the khakis, in the early days of our marriage, your father always told me to remember Captain Smithson.

"The camp was really a village of tents, rows and rows of round tents with streets in between. When we arrived, there was still grass here and there, but before long there was just red earth and dust, and thick red mud when it rained. It was hot in the daytime, but I liked that. Even summer nights, in the tents, were cold, and in the winter I used to be too cold to sleep. Our family had a small tent to ourselves. A lot of time I had to go and queue for our rations, meat one day, meal the next, candles after that. I was big enough, Mamma said, and she had other work. Lena had to help her with the little boys. The standing made me tired because I was so hungry. I also helped with the washing, and I dusted the tent and kept it tidy. There was very little time for playing.

"The meat was bad. Sometimes when I brought it back it smelt so that Mamma just made a hole next to the tent and buried it. If the joiners had seen her do that we wouldn't have been given meat for a month. In the tent next to ours there was a Mrs Van Niekerk from the Free State. She was a thin woman with dark hair and sad brown eyes like those of a collie dog. She had her six children with her. Her second husband had recently been killed at Gatsrand, with Commandant Danie Theron. She cried a lot. One day when the meat was very bad she cried and threw it at the tent wall, and it stuck there in a lump instead of falling to the ground.

"Mamma said Mrs Van Niekerk was a feckless woman. When she got her ration of coarse meal she sifted out all the bran and threw it away. Then she made vetkoekies and all her children ate as much as they wanted. Sarel van Niekerk used to bring me a few cakes too. The next day the little ones cried with hunger because all the meal was finished and they had no bread. Mrs Van Niekerk cried aloud, cursing the khakis between her sobs, and saying: 'They are killing all the women and children by starvation. They won't give us food to eat.'

"If the meal was given out on a Friday, Mamma said, and she knew there would be no more till the next Tuesday, she divided it into four portions and used just one part each day. She used it as it was, with the coarse bran in it. So we always had food, though not as much as we wanted, and it wasn't as good as the Van Niekerks' vetkoekies. When Sarel was hungry I gave him some of my food, but he wouldn't take much and I was glad, as I wanted it myself.

"Sarel and I used to invent games to play while we were in the queue waiting for the rations. He was a thin little boy with brown eyes like his mother's, but his hair was fair and he was always smiling. He was clever at thinking up things to do. He invented guessing and counting games which we could play without having to run about, but while we were well we also played hop-scotch between the tents, and we played the throwing game with pebbles which little native children play.

"Mrs Van Niekerk wouldn't be careful, as my mother was. She said the bran was fit only for pigs, and she threw it away in the mud or the red dust outside her tent door. She threw paper and bones and other rubbish there too. She wouldn't use the pit provided for our tents, which the kaffirs cleaned out once a week, piling the rubbish into a scotchcart. When they came to spray with the disinfectant, she wouldn't tie up the folds of her tent, so that everything got wet and messy. When the handsuppers and the joiners came round she used to cry and curse them, so that they were always harder on her than on us. After her little Daantjie died of the measles she got much worse. She was always in trouble. Once she was made to stand for a whole day in a barbed-wire enclosure in the baking sun. Sarel and I spent most of the day there too, talking to her and trying to soothe her. Sarel was the only person who could sometimes quiet his mother, when she was in one of her worst moods.

"It wasn't the khakis who treated us so badly. Your father always said many of them did not know what was happening in the camps. It was the handsuppers and the joiners, our own people working for the English. It was they who were so hard on the women. I heard them talking to Mrs Van Niekerk as I would never talk to a servant. Sometimes they threw her meat ration in the dirt and made her pick it up there. For a while there was a joiner in charge of the camp. It was he who made a small barbed-wire enclosure, with no shade and no protection from the wind, and there he put the women who had broken the rules. Their children used to stand and cry outside the wire. After Miss Hobhouse came they stopped all that. I saw Miss Hobhouse myself. She was a tall thin Englishwoman with long feet. We used to laugh about her feet, but she was very good to us women and children.

"None of my family got the measles, we'd all had it at home the year the war started, but many, many children died of it in the camp. Our baby was already dead. I don't remember exactly when he died, but it was soon after we got there. Both my little brothers got the stomach sickness. It was because of the bad food that was too heavy for their stomachs. Koosie was the worst. First he couldn't walk any more and went back to crawling like a year-old boy, then he couldn't even crawl but just lay still, or sat propped up. The nurses came round and brought medicines from the doctors, but nothing helped. When he lay on his side his cheeks were so fallen in that we could see the shape of each one of his teeth. His shoulder and knee joints looked enormous and his legs were like little sticks. They took him away to the hospital before he died and I was glad. I was a selfish child. I knew it was wrong of me, but I was glad that I could no longer see him breathing or hear his thin little cry. I don't remember anything more about him, only how my mother wept when he was dead.

"At that time thirty children were dying every day. Sarel and I used to watch the carts that took them to the cemetary. But Sarel got ill too and could not walk so far. There were no more children to be seen in the camp. I was quite well, but there was nobody to play with me when I had finished my work. After a while Sarel just stayed in bed and Jan and Anna van Niekerk were dead. Sarel was thinner than ever. He did not smile except when I talked to him and tried to make jokes. One day I saw that he was beginning to have the same look as my brother Koosie. Mrs Van Niekerk just sat and cried, or wailed and cursed the khakis and the handsuppers. My other brother, Dirk, was getting just like Koosie had been.

"Then my mother took the 'wonderdruppels' that she had for her pain in her side, and she began to give them to Dirk. And he didn't get worse. After a week he was even a little better. But I was very unhappy because Sarel van Niekerk couldn't stand up any longer, and he had always been such a strong little boy, and his mother's right hand. And, though he was seven months younger than me, he had always looked after me. I have had many troubles, and they say a child can't suffer as much as a grown-up person, but I have never in my life been as unhappy as when I thought Sarel would die. Mrs Van Niekerk did nothing for him. She just sat with her apron thrown over her head, wailing for her children who were already dead.

"So when Dirk was definitely getting better I begged a little bottle from Tant Hessie Swanepoel, that had the tent on the other side of us, and I stole half of what was left of Mamma's 'wonderdruppels'. Mamma was very angry and I got very frightened, but she never found out what had happened to the drops. She worried and worried about it, but she never guessed that I had taken them. And three times a day I gave a few drops to Sarel, just as I had seen Mamma do for Dirk. Whenever I could I also coaxed him to eat a little of my food. And slowly, slowly, Sarel got better. By then we were getting quite good food and sometimes even vegetables, and in time both Dirk and Sarel were well again.

"But then I got ill with the fever that came to the camps, and I don't remember much more. I don't even remember how we went home. What I'll never forget is the smell of the coffee and sugar, as the khakis burnt them in the market-place, and the anguish in my heart when I thought Sarel van Niekerk was going to die.

"Years later, years after Union, I married Sarel. Did you realise he was your father? In those days he was always called by his stepfather's name, but later, of course, he used his own. Mrs Van Niekerk was dead by the time we married. I often wonder what she would have said if she knew her grandchildren had worn khaki, and that her son died in Italy, fighting with the English. I could have felt like Mrs Van Niekerk, but your father said we had to change with the times, that we couldn't have kept our republic and were better off as the Union of South Africa. He said that the people who were most bitter about the war were the sons of the handsuppers and the joiners, and that we had to understand and forgive them. While he was alive I never liked to think about the concentration camp, but now I treasure every memory of him, and I can remember it all without bitterness. I remember only how grieved he was whenever I spoke rashly and unkindly. When I long for him and wonder why he died so young, I tell myself that he nearly died in 1902, and I am grateful for the forty years longer that he was spared, and for all the happy years that we were together."

Source:
Sampie de Wet: *Nine Stories*. Cape Town: A.A Balkema: 1948.

PEACE

J.C. STEYN

No, don't expect anything. We will lose. Don't expect *anything*. We *will* lose. Expect nothing. We are the losers, we will be the conquered, the downtrodden of Africa, even if our cause is just. We have never won, we always lose, always. But President Steyn did say he would never sign away our freedom? No, it doesn't help to believe in miracles. But we prayed? No, God sleeps in Africa. But our cause? Yes, our cause is just but right is not yet might? Peace must surely come? Peace, yes, the peace! That is coming. One day someone will come and say the war is over and we have lost. It can't be any other way. Expect nothing, absolutely nothing. Rather expect to lose everything. We've just about lost it all by now. Well? Understood? Now expect to lose everything, every single thing, to lose it all. Then the real loss won't be so difficult when peace comes.

"Daniel, are you coming?"

"Yes, Ma, now!"

As if we were still on the farm: "Come in out of the cold wind!"; "Come now, the food is ready"; "Let us read a passage from the Bible!"; "Let us pray", "Let us go to bed now because tomorrow . . ."

Tomorrow there may already be peace. One morning there will be peace. One morning will come when I won't have to wish: Maybe *tomorrow* there will be peace.

And don't forget the prayers: Our Father, please don't get tired of all the prayers – I know it seems to be an empty repetition of words, but I beg thee, o, I beg thee, I beg thee, don't let us lose our freedom! Thou bring about wonders: let us remain a free state, don't let us lose. Would that this winter may be the last of the War and help the poor and the ill, comfort the distressed, comfort Pa and Ma now that so many of their children and grandchildren have died and the farm destroyed! And let Freek be spared. Please, please, don't let me lose my only brother? Thy will be done, certainly, but let it be thy will and look after him on Bermuda. Wipe our sins from the face of the earth and . . . and . . . wipe out all the English, Amen. And don't let me stop praying, I can't pray the way I used to, it's as if Thou . . .

"Daniel, for the last time, come!"

As if it matters when I come. It's only a few yards and then you're in the same old cold camp tent and . . .

Bean soup?

"Ma, what is it? Why do you look so happy? Where do the beans come from?"

"Aunt Martha Snijders was given a pass to go to the village occasionally and she brought back some beans yesterday."

"But Ma, you're looking so cheerful today as if something else is going on. Hey? Yes, it seems like it. Tell! You won't smile like that for no good reason!"

"No! It's your imagination . . ."

"Do tell, please!"

Have they perhaps heard something from Bermuda?

"Have you had a message from Freek?"

"What do you know about Freek?"

"No, nothing, of course, Ma, but I thought . . ."

"I had such a lovely dream last night."

"Dreams are a deception."

Pa had probably forgotten that he had also said it the previous time.

"What did you dream, Ma?"

"I dreamt it was an afternoon like today. A bell rang and when we reached the camp commandant, we could see that he looked pretty dejected. Some of the women immediately started talking among themselves, wondering if there was news of peace. He climbed onto a cart drawn by two mules, picked up a blue gum twig and said: 'It's peace!' Of course, all of us were so happy that our prayers had been answered and that we hadn't suffered in vain. Some of the men threw their hats into the air and shouted: 'Hip, hip hurray!' When we had calmed down slightly, the commandant said there was post. And at last there was a letter from Freek who said that he'd had the fever but was much better now."

"Oh no, if it's a good dream, it won't come true. The opposite, rather."

"And what about Pharaoh's dream and Joseph and the cupbearer and the baker?"

"No, put it out of your mind, Ma. One only gets disappointed. I'd rather expect nothing. I won't believe that Freek is back until I've seen him in the flesh."

"Do you remember the last time?"

Yes, unfortunately I remembered it. Such terrible days have no end in one's thoughts. It was the same day that Pa broke his leg, everything always happens at once. If only I could have been gone to fight! But no, all I ever had to do was look after the farm, look after the farm. Many boys went who were also about fourteen, fifteen years old but there was always something to keep me from going.

"So, Daniel, at the time you wouldn't believe me either?"

No, that was true, we didn't want to. But why couldn't she stop going on about it? It wasn't pleasant to remember. Ma, totally despondent at table that morning, barely listening to our conversation.

"What's wrong, Ma?" I asked.

"Nothing, Daniel."

"No, it can't be nothing."

It was probably because she was born with a caul, giving her second sight, that one immediately became suspicious when she looked like that. Oddly enough, little Leentjie was also very sensitive to such things, especially when it seemed as if Ma had had an omen. An immediate blubbering, and Pa very cross.

"Be quiet!"

He had no time for the crying or giggling of children at table. Children should be seen and not heard.

"What's the matter, Lena, speak!"

"I dreamt about Frans last night. I saw Freek come riding up to us. I saw him from far off and I immediately asked: 'But where is Frans?' But somehow or other I knew that he was dead. He was shot in the head while they were attacking the Khakies. Freek only looked at me, for a while he didn't know what to say. 'Ma, you must prepare yourself, I have bad news.' 'Never mind,' I said to him, 'I know, he was shot in the head, wasn't he?'"

"Look, I don't want a vale of tears at table, do you hear me? If you want to cry, go and cry outside! Are you listening, Leentjie? Grandfather is telling you to be quiet! At once! We can't live according to dreams, dreams are a deception."

But towards evening a horseman came riding up. Freek, who barely looked up, his shoulders hanging, at a slow gait on a thin horse white with salpetre from the pace at which it had been ridden. Ma and I immediately went to him. Freek took off his hat and wiped his hand over his face and eyes.

"Freek, and where is Frans?"

"Ma, you must prepare yourself, I bring bad news."

"Never mind, I know. He was shot in the head?"

"Has someone already come to tell you?"

"Ma dreamt it last night."

"He was killed while he was on patrol."

That evening we sang Psalm 146:

Zalig hy die in het leven . . . Happy is the man who in this life has the God of Jacob to help him and depends on the Lord his God . . . He always keeps his promises: he judges in favour of the oppressed and gives food to the hungry.

The words half-comforted me, probably the others as well. Pa delivered a little sermon for the grandchildren's sake – Sannie's children – and probably for the older people as well. "We must hope and pray. Things cannot always only go well. These are desperate times as the psalm verse says, and we're fortunate that we've only lost one member of the family. And fortunately he died without suffering. All we can do is pray that we may be preserved. The Bible also says: 'Pray and you will be given, because everyone who prays receives . . .'"

"What is 'receive', Grandfather?"

It was fortunate that Ma didn't dream about the death of the others, or had she simply kept quiet?

"Right, Ma, this isn't the first time we didn't want to believe you. But do you really think that peace will come and that we'll hear good news from Freek, all in one day? Only mishaps have struck us here."

"You're lacking in faith. One musn't lack faith."

What could have caused the camp bell to ring so suddenly at this odd time, early in the afternoon? Could it possibly be . . .? Ma smiled. She probably thought she already knew.

"We might as well go."

No, don't expect anything. I *won't* expect anything. Oh, Lord, please help me not to expect anything good! Don't let us hope, don't let the old people expect that it's peace and that Freek is well! And yet: if it could all be true and there could be peace! We could go back to the farm. True, everything had been destroyed but one could start again. And when Freek was here one day . . .

If we worked hard, I'd be able to forget all the terrible events of the War, the way in which the Republic's flag was torn down in the village and the Union Jack hoisted while the English and even some of our own people sang "God save the Queen"; the day the English loaded us onto the wagon to bring us to the camp and burnt down the farm, took the cattle, stabbed the chickens and the geese in the yard, how Sannie looked after the two small ones until . . .

And almost the worst was Teacher. He was present the day the flag was torn down and he felt very bad.

"We'll have to accept, I suppose, Teacher. It's God's will."

It was a silly thing to say but one wanted to say something which was a sort of comfort when you could see someone was upset, even to a grown-up? I had heard what adults said to one another and I suppose I was too free with my remarks.

"God's will? My dear boy, I don't wish to hurt you but one can't solve any problems by saying every time: it's God's will. When it rains, we say, no I never say it, you say: We thank thee, it is thy will and when it's dry, we thank thee, thy will be done. If we win the war, we'll pray, We thank thee, it's thy will that we have kept our country, and if we lose, It is thy will that this has happened to us, thy will be done. We try to convince ourselves that there is something like the will of God."

Teacher who could speak so sensibly about everything, did not believe in God!

Had Teacher been right? We prayed for Leentjie; she died of whooping-cough. Prayed for Susan; she died of the wasting disease. Begged that Dolf might be saved; killed. Beseeched that Sannie . . . died of a broken heart. Maria . . . murdered by the blacks. Should one rather not pray? Does God not listen to his children?

Yes, it was almost like Ma's dream. There was a cart with, really and truly, two mules! And yes, the commandant looked down in the mouth. He who was always so contrary and disagreeable! Was it perhaps true that . . . Surely someone who had to bring bad news looked like this? In his right hand he had . . . what was it, a cypress twig! The clock struck. He waved his twig, now he'd probably speak.

"It's peace. It's peace. The Boers have lost their country."

So we'd lost.

God, is this the way thou answer prayers? Is that how thou listen to our praying? Had thou in fact never taken notice of us? While we were suffering, here in the camp, were ill and starving . . . we were hungry and thou did not feed us, we were strangers, strangers in our own land and thou gave us no shelter? We were ill, we had whooping-cough. Fever, the wasting disease and thou, did thou perhaps visit us? Yes, thou came, but in a different way – with disease, with suffering and death. We were confined, we are confined and did thou come to us?

We were confined and thou, thou chose the side of injustice! The side of the oppressor! Are thou still our God?

Yes, you poor buggers, crying like that, what's the use of tears? As useless as our prayers! The women who crawled on their knees? What moved them to do that? What good was it all? But there is one comfort and my goodness, what a comfort! It's not only I who feel like this: Uncle Lodewyk has torn his Bible to pieces: "I don't believe in anything any longer! This blow is too unfair!"

The joiners threw their hats into the air and shouted: "Hip, hip, hurrah!" Our own people and they shouted: "Hurrah!" Our own God and He was on their side?

"Come, Daniel, let us go."

To do what? To do what, perhaps? Surely not to go on eating? Or yes, the funeral meal! Funeral bean soup! A funeral meal for the end of the Boer Republics!

Very well, we might as well go – these dejected people I neither want to see nor hear. Why are they swearing now? Couldn't they have known beforehand?

They're handing out letters. No, no, it's sure to be bad news especially if there's something for us.

Yes, there they are reading out our name.

"News about Freek?"

"I don't know, I don't recognise the writing. 'My dearest Uncle Org and Tante Lena . . .' It's from Freek, of Slypklip. 'I set myself down to inform you that Freek, your son, died of fever this morning, oh, we tried everything that we could but it was the will of our Father that he should be taken. Shortly before he died he asked me to send you his regards and to say that Uncle Org and all of you musn't lose hope, and to tell Daniel in particular that what God does is well done, his will is wise and holy . . .'"

"Come, Daniel, let us go to the tent and read from the Bible."
Read!
"God is the true keeper of his people."
Keeper! Today we were totally vanquished and God is the keeper! Everything, everything He has taken from us – everyone, my brothers and my sisters, and their children, nearly our whole family has been wiped out. Our house has been burnt down, the whole farm destroyed. Our freedom has been taken from us and thou are the faithful keeper of our nation?

"I will lift up mine eyes unto the hills, from whence cometh my help? . . ."

"Help? Cometh?" The mountains are no longer ours, nor the plains, the marshes, the land, nothing belongs to us any more.

"Behold, He that keepeth Israel shall neither slumber nor sleep . . ."

Oh, doesn't sleep? But heard, and preferred to listen to the Khakies?

I suppose we have to sing now. What will it be this afternoon? This?

Can my parents really sing that?
Do they believe that? Do they mean that?

"Wij zegenen, o Heer, u goedheid al den dag!" We bless, oh Lord, your goodness all through the day; grant that age after age, your goodness we may praise; grant that when you come we may be freed from sin, that you will cover us with your blessing, in you we trust, never ashamed to rest in your goodness.

They were . . . really? They were even happy? Comforted? Ma was even smiling and Pa held her hand while he prayed. That voice wasn't the voice of someone who thought he had lost something. Could it be true? They couldn't be feeling the loss? They weren't crying, they're sitting there peacefully as if nothing had happened, as if everything remained the way it had been this morning or the way it had been before the War. And Freek was dead. Didn't they understand? Was all the bad news too sudden? We surrendered our country to death and everything was carrying on the way it did before? Ma smiled! Wasn't it terrible? She smiled when everything had happened so differently to what she had expected?

Or . . .

Do thou comfort after all?

Have thou indeed come to us?

Those who believe don't stand alone?

Is that how thou . . . ?

Have mercy, oh Lord, have mercy.

Source:
J.C. Steyn: *Op pad na die grens*. Cape Town: Tafelberg: 1976.
Translated by Madeleine van Biljon

The Brunt of the War . . .

Elsa Joubert

This extract from Joubert's novel Die reise van Isobelle *(The Journeys of Isobelle) is about the visit of the Reverend Josias van Velde to the concentration camp at Springfontein.*

Josias van Velde was one of the first Cape ministers of religion to visit the women and children in the concentration camps. Travel opportunities to the besieged republics were rare. It took him half a month to travel to the Springfontein camp where he had been assigned. There were more than enough troop trains. They steamed past the stations. Trains in which he eventually found accommodation, were shunted onto sidings to clear the tracks for the supply trains racing past. The Karoo stations were hot. Nelspoort, Hutchinson, Richmond Road. At each station he had to alight, show papers, permits, passes and passes yet again. Sometimes it seemed to him that no matter where he looked, there were Khakies; they appeared from behind every ridge, poured out of the small station buildings – singing, foul-mouthed Khakies, sent to wipe out his people.

In some of the south-bound trains, he encountered Boer families. At De Aar a woman grabbed his arm and begged: "Dominee, you must pray for us, it's my husband who is sending us away, he's joined the English. Dominee, it would've been better had he been killed."

"Where are you going?"

"To my brother's farm in the Stellenbosch district. How will my children and I survive the shame?"

He held her hands in both his and comforted her: "These troubled times will also pass."

That night he travelled far off his course. The conductor fetched him in the waiting room, bundled him onto a train, and he woke up at Hopetown. There he had to wait for a train to the south. "Dominee can come and sit in the caboose." He had only one suitcase with him and a food basket. Their doctor had given him medical supplies, as much as he could cram into the basket.

"I know it's only a drop in the ocean," the doctor had said, "but perhaps it will help someone, somewhere."

After a few days his food was finished. Sometimes, when the train was shunted off the main line at a small railway village and he could alight, he walked into the village and bought milk or bread. Often the villages were deserted and he bought from a handful of black men who tried to keep the neglected vegetable gardens going, a few carrots or turnips, or a fruit. But these were scarce. He washed the carrots at the station tap and ate. At Naauwpoort, where he could eventually alight again, he was given a share of the rations doled out to the soldiers. He ate this with greater reluctance than he did the raw food. Naauwpoort, Colesberg, Norvalspont. The countryside was grey and dry, the Orange River pools of mud.

He was a tidy man and the lack of washing facilities, even of water, was a trial. His black broadcloth suit was red with dust, his shirt collar and white bands dirty. He could remove his black hat and dust it with the white handkerchief until the handkerchief was brown with dust. His moustache and his beard felt hot and scratchy. He itched. The carriages in which he travelled were riddled with lice.

Whenever he took out his Bible and tried to read, it evoked so much catcalling and hurtful blasphemy from the soldiers, that he preferred to leave it. Prayer could not be denied him, his chin on his breast, his eyes closed as if he were asleep, his hands hidden under the hat which he kept on his lap. But he felt that his prayers were no more than meaningless words. God, give me the strength to do your work; of my own ability I cannot.

Eventually he reached Springfontein station where he had to get off the train. He was surprised to see, so close to the station and at an angle to the village, the stretch of tents. No arrangements had been made for him to be met. Slowly he started walking but after a while an old black man in a donkey cart picked him up. He sat in front on the wooden bench next to him.

It was April and a dry dusty wind was blowing. With the handkerchief, already dirty, he tried to wipe the sweat from his forehead. The narrow watercourses through which the cart rode, were as dry as dust. He saw no animals; eventually a group of white children gathering wood. The donkey trotted past a deserted farmyard. The few blue gum trees in the yard had a battered look. The old man muttered: "Those leaves I knocked down with my whip, oh, my dear Lord, the old mistress at the camp begged me so nicely. They soak the leaves in boiling water for the children's croup, yes."

The guards must've known the old black man because they allowed him to pass. The commandant in charge of the camp was red and sweaty behind his desk, the heat in the tent was worse than outside. He was to share quarters with two noncommissioned officers. On request, the orderly brought him a half pail of water, which he paid for. He also brought a camp bed to be erected.

Apart from the children gathering wood, he had been unaware up to now of any of the inhabitants of the camp. No matter in which direction he looked, the tents lay immobile in their white rows, the passageways empty. The heat of the midday hour was intense, the air heavy.

He must have dozed off on the camp bed because when he woke he heard people singing. His shirt was soaked with perspiration, but the atmosphere seemed to be cooler. Judging from the shadow in the tent, the sun was setting. He got up, summarily washing his hands and face with the water he'd used before, smoothing his hair. The singing came nearer. When he stepped out of the tent, he saw a crowd of women, children as well, some of the children on the arm, others clinging to their mothers' skirts. Some of the older children ran ahead, others dragged behind as if they were tired. There were old men with them.

They were singing a High Dutch hymn: "*Diep, o God in 't stof gebogen*": Deeply bowing in the dust, o God; guilty 'fore thy judgment high; tears are pouring from our eyelids, faces covered with our shame.

When they saw the dominee emerge, the group stood still. But they kept on singing. They're welcoming me, he thought. These weren't women like the ones he knew in the towns of the Boland. They had a neglected appearance, the dresses dragging in the red sand were no longer clean. The big bonnets on their heads weren't starched and hung so limply that very often he couldn't see the faces. Where a bonnet had been folded back and the face exposed, the sadness in the eyes and around the mouth dismayed him. The children, too, were thin and neglected. These are lower-class people, he thought and was ashamed of the thought.

A few of the guards approached, suspicious of this unusual gathering. The sight of the soldiers enraged him to such an extent that he felt something tear in him. He walked towards the group and joined them in song, his voice low and strong amongst the shriller female voices.

He struck up the second verse:

"*Vader vol van mededoogen! Zie ons arme zondaars aan*": Compassionate Father, gaze upon your poor sinners, cast on us your loving eyes. Jesus died for us, yes died for us; God accept us all as sinners, on his death give us eternal life.

His uplifted hands signalled them to stop singing.

The dominee bowed his head. "Let us pray."

The old men in the group said: "Amen, amen," when he had finished praying. A few of the women were weeping loudly. He, too, was deeply moved.

For the next few days he went from tent to tent. He became

acquainted, wrote down names, gave advice, encouragement. There was illness in virtually every tent. An old person, or a child, a baby, or a pregnant mother. On Sunday he held a service in the open air. Sick babies were brought to be christened.

The warm weather suddenly changed. Unseasonably the rain sluiced down. It rained right through the night, water poured into the tent, some of his possessions floated on the water. The two orderlies were using shovels to dig ditches around the tents. He dressed, hurried outside. It was getting light. Women and young girls, blankets around their shoulders, knelt in the mud trying to push the ground into little furrows so that the water could run off. He demanded a spade from the orderly who handed it over in surprise, and tried to help at the tents. He made retaining mounds, dug the furrows deeper. When things improved slightly at one tent, he moved to the next, but he felt powerless in the face of the sheer number of tents. One young child who was digging, began to cry when she saw him. She held up her hands, "Uncle," she wept, "my hands have become so stupid." She wiped the tears from her face with her wet forearms, her hands coated with mud. "They won't do what I tell them to, they're too stiff." She looked at her fingers which she had spread open.

"Go inside," he said, "I'll finish the digging. Tell your mother to rub your hands, then the feeling will come back."

By eleven o'clock the rain had stopped and the sun came out. The sick lay on soaked mattresses because there were no beds. Where they could, women dragged mattresses and bedding into the sun. Here and there someone put kettles on to boil for coffee but the wood was wet, the rations in the tents soaked.

"Run about," he said to the children, "run, move so that you can get warm and your wet clothes can dry out."

Sickness increased. He was taken from tent to tent. After the rain, cold weather set in, bringing fever, measles, diseases of the lung – sometimes he felt as if the camp was coughing itself to pieces. The gasping, croaking coughing of the old men went on all night; the dark coughing of women trying to stop the cough, holding blankets, pieces of clothing in front of their mouths so that only the muffled labouring for breath could be heard. And then the sad, monotonous coughing of children.

He wanted to cover his ears at night.

Often during his morning rounds, he found more than one body in a tent, then he said a prayer and sent a message for the bodies to be taken away. The rebellion and bitter clutching at the body of the first child who died, made way for a deadly resignation among the women. "Take him, Dominee." Evidently it comforted them if he carried the child to the tent of the dead.

One mother lost all four her children. And only then did she take to her bed. She burned with fever. Some of the women who shared the tent, kept vigil next to her all night. Two days later she died. There were no planks for coffins. The blanket in which an ill person died, served as both shroud and coffin. On one day eight women were buried, wrapped only in the blankets in which they had died.

"She was such a proud woman, Dominee, thought she was better than the rest of us. If only she knew . . ." He didn't reprimand her. Who was without sin?

He spoke to the commandant; asked for more blankets, medicines, doctors, better food, more latrines. Did the officer realise that latrines meant for five hundred people were now being used by two thousand?

His gentle pleading was useless. He became angry, accused the British authorities of murder on a massive scale. The commandant became angry in turn. "Who gave you the right to address me in this fashion? I am the representative of Her Majesty the Queen!"

"And I, sir, however weak and unworthy, am the representative of God."

And in a strange manner, Josias van Velde thought this was true.

These suffering women and children seemed to have brought him nearer to God than he had ever been. It was as if the thin line between death and life which he was experiencing here, had brought him to the edge of the Unseen. He got little sleep, every night he kept vigil. The old men, especially, moved him, dying with a verse from the Bible on their lips; and the soft, sad singing of the women.

Newcomers arrived endlessly and the tents were overcrowded, fourteen, twenty to a tent.

During the day he tried to tidy himself, took his Bible and hymnal and led the people to the piece of ground fenced off with wire, which served as a graveyard. When the graves were dug, the little boys or the women, whoever had the strength, dragged the little wagon with the body. Sometimes he simply remained standing there because scarcely was the one grave covered or the next group with their wagon of death were on the way. On one day he buried sixteen corpses.

That night he was called to the bedside of Aunt Hester Prinsloo. There were eight people ill in the tent.

"Oh, Dominee, we don't know whom to help when we come here. Four are so serious that we can't leave them. There's hardly room for us in the tent."

Aunt Hester was dying. She no longer paid any attention to those around her, not to her ill children, nor to her daughter who sat on the ground next to her bed. "She was our pillar of strength, Dominee. She always gave us courage. Taking leave of her is very hard."

He could smell death in the tent. He sat on a little chest and opened his Bible. He paged in the Bible, unsure of what he should read. Lord, where to, to what purpose, he pleaded wordlessly.

And suddenly the smell of death was no longer there and something like the lovely smell of tuberoses filled the tent.

The dying children on their mattresses were quiet and their eyes opened, suddenly clear. The dying woman opened her eyes. She said in her old, sweet voice, but very softly: "How beautiful it is, and see the many angels gathered around us." Then she closed her eyes and died.

No one spoke a single word. Tears ran out of Dominee van Velde's eyes but he didn't raise his hands to his face to wipe them.

The others who had watched, were deathly quiet as though they, too, felt the presence of angels. How long this silence lasted they could not remember later. But slowly, as the soul took leave of the body, the sweet smell of tuberoses and the presence of the Unseen gradually lessened.

Those who watched, and those who were ill, became aware of the cold in the tent once again, of the darkness of the night outside. Even so, they didn't move.

They began singing, softly but with great love.

"Middelpunt van ons verlangen, trooster van 't onrust gemoed": Centre of our greatest longing, comfort of a restless soul, Jesus, all our thankful singing, is in praise of your love's glow.

At last the Dominee took his handkerchief out of his pocket and dried his eyes. Is suffering the price of the awareness of God? he thought as he walked to his tent. Is it true, then, that suffering is the instrument with which God brings his children to Him?

Source:
Elsa Joubert: *Die reise van Isobelle*. Cape Town: Tafelberg: 1995.

The Rooinek

Herman Charles Bosman

Rooineks, said Oom Schalk Lourens, are queer. For instance, there was that day when my nephew Hannes and I had dealings with a couple of Englishmen near Dewetsdorp. It was shortly after Sanna's Post, and Hannes and I were lying behind a rock watching the road. Hannes spent odd moments like that in what he called a useful way. He would file the points of his Mauser cartridges on a piece of flat stone until the lead showed through the steel, in that way making them into dum-dum bullets.

I often spoke to my nephew Hannes about that.

"Hannes," I used to say. "That is a sin. The Lord is looking at you."

"That's all right," Hannes replied. "The Lord knows that this is the Boer War, and in war-time he will always forgive a little foolishness like this, especially as the English are so many."

Anyway, as we lay behind that rock we saw, far down the road, two horsemen come galloping up. We remained perfectly still and let them approach to within four hundred paces. They were English officers. They were mounted on first-rate horses and their uniforms looked very fine and smart. They were the most stylish-looking men I had seen for some time, and I felt quite ashamed of my own ragged trousers and veldskoens. I was glad that I was behind a rock and they couldn't see me. Especially as my jacket was also torn all the way down the back, as a result of my having had, three days before, to get through a barbed-wire fence rather quickly. I just got through in time, too. The veldkornet, who was a fat man and couldn't run so fast, was about twenty yards behind me. And he remained on the wire with a bullet through him. All through the Boer War I was pleased that I was thin and never troubled with corns.

Hannes and I fired just about the same time. One of the officers fell off his horse. He struck the road with his shoulders and rolled over twice, kicking up the red dust as he turned. Then the other soldier did a queer thing. He drew up his horse and got off. He gave just one look in our direction. Then he led his horse up to where the other man was twisting and struggling on the ground. It took him a little while to lift him on to his horse, for it is no easy matter to pick up a man like that when he is helpless. And he did all this slowly and calmly, as though he was not concerned about the fact that the men who had shot his friend were lying only a few hundred yards away. He managed in some way to support the wounded man across the saddle, and walked on beside the horse. After going a few yards he stopped and seemed to remember something. He turned round and waved at the spot where he imagined we were hiding, as though inviting us to shoot. During all that time I had simply lain watching him, astonished at his coolness.

But when he waved his hand I thrust another cartridge into the breach of my Martini and aimed. At that distance I couldn't miss. I aimed very carefully and was just on the point of pulling the trigger when Hannes put his hand on the barrel and pushed up my rifle.

"Don't shoot, Oom Schalk," he said. "That's a brave man."

I looked at Hannes in surprise. His face was very white. I said nothing, and allowed my rifle to sink down on to the grass, but I couldn't understand what had come over my nephew. It seemed that not only was that Englishman queer, but that Hannes was also queer. That's all nonsense not killing a man just because he's brave. If he's a brave man and he's fighting on the wrong side, that's all the more reason to shoot him.

I was with my nephew Hannes for another few months after that. Then one day, in a skirmish near the Vaal River, Hannes with a few dozen other burghers was cut off from the commando and had to surrender. That was the last I ever saw of him. I heard later on that, after taking him prisoner, the English searched Hannes and found dum-dum bullets in his possession. They shot him for that. I was very much grieved when I heard of Hannes's death. He had always been full of life and high spirits. Perhaps Hannes was right in saying that the Lord didn't mind about a little foolishness like dum-dum bullets. But the mistake he made was in forgetting that the English did mind.

I was in the veld until they made peace. Then we laid down our rifles and went home. What I knew my farm by was the hole under the koppie where I quarried slate-stones for the threshing-floor. That was about all that remained as I left it. Everything else was gone. My home was burnt down. My lands were laid waste. My cattle and sheep were slaughtered. Even the stones I had piled for the kraals were pulled down. My wife came out of the concentration camp, and we went together to look at our old farm. My wife had gone into the concentration camp with our two children, but she came out alone. And when I saw her again and noticed the way she had changed, I knew that I, who had been through all the fighting, had not seen the Boer War.

Neither Sannie nor I had the heart to go on farming again on that same place. It would be different without the children playing about the house and getting into mischief. We got paid out some money by the new Government for part of our losses. So I bought a wagon and oxen and left the Free State, which was not even the Free State any longer. It was now called the Orange River Colony.

We trekked right through the Transvaal into the northern part of the Marico Bushveld. Years ago, as a boy, I had trekked through that same country with my parents. Now that I went there again I felt that it was still a good country. It was on the far side of the Dwarsberge, near Derdepoort, that we got a Government farm. Afterwards other farmers trekked in there as well. One or two of them had also come from the Free State, and I knew them. There were also a few Cape rebels whom I had seen on commando. All of us had lost relatives in the war. Some had died in the concentration camps or on the battlefield. Others had been shot for going into rebellion. So, taken all in all, we who had trekked into that part of the Marico that lay nearest the Bechuanaland border were very bitter against the English.

Then it was that the rooinek came.

It was in the first year of our having settled around Derdepoort. We heard that an Englishman had bought a farm next to Gerhardus Grobbelaar. This was when we were sitting in the voorkamer of Willem Odendaal's house, which was used as a post office. Once a week the post-cart came up with letters from Zeerust, and we came together at Willem Odendaal's house and talked and smoked and drank coffee. Very few of us ever got letters, and then it was mostly demands to pay for the boreholes that had been drilled on our farms or for cement and fencing materials. But every week regularly we went for the post. Sometimes the post-cart didn't come, because the Groen River was in flood, and we would most of us have gone home without noticing it, if somebody didn't speak about it.

When Koos Steyn heard that an Englishman was coming to live amongst us he got up from the riempies-bank.

"No, kêrels," he said. "Always when the Englishman comes, it means that a little later the Boer has got to shift. I'll pack up my wagon and make coffee, and just trek first thing tomorrow morning."

Most of us laughed then. Koos Steyn often said funny things like that. But some didn't laugh. Somehow, there seemed to be too much truth in Koos Steyn's words.

We discussed the matter and decided that if we Boers in the Marico could help it the rooinek would not stay amongst us too long. About half an hour later one of Willem Odendaal's children came in and said that there was a strange wagon coming along the big road. We went to the door and looked out. As the wagon came nearer we saw that it was piled up with all kinds of furniture and also sheets of iron and farming implements. There was so much stuff on the wagon that the tent had to be taken off to get everything on.

The wagon rolled along and came to a stop in front of the house. With the wagon there were one white man and two kaffirs. The white man shouted something to the kaffirs and threw down the whip. Then he walked up to where we were standing. He was dressed just as we were, in shirt and trousers and veldskoens, and he had dust all over him. But when he stepped over a thorn-bush we saw that he had got socks on. Therefore we knew that he was an Englishman.

Koos Steyn was standing in front of the door.

The Englishman went up to him and held out his hand.

"Good afternoon," he said in Afrikaans. "My name is Webber."

Koos shook hands with him.

"My name is Prince Lord Alfred Milner," Koos Steyn said.

That was when Lord Milner was Governor of the Transvaal, and we all laughed. The rooinek also laughed.

"Well, Lord Prince," he said, "I can speak your language a little, and I hope that later on I'll be able to speak it better. I'm coming to live here, and I hope that we'll all be friends."

He then came round to all of us, but the others turned away and refused to shake hands with him. He came up to me last of all; I felt sorry for him, and although his nation had dealt unjustly with my nation, and I had lost both my children in the concentration camp, still it was not so much the fault of this Englishman. It was the fault of the English Government, who wanted our gold mines. And it was also the fault of Queen Victoria, who didn't like Oom Paul Kruger, because they say that when he went over to London Oom Paul spoke to her only once for a few minutes. Oom Paul Kruger said that he was a married man and he was afraid of widows.

When the Englishman Webber went back to his wagon Koos Steyn and I walked with him. He told us that he had bought the farm next to Gerhardus Grobbelaar and that he didn't know much about sheep and cattle and mealies, but he had bought a few books on farming, and he was going to learn all he could out of them. When he said that I looked away towards the poort. I didn't want him to see that I was laughing. But with Koos Steyn it was otherwise.

"Man," he said, "let me see those books."

Webber opened the box at the bottom of the wagon and took out about six big books with green covers.

"These are very good books," Koos Steyn said. "Yes, they are very good for the white ants. The white ants will eat them all in two nights."

As I have told you, Koos Steyn was a funny fellow, and no man could help laughing at the things he said.

Those were bad times. There was drought, and we could not sow mealies. The dams dried up, and there was only last year's grass on the veld. We had to pump water out of the borehole for weeks at a time. Then the rains came and for a while things were better.

Now and again I saw Webber. From what I heard about him it seemed that he was working hard. But of course no rooinek can make a living out of farming, unless they send him money every month from England. And we found out that almost all the money Webber had was what he had paid on the farm. He was always reading in those green books what he had to do. It's lucky that those books are written in English, and that the Boers can't read them. Otherwise many more farmers would be ruined every year. When his cattle had the heart-water, or his sheep had the blue-tongue, or there were cut-worms or stalk-borers in his mealies, Webber would look it all up in his books. I suppose that when the kaffirs stole his sheep he would look that up too.

Still, Koos Steyn helped Webber quite a lot and taught him a number of things, so that matters did not go as badly with him as they would have if he had only acted according to the lies that were printed in those green books. Webber and Koos Steyn became very friendly. Koos Steyn's wife had had a baby just a few weeks before Webber came. It was the first child they had after being married seven years, and they were very proud of it. It was a girl. Koos Steyn said that he would sooner it had been a boy; but that, even so, it was better than nothing. Right from the first Webber had taken a liking to that child, who was christened Jemima after her mother. Often when I passed Koos Steyn's house I saw the Englishman sitting on the front stoep with the child on his knees.

In the meantime the other farmers around there became annoyed on account of Koos Steyn's friendship with the rooinek. They said that Koos was a hendsopper and a traitor to his country. He was intimate with a man who had helped to bring about the downfall of the Afrikaner nation. Yet it was not fair to call Koos a hendsopper. Koos had lived in the Graaff-Reinet District when the war broke out, so that he was a Cape Boer and need not have fought. Nevertheless, he joined up with a Free State commando and remained until peace was made, and if at any time the English had caught him they would have shot him as a rebel, in the same way that they shot Scheepers and many others.

Gerhardus Grobbelaar spoke about this once when we were in Willem Odendaal's post office.

"You are not doing right," Gerhardus said; "Boer and Englishman have been enemies since before Slagtersnek. We've lost this war, but some day we'll win. It's the duty we owe to our children's children to stand against the rooineks. Remember the concentration camps."

There seemed to me to be truth in what Gerhardus said.

"But the English are here now, and we've got to live with them," Koos answered. "When we get to understand one another perhaps we won't need to fight any more. This Englishman Webber is learning Afrikaans very well, and some day he might almost be one of us. The only thing I can't understand about him is that he has a bath every morning. But if he stops that and if he doesn't brush his teeth any more you will hardly be able to tell him from a Boer."

Although he made a joke about it, I felt that in what Koos Steyn said there was also truth.

Then, the year after the drought, the miltsiek broke out. The miltsiek seemed to be in the grass of the veld, and in the water of the dams, and even in the air the cattle breathed. All over the place I would find cows and oxen lying dead. We all became very discouraged. Nearly all of us in that part of the Marico had started farming again on what the Government had given us. Now that the stock died we had nothing. First the drought had put us back to where we were when we started. Now with the miltsiek we couldn't hope to do anything. We couldn't even sow mealies, because, at the rate at which the cattle were dying, in a short while we would have no oxen left to pull the plough. People talked of selling what they had and going to look for work on the gold mines. We sent a petition to the Government, but that did no good.

It was then that somebody got hold of the idea of trekking. In a few days we were talking of nothing else. But the question was where we could trek to. They would not allow us into Rhodesia for fear we might spread the miltsiek there as well. And it was useless going to any other part of the Transvaal. Somebody mentioned German West Africa. We had none of us been there before, and I suppose that really was the reason why, in the end, we decided to go there.

"The blight of the English is over South Africa," Gerhardus Grobbelaar said. "We'll remain here only to die. We most go away somewhere where there is not the Englishman's flag."

In a few week's time we arranged everything. We were going to trek across the Kalahari into German territory. Everything we had we loaded up. We drove the cattle ahead and followed behind on our wagons. There were five families: the Steyns, the Grobbelaars, the Odendaals, the Ferreiras and Sannie and I. Webber also came with us. I think it was not so much that he was anxious to leave as that he and Koos Steyn had become very much attached to one another, and the Englishman did not wish to remain alone behind.

The youngest person in our trek was Koos Steyn's daughter Jemima, who was then about eighteen months old. Being the baby, she was a favourite with all of us.

Webber sold his wagon and went with Koos Steyn's trek.

When at the end of the first day we outspanned several miles inside the Bechuanaland Protectorate, we were very pleased that we were done with the Transvaal, where we had had so much misfortune. Of course, the Protectorate was also British territory, but all the same we felt happier there than we had done in our country. We saw Webber every day now, and although he was a foreigner with strange ways, and would remain an Uitlander until he died, yet we disliked him less than before for being a rooinek.

It was on the first Sunday that we reached Malopolole. For the first part of our way the country remained Bushveld. There were the same kind of thorn-trees that grew in the Marico, except that they became fewer the deeper into the Kalahari that we went. Also, the ground became more and more sandy, until even before we came to Malopolole it was all desert. But scattered thorn-bushes remained all the way. That Sunday we held a religious service. Gerhardus Grobbelaar read a chapter out of the Bible and offered up a prayer. We sang a number of psalms, after which Gerhardus prayed again. I shall always remember that Sunday and the way we sat on the ground beside one of the wagons, listening to Gerhardus. That was the last Sunday that we were all together.

The Englishman sat next to Koos Steyn and the baby Jemima lay down in front of him. She played with Webber's fingers and tried to bite them. It was funny to watch her. Several times Webber looked down at her and smiled. I thought then that although Webber was not one of us, yet Jemima certainly did not know it. Maybe in a thing like that the child was wiser than we were. To her it made no difference that the man whose fingers she bit was born in another country and did not speak the same language that she did.

There are many things that I remember about that trek into the Kalahari. But one thing that now seems strange to me is the way in which, right from the first day, we took Gerhardus Grobbelaar for our leader. Whatever he said we just seemed to do without talking very much about it. We all felt that it was right simply because Gerhardus wished it. That was a strange thing about our trek. It was not simply that we knew Gerhardus had got the Lord with him for we did know that but it was rather that we believed in Gerhardus as well as in the Lord. I think that even if Gerhardus Grobbelaar had been an ungodly man we would still have followed him in exactly the same way. For when you are in the desert and there is no water and the way back is long, then you feel that it is better to have with you a strong man who does not read the Book very much, than a man who is good and religious, and yet does not seem sure how far to trek each day and where to outspan.

But Gerhardus Grobbelaar was a man of God. At the same time there was something about him that made you feel that it was only by acting as he advised that you could succeed. There was only one other man I have ever known who found it so easy to get people to do as he wanted. And that was Paul Kruger. He was very much like Gerhardus Grobbelaar, except that Gerhardus was less quarrelsome. But of the two Paul Kruger was the bigger man.

Only once do I remember Gerhardus losing his temper. And that was with the Nagmaal at Elandsberg. It was on a Sunday, and we were camped out beside the Crocodile River. Gerhardus went round early in the morning from wagon to wagon and told us that he wanted everybody to come over to where his wagon stood. The Lord had been good to us at that time, so that we had had much rain and our cattle were fat. Gerhardus explained that he wanted to hold a service, to thank the Lord for all His good works, but more especially for what He had done for the farmers of the northern part of the Groot Marico District. This was a good plan, and we all came together with our Bibles and hymn-books. But one man, Karel Pieterse, remained behind at his wagon. Twice Gerhardus went to call him, but Karel Pieterse lay down on the grass and would not get up to come to the service. He said it was all right thanking the Lord now that there had been rains, but what about all those seasons when there had been drought and the cattle had died of thirst. Gerhardus Grobbelaar shook his head sadly, and said there was nothing he could do then, as it was Sunday. But he prayed that the Lord would soften Brother Pieterse's heart, and he finished off his prayer by saying that in any case, in the morning, he would help to soften the brother's heart himself.

The following morning Gerhardus walked over with a sjambok and an ox-riem to where Karel Pieterse sat before his fire, watching the kaffir making coffee. They were both of them men who were big in the body. But Gerhardus got the better of the struggle. In the end he won. He fastened Karel to the wheel of his own wagon with the ox-riem. Then he thrashed him with the sjambok while Karel's wife and children were looking on.

That had happened years before. But nobody had forgotten. And now, in the Kalahari, when Gerhardus summoned us to a service, it was noticed that no man stayed away.

Just outside Malopolole is a muddy stream that is dry part of the year and part of the year has a foot or so of brackish water. We were lucky in being there just at the time when it had water. Early the following morning we filled up the water-barrels that we had put on our wagons before leaving the Marico. We were going right into the desert, and we did not know where we would get water again. Even the Bakwena kaffirs could not tell us for sure.

"The Great Dorstland Trek," Koos Steyn shouted as we got ready to move off. "Anyway, we won't fare as badly as the Dorstland Trekkers. We'll lose less cattle than they did because we've got less to lose. And seeing that we are only five families, not more than about a dozen of us will die of thirst."

I thought it was bad luck for Koos Steyn to make jokes like that about the Dorstland Trek, and I think that others felt the same way about it. We trekked right through that day, and it was all desert. By sunset we had not come across a sign of water anywhere. Abraham Ferreira said towards evening that perhaps it would be better if we went back to Malopolole and tried to find out for sure which was the best way of getting through the Kalahari. But the rest said that there was no need to do that, since we would be sure to come across water the next day. And, anyway, we were Doppers and, having once set out, we were not going to turn back. But after we had given the cattle water our barrels did not have too much left in them.

By the middle of the following day all our water had given out except a little that we kept for the children. But still we pushed on. Now that we had gone so far we were afraid to go back because of the long way that we would have to go without water to get back to Malopolole. In the evening we were very anxious. We all knelt down in the sand and prayed. Gerhardus Grobbelaar's voice sounded very deep and earnest when he besought God to have mercy on us, especially for the sakes of the little ones. He mentioned the baby Jemima by name. The Englishman knelt down beside me, and I noticed that he shivered when Gerhardus mentioned Koos Steyn's child.

It was moonlight. All around us was the desert. Our wagons seemed very small and lonely; there was something about them that looked very mournful. The women and children put their arms round one another and wept a long while. Our kaffirs stood some distance away and watched us. My wife Sannie put her hand in mine, and I thought of the concentration camp. Poor woman, she had suffered much. And I knew that her thoughts were the same as my own: that after all it was perhaps better that our children should have died then than now.

We had got so far into the desert that we began telling one another that we must be near the end. Although we knew that German West was far away, and that in the way we had been travelling we had got little more than into the beginning of the Kalahari, yet we tried to tell one another lies about how near water was likely to be. But, of course, we told those lies only to one another. Each man in his own heart knew what the real truth was. And later on we even stopped telling one another lies about what a good chance we had of getting out alive. You can understand how badly things had gone with us when you know that we no longer troubled about hiding our position from the women and children. They wept, some of them. But that made no difference then. Nobody tried to comfort the women and children who cried. We knew that tears were useless, and yet somehow at that hour we felt that the weeping of the women was not less useless than the courage of the men. After a while there was no more weeping in our camp. Some of the women who lived through the dreadful things of the days that came after, and got safely back to the Transvaal, never again wept. What they had seen appeared to have hardened them. In this respect they had become as men. I think that is the saddest thing that ever happens in this world, when women pass through great suffering that makes them become as men.

That night we hardly slept. Early the next morning the men went out to look for water. An hour after sun-up Ferreira came back and told us that he had found a muddy pool a few miles away. We all went there, but there wasn't much water. Still, we got a little, and that made us feel better. It was only when it came to driving our cattle towards the mudhole that we found our kaffirs had deserted us during the night. After we had gone to sleep they had stolen away. Some of the weaker cattle couldn't get up to go to the pool. So we left them. Some were trampled to death or got choked in the mud, and we had to pull them out to let the rest get to the hole. It was pitiful.

Just before we left one of Ferreira's daughters died. We scooped a hole in the sand and buried her.

So we decided to trek back.

After his daughter was dead Abraham Ferreira went up to Gerhardus and told him that if we had taken his advice earlier on and gone back, his daughter would not have died.

"Your daughter is dead now, Abraham," Gerhardus said. "It is no use talking about her any longer. We all have to die some day. I refused to go back earlier. I have decided to go back now."

Abraham Ferreira looked Gerhardus in the eyes and laughed. I shall always remember how that laughter sounded on the desert. In Abraham's voice there was the hoarseness of the sand and thirst. His voice was cracked with what the desert had done to him; his face was lined and his lips were blackened. But there was nothing about him that spoke of grief for his daughter's death.

"Your daughter is still alive, Oom Gerhardus," Abraham Ferreira said, pointing to the wagon wherein lay Gerhardus's wife, who was weak, and the child to whom she had given birth only a few months before. "Yes, she is still alive . . . so far."

Ferreira turned away laughing, and we heard him a little later explaining to his wife in cracked tones about the joke he had made.

Gerhardus Grobbelaar merely watched the other man walk away without saying anything. So far we had followed Gerhardus through all things, and our faith in him had been great. But now that we had decided to trek back we lost our belief in him. We lost it suddenly, too. We knew that it was best to turn back, and that to continue would mean that we would all die in the Kalahari. And yet, if Gerhardus had said we must still go on we would have done so. We would have gone through with him right to the end. But now that he as much as said he was beaten by the desert we had no more faith in Gerhardus. That is why I have said that Paul Kruger was a greater man than Gerhardus. Because Paul Kruger was that kind of man whom we still worshipped even when he decided to retreat. If it had been Paul Kruger who told us that we had to go back we would have returned with strong hearts. We would have retained exactly the same love for our leader, even if we knew that he was beaten. But from the moment that Gerhardus said we must go back we all knew that he was no longer our leader. Gerhardus knew that also.

We knew what lay between us and Malopolole and there was grave doubt in our hearts when we turned our wagons round. Our cattle were very weak, and we had to inspan all that could walk. We hadn't enough yokes, and therefore we cut poles from the scattered bushes and tied them to the trek-chains. As we were also without skeis we had to fasten the necks of the oxen straight on to the yokes with strops, and several of the oxen got strangled.

Then we saw that Koos Steyn had become mad. For he refused to return. He inspanned his oxen and got ready to trek on. His wife sat silent in the wagon with the baby; wherever her husband went she would go, too. That was only right, of course. Some women kissed her goodbye, and cried. But Koos Steyn's wife did not cry. We reasoned with Koos about it, but he said that he had made up his mind to cross the Kalahari, and he was not going to turn back just for nonsense.

"But, man," Gerhardus Grobbelaar said to him, "you've got no water to drink."

"I'll drink coffee then," Koos Steyn answered, laughing as always, and took up the whip and walked away beside the wagon. And Webber went off with him, just because Koos Steyn had been good to him, I suppose. That's why I have said that Englishmen are queer. Webber must have known that if Koos Steyn had not actually gone wrong in the head, still what he was doing now was madness, and yet he stayed with him.

We separated. Our wagons went slowly back to Malopolole. Koos Steyn's wagon went deeper into the desert. My wagon went last. I looked back at the Steyns. At that moment Webber also looked round. He saw me and waved his hand. It reminded me of that day in the Boer War when that other Englishman, whose companion we had shot, also turned round and waved.

Eventually we got back to Malopolole with two wagons and a handful of cattle. We abandoned the other wagons. Awful things happened on that desert. A number of children died. Gerhardus Grobbelaar's wagon was in front of me. Once I saw a bundle being dropped through the side of the wagon-tent. I knew what it was. Gerhardus would not trouble to bury his dead child, and his wife lay in the tent too weak to move. So I got off the wagon and scraped a small heap of sand over the body. All I remember of the rest of the journey to Malopolole is the sun and the sand. And the thirst. Although at one time we thought that we had lost our way, yet that did not matter much to us. We were past feeling. We could neither pray nor curse, our parched tongues cleaving to the roofs of our mouths.

Until today I am not sure how many days we were on our way back, unless I sit down and work it all out, and then I suppose I get it wrong. We got back to Malopolole and water. We said we would never go away from there again. I don't think that even those parents who had lost children grieved about them then. They were stunned with what they had gone through. But I knew that later on it would all come back again. Then they would remember things about shallow graves in the sand, and Gerhardus Grobbelaar and his wife would think of a little bundle lying out in the Kalahari. And I knew how they would feel.

Afterwards we fitted out a wagon with fresh oxen; we took an abundant supply of water and went back into the desert to look for the Steyn family. With the help of the Sechuana kaffirs, who could see tracks that we could not see, we found the wagon. The oxen had been outspanned; a few lay dead beside the wagon. The kaffirs pointed out to us footprints on the sand, which showed which way those two men and that woman had gone.

In the end we found them.

Koos Steyn and his wife lay side by side in the sand; the woman's head rested on the man's shoulder; her long hair had become loosened, and blew about softly in the wind. A great deal of fine sand had drifted over their bodies. Near them the Englishman lay, face downwards. We never found the baby Jemima. She must have died somewhere along the way and Koos Steyn must have buried her. But we agreed that the Englishman Webber must have passed through terrible things; he could not even have had any understanding left as to what the Steyns had done with their baby. He probably thought, up to the moment when he died, that he was carrying the child. For, when we lifted his body, we found, still clasped in his dead and rigid arms, a few old rags and a child's clothes.

It seemed to us that the wind that always stirs in the Kalahari blew very quietly and softly that morning.

Yes, the wind blew very gently.

Source:
Herman Charles Bosman: *Mafeking Road and Other Stories: The Anniversary Edition,* Craig MacKenzie (ed). Cape Town: Human & Rousseau: 1998, written c. 1947.

THE BLACK CAT

MICHAEL RICE

The visitor paused at the top of the steps leading into the Palace of Justice recently converted into a temporary military hospital. Across the square a breeze stirred the Union Jack above the entrance to the Raadzaal. The National and Netherlands banks presented bland façades decorated with red, white and blue bunting to the holiday crowds. Young clerks jostled in the windows to get a good view of the parade. In the distance, along Church Street, a brass band playing Rule Britannia announced the approaching columns of cavalry and marching infantry, lances and bayonets gleaming in the sun. A sergeant at the head of the parade led an angora goat decked with regimental colours. Just as the procession was about to enter the square a gun carriage careered wildly out of the cavalcade, its horses bolting, churning dust and grit up into the already stifling air. A wag in the crowd cheered ironically as it disappeared behind the public grandstand where the dignatories and their wives were beginning to assemble.

The orderly looked up from his desk: "Yer want to interview one of the wounded? Well, we've got plenty as'll be willin'. Give 'em somethin' to do, like. No parades for 'em. Make the blighters feel like bleedin' heroes – that the idea? From the ranks: a personal account of a memorable experience? Right? Trooper Hancock'll be able to help you. Talkative blighter. Straight down the hall. Third on the left."

The visitor passed into the deeper gloom of the hospital, beyond the sounds of trumpets and drums and neighing horses. "The newspapers? Yer 'aven't brought 'em? Not even 'ome comforts? Last Christmas I got a tin of biscuits with a picture of the King on it. Yer from . . . *The Morning Post*. An exclusive interview? What, with the likes of me? . . . A yuman story . . . I was there and this is what it was like? Go on. Who'd read it?"

"I was there alright. That's why I'm here. Depends what piece of veld yer talkin' about. What a bloody country! Flies and ticks and dust. No water in the rivers. Leastways, not when yer want it. Bleedin' things come down in flood when yer least expect it. Not a cloud in the sky. 'eard of a platoon what camped in a dry river bed one night. The next mornin' their bodies was found on some rocks 'alf a mile down stream. The flood 'ad bin and gone. Not a sign of water anywhere. Unpredictable, that's what it is. Like the bleedin' Boers. Yer never know what they'll do next.

"Yes, I've known a Boer or two in my time. A funny bunch. White men . . . Christians . . . too excitable and emotional . . . no sense of proportion. Just look at this 'ere war. Anyone with any sense in their 'ead would 'ave made peace long ago. Can't 'elp admirin' 'em though. Damned fools. Think of all the sufferin' what could 'ave bin avoided if they'd given in when the writin' was on the wall. After Pretoria, that is.

"Spent eighteen months trackin' Van der Berg's commando from Bandolier Kop to the Wolkberg. Got him in the end. At Chuniespoort. Led us a merry dance. No 'eroics in the end, though. Not the sort of thing what gets into the papers back 'ome.

"Yes, I've known a Boer or two in my time. They say it's their women what kept 'em going. And I believe 'em. I remember sittin' down with me pack in the square outside the mornin' we took Pretoria and sayin' to me mate Jock: 'Thank God, the war's over.' And this Boer woman, she was pretty, too, turns to me, her eyes ablaze: 'Tommy Atkins,' they call us all Tommy Atkins, can't think why; 'Tommy Atkins,' she says, 'the war's just begun.'

"I'll say this too: I've a damned sight more respect for those what stayed out than those what joined and fought against their own kind. National Scouts. That's what they're called in some circles. That was Kitchener's doin'. Five bob a day. The wonder is so few of 'em joined. I'm gettin' 'alf that.

"Mounted infantry! Only the army could think that one up. Took us out of the lines; out us on mules and 'alf broken 'acks from the Argentine what 'adn't found their land legs yet and sent us off to tackle the bleedin' Boers at their own game! Fer the first two months I was more out of the saddle than in it. Could 'ardly move. The nearest I'd bin to an 'orse was the five quid I won on Flyin' Fox in the Derby. Not that I'm what yer might ordinarily call a bettin' man, yer understand. Though, when I mounted that mule for the first time I wouldn't 'ave minded givin' even money that it would get me afore the Boers did.

"The National Scouts? Oh yes. Many of 'em joined jist to get 'emselves fitted out again and then disappeared to rejoin their commandos. Many stayed, though. A scruffy lot with an eye to the main chance. Didn't seem to believe in nothin' except savin' their own skins. Kept out of the action; mostly only joinin' in when they was sure their brothers was runnin' fer it. Don't know that any of the men 'as any respect fer 'em, either. Their brothers even less. Shot 'em out of 'and if they caught 'em. I'd 'ave done the same if I was in their shoes.

"We 'ad one attached to our squad. Piet Venter was 'is name. Funny bloke. Fond of cats 'e was. Always pickin' 'em up and fondlin' 'em. 'e found this black kitten. Abandoned it was in a burnt-out farmhouse. Carried it around with 'im wherever 'e went, curled up inside 'is shirt. Slept there as safe as anythin'. We used to kid 'im about it. Me mate Jock said 'e slept with it as 'is wife wouldn't 'ave nothin' to do with 'im since 'e joined. It grew into a big, black, wicked lookin' tom. Fair give me the creeps it did. Always rubbin' itself against yer legs. Jumpin' onto yer lap. And steal? Yer daren't leave nothin' lyin' around. Don't see what 'e saw in it. Not like a dog. No loyalty, like.

"The wife, she stayed on the farm about a day's ride from our camp. No we didn't burn it. Served us pretty well in the end. We kept an eye on 'er fer 'im yer might say. Sarie was 'er name. Pretty figure of a woman. They'd bin married about three years. No kids as yet, what with the war and all. When Piet 'andsup she wouldn't 'ave nothin' more to do with 'im. Though it wasn't from want of tryin' on 'is part. 'e saw 'er whenever we was in the district, but she never relented. Plenty of families 'ave bin split like that. I hear tell even De Wet's brother 'andsupped and joined. Can't be much love lost there. Sergeant Walker, that's our NCO, let 'er stay on the farm instead of burnin' it down, 'opin' to lure 'er father, old Van der Berg, and 'er brothers fer forage and provisions in the winter. We suspected she was supplyin' 'em but couldn't catch 'er. But we was prepared to play a waitin' game. Piet was pretty bitter. Claimed it was 'er father what put 'er up to it. From what I saw she 'ad a mind of 'er own. Though I never could understand why she married Piet in the first place. But then who knows what makes a woman choose 'er mate? Or throw 'im out?

"Surly bugger; Piet, that is. I was never sure of 'im. 'is English were too good. Spoke me own language better than me. Never a smile or a pleasant 'ow d'you do for anyone. Jist crooned over that damned cat all day, ticklin' its neck and ears.

"We was tryin' to clear Van der Berg's commando out of the Chuniespoort district. 'ardly a convoy came through to Pietersburg last year what 'e didn't attack. The broken country give 'im plenty of cover, but we was sure that 'e was getting' information about our movements. Otherwise 'e 'ad the damndest luck. We tried everythin' to surprise 'im. Night rides. Sudden changes of plan. False rumours. All that sort of thing. Nothin' seemed to work until early one mornin' jist as the sun was comin' up, we was passin' Piet's place hopin' to stop in fer a cup of coffee, as yer might say. It was that cold. There weren't no sign of life except fer a couple of fowls scratchin' in the yard and a dog asleep at the end of a rope. And that was odd. Not even the sight of smoke comin' from the chimney. Somewhere a calf was bawlin' fer its mother. An 'orse tethered to a thorn tree jerked its 'ead up and snorted. It must 'ave 'eard or smelled us. Jist then the kitchen door opened and a man and a girl came out onto the back stoep. They walked over to the 'orse which was saddled up and ready, their arms about each other, like lovers. They kissed before 'e mounted. It was almost indecent like, watchin' 'em and all. The man took off 'is 'at as 'e bent down to kiss 'er again. I noticed that 'at because it 'ad a peacock feather stuck in the band. We all recognised the girl. It was Sarie, Piet's wife. She stood there fer a while as 'e rode away, the mornin' sun catchin' 'er black 'air shinin' down the length of 'er back. I can tell yer the sight of 'er did somethin' to me, not 'avin' seen a decent women in eighteen months. A man begins to miss female company after a while out there in the veld. Especially when the nights is cold.

"We kept cover fer a while before Piet crossed the yard to the 'ouse, us keepin' 'im covered all the while. 'e said it was 'is affair. Didn't want no interference from anybody. 'e was gone about an 'our. A couple of times I thought I 'eard raised voices but mainly I was chilled and stiff from not movin'. A nasty cold wind that the sun did nothin' to warm 'ad sprung up. Yer wouldn't think the winters could be that cold in Africa.

"I'll never forget that first winter outside Bloemfontein. I fair froze to death. I've never bin that cold. Sleepin' out in the open, like. Wakin' in the mornin', me blankets white with frost.

"Anyway, we mounted up as soon as Piet got back. There's no tellin' what a man will do in a situation like that. Never did work out what passed between 'em. The look on 'er face as she stood in the doorway was like it always was. We was never in any doubt what she thought of us. Now we knew what she thought of 'er 'usband. If ever we 'ad any doubts about 'im we 'ad none now. What I couldn't work out was if 'e'd let on to 'er what we'd seen that mornin'. As fer 'er, she stood there pale and silent in the early mornin' sun, the winter wind tuggin' at 'er dress.

"When we reached the poort later that mornin' we dismounted and settled amongst the rocks and aloes out of the wind and waited. There wasn't a round but fer the go-away birds and a troop of monkeys arsin' about in the trees a little way off. It was that peaceful. Yer almost forgot there was a war on. A couple of 'ours later a small commando came into view. It's uncanny 'ow quiet an 'orse can be in the veld. They was almost on top of us before we knew it. An old grey-beard who looked as if 'e'd be better occupied dozin' on 'is stoep in the sun and four or five younger men passed through the defile. I recognised the outrider by the peacock feather wavin' from 'is 'atband.

"It weren't a pleasant business. But it's all in the game. If it 'adn't bin them it might jist as easily 'ave bin us. It only struck me later as odd that Piet should 'ave led us straight to the place where we set up the ambush. After all those months. Oh, it was Van der Berg's commando, all right.

"The followin' mornin' on our way back to camp we passed through Piet's farm again and stopped off at the 'ouse. This time the smoke was risin' from the chimney. Sarie came to the front door as we rode up. Piet nudged 'is 'orse ahead of the rest of us and flung somethin' in her face. As it fell to the ground I recognised the peacock feather in the 'atband. Without a word 'e turned 'is 'orse and galloped out of the yard.

"When we got back to camp that evenin' 'e was sittin' beside the fire strokin' the cat on 'is lap, starin' into the flames.

"That night we all got a double ration of rum. I was glad of it, I can tell you. The wind 'and't let up. I was that chilled. Later I was even more glad to get into me blanket roll and get a few 'ours sleep at last. I 'ad a restless night of it. What with the calls to change guard and the wind flappin' the tent, I drifted from one dream to another. In one of my dreams I dreamed of Sarie as I'd last seen 'er that mornin' clutchin' that old felt 'at to 'er breast. In me dream she come to me, her 'air black against 'er white skin, tumblin' over 'r breast, like. She seemed to stoop over me as if she were searchin' fer somethin'. In me dream it felt as if 'er 'air brushed over me face. I wanted to ask 'er what she wanted, but as always 'appens in a dream 'er image faded and I woke shiverin', me blankets off me.

"The followin' mornin' Piet didn't appear at roll-call. 'e always slept apart from us under a small lean-to 'e'd rigged up. I went across to see if anythin' was amiss. As I moved the canvas flap aside the cat looked up at me for a moment and then went on lappin' the blood from the cut across 'is throat.

"Yes. I've known a Boer or two in me time. Jist the same as us really, but no sense of proportion. Strange what a man will do because of a woman. Can't say I understand it; not bein' a marryin' man, as yer might say."

When the visitor emerged from the gloom of the hospital into the glare of the noon sun, the procession was over and the crowds had gone home. The flags hung limply in the still air and because he had nothing to celebrate he turned to his own affairs.

Source:
Contrast 66, 17:2: December 1988.

The Traitor's Wife

Herman Charles Bosman

We did not like the sound of the wind that morning, as we cantered over a veld trail that we had made much use of, during the past year, when there were English forces in the neighbourhood.

The wind blew short wisps of yellow grass in quick flurries over the veld and the smoke from the fire in front of a row of kafir huts hung low in the air. From that we knew that the third winter of the Boer War was at hand. Our small group of burghers dismounted at the edge of a clump of camel-thorns to rest our horses.

"It's going to be an early winter," Jan Vermeulen said, and from force of habit he put his hand up to his throat in order to close his jacket collar over in front. We all laughed, then. We realized that Jan Vermeulen had forgotten how he had come to leave his jacket behind when the English had surprised us at the spruit a few days before. And instead of a jacket, he was now wearing a mealie sack with holes cut in it for his head and arms. You could not just close over in front of your throat, airily, the lapels cut in a grain bag.

"Anyway, Jan, you're all right for clothes," Kobus Ferreira said, "but look at me."

Kobus Ferreira was wearing a missionary's frock-coat that he had found outside Kronendal, where it had been hung on a clothes-line to air.

"This frock-coat is cut so tight across my middle and shoulders that I have to sit very stiff and awkward in my saddle, just like the missionary sits on a chair when he is visiting at a farmhouse," Kobus Ferreira added. "Several times my horse has taken me for an Englishman, in consequence of the way I sit. I am only afraid that when a bugle blows my horse will carry me over the rant into the English camp."

At Kobus Ferreira's remarks the early winter wind seemed to take on a keener edge.

For our thoughts went immediately to Leendert Roux, who had been with us on commando a long while and who had been spoken of as a likely man to be veldkornet – and who had gone out scouting, one night, and not come back with a report.

There were, of course, other Boers who had also joined the English. But there was not one of them that we had respected as much as we had done Leendert Roux.

Shortly afterwards we were on the move again.

In the late afternoon we emerged through the Crocodile Poort that brought us in sight of Leendert Roux's farmhouse. Next to the dam was a patch of mealies that Leendert Roux's wife had got the kafirs to cultivate.

"Anyway, we'll camp on Leendert Roux's farm and eat roast mealies, tonight," our veldkornet, Apie Theron, observed.

"Let us first rather burn his house down," Kobus Ferreira said. And in a strange way it seemed as though his violent language was not out of place, in a missionary's frock-coat. "I would like to roast mealies in the thatch of Leendert Roux's house."

Many of us were in agreement with Kobus.

But our veldkornet, Apie Theron, counselled us against that form of vengeance.

"Leendert Roux's having his wife and farmstead here will yet lead to his undoing," the veldkornet said. "One day he will risk coming out here on a visit, when he hasn't got Kitchener's whole army at his back. That will be when we will settle our reckoning with him."

We did not guess that that day would be soon.

The road we were following led past Leendert Roux's homestead. The noise of our horses' hoofs brought Leendert Roux's wife, Serfina, to the door. She stood in the open doorway and watched us riding by. Serfina was pretty, taller than most women, and slender, and there was no expression in her eyes that you could read, and her face was very white.

It was strange, I thought, as we rode past the homestead, that the sight of Serfina Roux did not fill us with bitterness.

Afterwards, when we had dismounted in the mealie-lands, Jan Vermeulen made a remark at which we laughed.

"For me it was the worst moment in the Boer War," Jan Vermeulen said. "Having to ride past a pretty girl, and me wearing just a sack. I was glad there was Kobus Ferreira's frock-coat for me to hide behind."

Jurie Bekker said there was something about Serfina Roux that reminded him of the Transvaal. He did not know how it was, but he repeated that, with the wind of early winter fluttering her dress about her ankles, that was how it seemed to him.

Then Kobus Ferreira said that he had wanted to shout out something to her when we rode past the door, to let Serfina know how we, who were fighting in the last ditch – and in unsuitable clothing – felt about the wife of a traitor. "But she stood there so still," Kobus Ferreira said, "that I just couldn't say anything. I felt I would like to visit her, even."

That remark of Kobus Ferreira's fitted in with his frock-coat also. It would not be the first time a man in ecclesiastical dress called on a woman while her husband was away.

Then, once again, a remark of Jan Vermeulen's made us realize that there was a war on. Jan Vermeulen had taken the mealie sack off his body and had threaded a length of baling-wire above the places where the holes were. He was now restoring the grain bag to the use it had been meant for, and I suppose that, in consequence, his views generally also got sensible.

"Just because Serfina Roux is pretty," Jan Vermeulen said, flinging mealie heads into the sack, "let us not forget who and what she is. Perhaps it is not safe for us to camp tonight on this farm. She is sure to be in touch with the English. She may tell them where we are. Especially now that we have taken her mealies."

But our veldkornet said that it wasn't important if the English knew where we were. Indeed, any kafir in the neighbourhood could go and report our position to them. But what did matter was that we should know where the English were. And he reminded us that in two years he had never made a serious mistake that way.

"What about the affair at the spruit, though?" Jan Vermeulen asked him. "And my pipe and tinder-box were in the jacket, too."

By sunset the wind had gone down. But there was a chill in the air. We had pitched our camp in the tamboekie grass on the far side of Leendert Roux's farm. And I was glad, lying in my blankets, to think that it was the turn of the veldkornet and Jurie Bekker to stand guard.

Far away a jackal howled. Then there was silence again. A little later the stillness was disturbed by sterner sounds of the veld at night. And those sounds did not come from very far away, either. They were sounds Jurie Bekker made – first, when he fell over a beacon, and then when he gave his opinion of Leendert Roux for setting up a beacon in the middle of a stretch of dubbeltjie thorns. The blankets felt very snug, pulled over my shoulders, when I reflected on those thorns.

And because I was young, there came into my thoughts, at Jurie Bekker's mention of Leendert Roux, the picture of Serfina as she had stood in front of her door.

The dream I had of Serfina Roux was that she came to me, tall and graceful, beside a white beacon on her husband's farm. It was that haunting kind of dream, in which you half know all the time, that you are dreaming. And she was very beautiful in my dream. And it was as though her hair was hanging half out of my dream and reaching down into the wind when she came closer to me. And I knew what she wanted to tell me. But I did not wish to hear it. I knew that if Serfina spoke that thing I would wake up from my dream. And in that moment, like it always happens in a dream, Serfina did speak.

"Opskud, kêrels!" I heard.

But it was not Serfina who gave that command. It was Apie Theron, the veldkornet. He came running into the camp with his rifle at the trail. And Serfina was gone. In a few minutes we had saddled our horses and were ready to gallop away. Many times during the past couple of years our scouts had roused us thus when an English column was approaching.

We were already in the saddle when Apie Theron let us know what was toward. He had received information, he said, that Leendert Roux had that very night ventured back to his homestead. If we hurried we might trap him in his own house. The veldkornet warned us to take no chances, reminding us that when Leendert Roux had still stood on our side he had been a fearless and resourceful fighter.

So we rode back during the night along the same way we had come in the afternoon. We tethered our horses in a clump of trees near the mealie-lands and started to surround the farmhouse. When we saw a figure running for the stable at the side of the house, we realized that Leendert Roux had been almost too quick for us.

In the cold, thin wind that springs up just before the dawn we surprised Leendert Roux at the door of his stable. But when he made no resistance it was almost as though it was Leendert Roux who had taken us by surprise. Leendert Roux's calm acceptance of his fate made it seem almost as though he had never turned traitor, but that he was laying down his life for the Transvaal.

In answer to the veldkornet's question, Leendert Roux said that he would be glad if Kobus Ferreira – he having noticed that Kobus was wearing the frock-coat of a man of religion – would read Psalm 110 over his grave. He also said that the did not want his eyes bandaged. And he asked to be allowed to say goodbye to his wife.

Serfina was sent for. At the side of the stable, in the wind of early morning, Leendert and Serfina Roux, husband and wife, bade each other farewell.

Serfina looked even more shadowy than she had done in my dream when she set off back to the homestead along the footpath through the thorns. The sun was just beginning to rise. And I understood how right Jurie Bekker had been when he said that she was just like the Transvaal, with the dawn wind fluttering her skirts about her ankles as it rippled the grass. And I remembered that it was the Boer women that kept on when their menfolk recoiled before the steepness of the Drakensberge and spoke of turning back.

I also thought of how strange it was that Serfina should have come walking over to our camp, in the middle of the night, just as she had done in my dream. But where my dream was different was that she had reported not to me but to our veldkornet where Leendert Roux was.

Source:
Herman Charles Bosman: *Unto Dust.* Cape Town: Human & Rousseau: 1963.

THE FLOOD

ETIENNE LEROUX

Leroux's novel Magersfontein, o Magersfontein! *is about a foreign team of film makers who come to South Africa to produce a film about the historic battle of Magersfontein, where the Boers defeated the British. In the extract, close to the end of the book, incessant rain has turned the whole area into a huge lake. All their carefully prepared plans are upset. Chaos erupts. The fragment is permeated by nihilism, satire, absurdity and humour.*

As far as the eye could see, to where the plain disappeared in a fogbank which blotted out Modder River station and the horizon, there was a sheet of water which shone a muddy brown in the weak sun. Against the background of the far-off fogbank, there was a rainbow which offered no reassurance. At first it was difficult to assess whether the whole battlefield was a sea above which Magersfontein Hill rose like an Ararat, but in the growing light, and as the illusions disappeared, a better idea of the scene could be formed. In the distance there were still the muddy yellow marquee tents of Headquarters Hill, which rose above the rippling ground level like a Moorish fortress. Further east Horse Artillery Hill showed its hump on which a single horse and rider were silhouetted. The whole battlefield was under water but it was a calm water which was slowly increasing as the flood was reaching its apex. A thirty-metre-high wall of water at the confluence of rivers coming from the endless plains of the Free State, came slowly, telegraphing its power like a dim-witted boxer.

In the beginning it had been difficult to measure the depth of the water. Here and there wire fences could be used as meters but that, too, was misleading. In some places the fences were a metre below the water, in others the fences had disappeared completely and that meant a depth of two metres or more. In some other places the fences were high and dry. From Headquarters Hill a line of human and mechanical objects could be seen, stretched in a northeasterly and then gradually northwesterly direction, virtually up to the trenches. It was actually Hans Winterbach who could see best through his binoculars.

For the first few thousand yards there were the bulldozers, cranes, etcetera of De Beers, bright yellow and thus easy to see, which appeared and disappeared at various heights in and above the water like a Loch Ness monster. In the distance, in the direction of the Modder River station, disappearing in the bank of fog, the bright green of Border Jones's trucks. It was some sort of mechanical connecting line via Headquarters Hill to Magersfontein Hill which suddenly ended in front of an evident lake of 30 000 square metres of white water. (Three hectares. Previously a little pan.) It was difficult to judge its depth. There was no wire fence which could establish the depth. In the centre there was a small yellow fleck which could well have been the top of one of De Beers' 200-ton trucks. With the necessary imagination a human figure could also be perceived who gave the impression that he was walking on water. For the sake of human mental health it must be assumed that it was the driver who was standing on his vehicle. On this side of the little lake, its arse in the water, was the television minibus of Amicus Achtung. The prow pointed in the direction of the sky. It looked like a tortoise which was on the point of emerging from the water.

Only then did the line of objects become nonmechanical and human.

The first column in the direction of Magersfontein Hill was possibly the MEC's, Members of the Executive Council, as well as a section of the older actresses and contemporaries, consisting of spectators from Kimberley with here and there a small grandchild holding the hand of a grandmother or grandfather, the impetuous father and mother having disappeared ahead already. They were on little islands of high ground between water more or less one-metre deep, stranded with a regularity which reminded one of the perforations on paper. If one didn't think about the fact that the water was only one-metre deep there it could have been heart-rending scenes. There were visions of greybeards being helped out of the depths by other greybeards. It was also obvious that the grey women seemed more energetic. The little children spoilt the heart-rending impression because they were constantly jumping back into the water and splashing away, paddling gaily to other little islands. The most astonishing aspect of the disaster, however, was that this fragile composition of old age and vulnerable tots had progressed further than all the mechanical objects.

Closer to the Boer lines and the trenches, were the Scots, supplemented by young men from Kimberley. Here and there there were youthful actresses and beauty queens who, often up their waists in the water and then suddenly on dry ground, were approaching Magersfontein Hill with the Scots. It goes without saying that they reached high ground, and safety as well.

Lord Seldom was in the lead, sword aloft, tired unto death, his face as pale as wax, and the blue veins of high blood pressure sketched like rivers on his forehead. He was surrounded by his ADC's, sturdy young men in Scottish dress who were enjoying this adventure to the utmost. They moved forward inexorably through half a metre of water. They stumbled over shrubs, became soaked and then stood up again and struggled through the mud directly to the white stones.

Behind them, already on dry ground, was Amicus Achtung with his cameras and assistants who carried the photographic and lighting equipment with superhuman strength. Photographers from the best-known Sunday papers were also present. Danger was their fate; they were fighting for their newspapers with the commitment and belief which Wauchope and De la Rey had had in the past. They fought for the untrammeled truth as they saw it. They were motivated. Perhaps they were also one of the few remnants of a Victorian tradition of commitment to an ideal. No one knew how they had landed at the forefront.

Hans Winterbach put down his binoculars and picked up his walkie-talkie. He held it in front of his lips, looked fixedly at the Scots, led by Lord Seldom who was now clearly visible to the naked eye. And then he gave the order: "Shoot!"

But it wasn't his cameras which went into action. All along the trenches fireworks exploded with an unusual intensity. Even the trajectory of the rockets had been set so low that they found their height only a few feet above the heads of the Scots, disappeared into the fog to explode in a halo of light in the mistiness.

The ensuing chaos was predictable. It was probably too much to expect of human nature which, on the wings of a flood and in rain and thunder throughout the entire night, had to enter the darkness for a television programme under the leadership of a semiblind man and then, in a moment of triumph, with the end in sight, to be virtually beheaded by maniacs who were arbitrarily shooting crackers, rockets and other demonic manifestations of firework factories. They had expected acclamation and afterwards tea and sandwiches at the very least because they had reached the end.

It was only at that stage that Hans Winterbach's cameras went into action. And at that precise moment, so did the cameras of Amicus Achtung. And they shot far back, across the water, up to Headquarters Hill.

The majority fell back into the water and trampled all over one another. A negligible group moved eastward and reached the foot of Magersfontein Hill. They climbed the hill, badly grazing their knees in going across ironstone to the heights.

But when they had reached the crest and safety, an appalling concentration of fireworks exploded right in front of them, causing them to stagger back and slip on smooth dolomite resulting in severe bruises and cracked and broken bones. At the same moment the cameras flashed and the rolls of intricate television apparatus began turning.

It was difficult to establish whose order it had been because both Amicus Achtung and Hans Winterbach were in control of the camera work with the aid of walkie-talkies. The collaboration of Amicus Achtung and Hans Winterbach in the realm of the film world and the television arena was legendary.

"That was superbly done," Dr F. Laird said admiringly to Hans Winterbach. "And it is historically correct. It is said that Lieutenant Wilson with about a hundred men of the Seaforths and the Black Watch found the gap and climbed the northeastern side of the Hill. And then they came upon General Cronjé who, with his staff, had lost his way on the Hill during an inspection tour. The Boers thought the strange-looking objects were ostriches until General Cronjé suddenly ordered: 'Shoot, Boers, shoot, they're not ostriches, they're Highlanders!'"

"Beautiful," said Hans Winterbach. "That will be put on the soundtrack."

"But perhaps it's not the whole truth," said Dr F. Laird. "Allegedly it was Free Staters under the leadership of Commandant P. de Villiers who were sent to close the gap between Magersfontein and the Scandinavians. They accidentally came upon the Highlanders and shot them."

"I find it less filmic, less tragically comic," said Hans Winterbach. "Is there another theory?"

"Well," said Dr Laird, "there is also the theory that by chance a group of Boers who had been on a raid had returned to Magersfontein, saw the Highlanders and methodically shot them."

"That's rather dull," said Hans Winterbach. "Anything else?"

"Well," said Dr F. Laird, "at that stage the British artillery had started bombarding Magersfontein Hill again, unaware of the fact that the Highlanders were climbing it. Whatever the reason, the Highlanders were either killed or captured. But it saved Magersfontein for the Boers."

"I understand," said Hans Winterbach. "Actually it means that if General Wauchope hadn't been killed, the British would have won the battle."

"Perhaps," said Dr F. Laird.

"In that case," said Hans Winterbach, "perhaps the time has come for us to concentrate on Lord Seldom as General Wauchope."

He gave orders over his walkie-talkie and the cameras fixed their multiple lenses on Lord Seldom who, sword aloft, was on the point of entering a pool of water on the way to Magersfontein Hill.

"How can I 'kill' him?" Hans Winterbach wondered. He held his cameras in readiness and brought the image of Lord Seldom onto the retinas of the intricate appliances.

Lord Seldom gave one step forward and disappeared under two metres of water.

At that precise moment the Man from the Department of Water Affairs got up. There was a time to arrive and a time to go, or the other way round. What he saw in front of him confirmed his darkest suspicions. Even the engineers with university degrees were not immune to the apparent arbitrariness of Providence. He was suddenly aware of Koestler's view of the inconsistency between the limited and the limitless; the everyday worldly simplicity of personal tragedy, set against the universal system, the destination of fate; the relative against the absolute; comedy in contrast with tragedy. It was time for Water Affairs to distance itself from the insignificant and to find reconciliation. Water Affairs should also be able, according to Kierkegaard, to combine the two: "Mind as it soars to the infinite, whilst existence binds it fast to the finite." Water Affairs also had a close affinity with Jung, meaning the search for the self; meaning the centre, the island, in the sea of egos.

The Man from Water Affairs got up and told Hans Winterbach that he had to leave now. But no one listened to him. Not even Dr Laird. The way of Water Affairs is a lonely one.

No one took any notice of any cultural-historical-philosophical aspects in the composition of pure science.

On the way he met Le Grange, the speed cop, and in a moment of weakness he aired his theory. In Le Grange he found a soul mate. He found that they were both filled with an existentialist fear. Symbols had become meaningless. The romanticism established in the composition of water and traffic which led to infinity had become a farce.

"We are irresistably coming to a condition of *nada*," said the Man from Water Affairs.

"What does *nada* mean?" asked Le Grange.

"Nothing," said the Man from Water Affairs.

"That's my feeling, too," said Le Grange.

They admired one another mutually.

"Sister Nagtegaal feels that way too," said Le Grange.

Sister Nagtegaal was exhausted and hung in the hollow of Le Grange's arm.

"I caught three babies tonight," said Sister Fiskaal.

There was a noisy procession of amateur nurses bringing various casualties with broken bones and suchlike. For the attention of Sister Nagtegaal. Bravely she straightened herself again. She looked at the sufferers and collapsed.

"We need helicopters," said Le Grange. "Urgently."

The Man from Water Affairs declared that he was willing to part with one helicopter and Sister Fiskaal and various victims of fireworks, dolomite and exhaustion disappeared in the direction of the Kimberley Hospital.

"I have three helicopters left," said the Man from Water Affairs.

He gazed at the panorama of water.

"It's my destination," he said.

Water Affairs disappeared with three helicopters in the direction of the flood.

Methodically Le Grange examined all the vehicles. His soul was filled with rage. He filled an entire notebook with summonses. Every vehicle was found to be defective. He defied the fury of the owners with a will of steel.

The word "nada" became a refrain every time he signed his name illegibly.

Nada, nada, nada . . .

Throughout the night the helicopters hovered and shot back and forth like dragonflies over the battlefield. Exhausted grateful ones, the aged, recalcitrant nursery tots and "volunteers" were picked up everywhere and transported to Kimberley.

As the water level slowly rose, the helicopters of Water Affairs found more and more "volunteers". But across the battlefield, there were also a great many Scots and civilians on a difficult terrain, in other words, up to their waists in water, temporarily safe but in the long term, in danger. It was a difficult decision for Water Affairs. The senior Man from Water Affairs had to make his own decisions without instructions from Pretoria. From his helicopter he looked at the growing lake and like God he had to decide where and whom. Obviously, his view was panoramic and naturally this made his choice more difficult. "Here!" he said. "There!" But it was a slow process, equal to the tempo of the flood which was just as slow. All in all, it came down to the fact that in terms of *time* and *motion*, there were going to be a great many victims. He remembered the English terms. This was no time to translate the English textbooks. In times of need, it was easiest to communicate in the babble of the composition of our nation. This was no time for purity. To find the correct verb or preposition or suchlike was a loss of precious time.

The senior Man from Water Affairs sent an urgent message to headquarters. "Send help. It's a fuck-up."

Reply from headquarters: "We don't read you."

Senior Man at the head of Water Affairs: "Condition chaotic. Rise of water level 3% more than computer-established figure. Waiting for instructions."

Within half an hour three Impala jets sheared across the waters and disappeared into the distance. From Kimberley came trucks filled with conscripts with machine guns in time to foil looters. That is, on the banks, at the hotel, the cafés.

The Crown Hotel once again became the headquarters.

Purely military.

Helicopters from the Defence Force arrived and joined Water Affairs. They were far more effective and faster.

"It's because they have the best equipment, of course," said the senior Man from Water Affairs to his junior while he jealously looked on to see twice as many victims being saved. "I see they're using rope ladders," he said, "so of course they needn't land."

They circled the battlefield looking for a place to land but the islands were diminishing.

Senior looked at Junior. It seemed as if they were thinking the same thing.

"I see there's a rope in the cabin," the Senior said.

"I'm ready," said the Junior.

"I have the greatest admiration for you," the Senior said. "Water Affairs is proud of you."

A helicopter from Water Affairs hovered low over an old MEC and a beloved bitch of the theatre who were standing knee-deep in water. They saw a rope descending from the cabin and swing to the surface, dangling and swaying. Then a man from Water Affairs appeared in a safari suit and with difficulty began climbing down the rope.

"Homage, homage," said the old MEC as he looked on anxiously.

Halfway the rope slipped through the hands of the Man from Water Affairs and he landed from a height of two metres into one metre of water. This injured his coccyx in the rocky mud below. Now there were three of them and they gazed cheerlessly at the rising heliocopter with its swinging rope.

The young man from Water Affairs comforted the MEC and the beloved bitch.

"There is no reason to panic," he said.

Within the radius of the walkie-talkie came the voice of someone who was evidently in charge of the main broadcast centre.

"Shipmaster, logistics here," he said. "I'm calling Water Affairs and Traffic. I'm calling, I repeat, Water Affairs and Traffic.

An angry voice came back.

"Get off the frequency, fuck you!"

On the walkie-talkie a soft little voice signalled:

"He's speaking English." And then loud and clear:

"This is Rosemary Golden Dawn. Repeat, this is Rosemary Golden Dawn. Over to Traffic and Water Affairs. Do you hear me?"

"Dear Rosemary," said the voice. "Please, dear, get off the frequency."

Over the airspace a girl giggled.

"I like your voice, Love. I'm Rosemary Dawn. Will you please come to Headquarters Hill? There is an awful lot of water here and I want to go back to the hotel."

"Will do," said the voice. "But, Rosemary dear, please put the instrument down."

The voices faded.

"Rosemary! Rosemary!" it came again.

"This Rosemary Golden Dawn. Please come in."

"Dear Rosemary, please press the button."

There was a click sound and then silence.

On the tarred road from Kimberley more or less at the Modder River station, there was probably one of the largest contingents of traffic police and their cars. They arrived with screaming sirens and flashing roof lights. Men in black with helmets and dark glasses jumped out and stood fearlessly in the centre of the road to stop the advancing stream of cars of the citizenry. Black gloves were uplifted and with a swing of the arm the cars were ordered to stop in an orderly row next to the road. The head of the traffic department had also arrived. His car had arrived at an unbelievable speed and stopped, with the screaming of rubber on tar, sideways across the road. The chauffeur got out briskly, saluted, and opened the door. The Head of Traffic climbed out slowly and calmly took off his gloves while he surveyed the scene.

"Who is in charge here?" he enquired.

Several traffic police announced themselves. It was actually an interprovincial gathering although the majority of the Free State traffic police was cut off by the flood.

The Head of Traffic nodded approvingly.

"Who is in charge of the flood area?"

"Le Grange," someone said.

"Where is he?"

"On Magersfontein Hill."

"Where is Magersfontein Hill?" enquired the Head of Traffic.

Magersfontein Hill was pointed out to him. It looked like a far-off island in the plains of rippling water.

"The right man in the right place," said the Head of Traffic. "An excellent man. I would like to contact him."

From the radios in the traffic police cars signals were sent to Magersfontein Hill. In vain.

"I hope there's nothing wrong," said the Head of Traffic. "Try again. He's totally alone. "

After a while someone reported back. "We've just established contact but it's not very clear. We can only hear certain words."

"Yes?"

"'Tyres and lights defective . . . Drunken driving'." The traffic policeman hesitated. "And then something that sounds like 'nada'."

"Is that a code?" the Head of Traffic asked.

"I suspect it is," said the traffic cop in charge of the transmitter.

"Anything else?" the Head asked.

The traffic policeman listened intently to the crackle on his set.

"Yes," he said. "I can hear quite clearly now. 'Send helicopters.'"

"It's only Water Affairs, Power Lines, the Air Force and suchlike who have helicopters," said the Head. "Contact public relations."

While they waited, a traffic cop said: "I see quite a few helicopters."

The Head looked at the sky and nodded in agreement.

"Cancel public relations. I think our first task is to stop all traffic from advancing any further. Put up roadblocks. Your task will be to get the traffic from the north, that is to say the rear, turned back to Kimberley."

Traffic police raced away at high speed to meet the oncoming stream of cars and to contain them in sections.

The Head of Traffic turned to the traffic cop in charge of radio service again.

"Get hold of Le Grange," he said. He picked up the receiver himself when Le Grange's voice came over the ether. "Congratulations, Le Grange. Excellent service. Carry on. Traffic is behind you. This is the Head speaking."

A voice came crackling back.

"Thank you, Chief."

The Head hesitated for a moment and then said meaningfully: "Nada!"

It seemed as though a sob came over the ether.

"Thank you, Chief. Nada."

"More power to your elbow," said the Head. There was a slight dampness in his steely eyes but he gave further orders with a cool calmness which was admirable. The traffic was properly organised and the oncoming cars forced to return to Kimberley.

He could do little about the cars which were already parked at the side of the road. He even felt helpless when he saw that some tourists were taking small boats off trailers and with the aid of oars and small engines were sailing off on Magersfontein Plains. He could also do very little when he saw various families picnicking and children in bathing suits paddling to and fro in the swirling water on the edge of the flood.

But he was wide awake when he barred his traffic officers from stopping a row of Landrovers manned by men in safari suits. He wasn't Head of Traffic for nothing.

He immediately recognised the presence of Water Affairs.

The men of Water Affairs opened a collapsible table in the middle of the tarred road with four chairs around upon which each one sat down immediately. Each one had a walkie-talkie and there was a portable transistor computer which worked with batteries. A few others were busy setting up theodolites and other forms of graphometers from which they could supply readings which were processed by the group at the table by means of the computer. They took very little notice of the Head of Traffic.

"We're at your disposal," said the Head of Traffic. "We can partition you off."

He was acknowledged with the wave of a hand.

The enigineer with a university degree spoke on the walkie-talkie.

"Come in," he said after he had obtained the correct frequency from the senior Man of Water Affairs in the helicopter. He listened attentively, then said to one of his colleagues: "We've lost one of our junior men."

"Who is he?"

"Sam Wannamaker."

"I don't know him."

"It's one of the most junior."

The engineer with a university degree struggled for a while and then connected up with the Senior again.

"How are things up there?" He listened attentively and then said to his colleague: "Senior says that almost the whole of the battlefield is covered in water and that there are only a few islands left on the level. Headquarters Hill, Horse Artillery Hill, and a few unknown hills. Depth of water varying from one metre to two metres." He looked at the figures on his computer fed in by the men of the theodolites. "That's more or less accurate." He spoke on the walkie-talkie again and then said: "Jesus Christ!"

"What now?" his colleague asked.

"Senior is under the impression that the rise of the water is 0,3% more than the calculations!"

There was great agitation.

"Put the facts too him," said his colleague.

"Come in, Senior," said the engineer. "Correction. Rise is 3,3% *more* than calculated."

At that moment the Head of Traffic approached.

"We have had further information over our radio from the Free State side. Reports from Traffic Services about the precipitation in the catchment area. Here are the figures."

The engineer listened closely. He fed the computer and went deathly pale.

"Listen, Senior," he said over the walkie-talkie. "Correction. According to latest information a correction. According to last information, figure now 7,7% more than calculation."

The walkie-talkie crackled as the voice of the Senior of Water Affairs commented.

"There is no reason to be upset," said the engineer with a university degree. He briefly glanced at the computer.

The walkie-talkie crackled. In the distance a helicopter took off high into the sky. The Senior wanted a better panoramic view. And then the helicopter dropped. The walkie-talkie crackled again.

"It is the Senior," the engineer said to his colleague. He listened attentively.

And then he reported to his colleague.

"The Senior says there was no proper reconnaissance. The Senior says that all hell is going to break loose when he comes to earth again. The Senior says that he's sick of water. The Senior says . . ." The engineer couldn't hear very well and then he suddenly smiled. "The Senior has a sense of humour. That is the way we know him. He said something like 'nearer to the rugby posts'."

"Are you sure?" his colleague asked.

"I definitely heard the word 'nader'[1]," said the engineer.

NOTES

1. Nearer. The Afrikaans word "nader" sounds like "nada".

Source:
Etienne Leroux: *Magersfontein, o Magersfontein!* Cape Town: Human & Rousseau: 1976.
Translated by Madeleine van Biljon

Mafeking Road

Herman Charles Bosman

When people ask me – as they often do – how it is that I can tell the best stories of anybody in the Transvaal (Oom Schalk Lourens said, modestly), then I explain to them that I just learn through observing the way that the world has with men and women. When I say this they nod their heads wisely, and say that they understand, and I nod my head wisely also, and that seems to satisfy them. But the thing I say to them is a lie, of course.

For it is not the story that counts. What matters is the way you tell it. The important thing is to know just at what moment you must knock out your pipe on your veldskoen, and at what stage of the story you must start talking about the School Committee at Drogevlei. Another necessary thing is to know what part of the story to leave out.

And you can never learn these things.

Look at Floris, the last of the Van Barnevelts. There is no doubt that he had a good story, and he should have been able to get people to listen to it. And yet nobody took any notice of him or of the things he had to say. Just because he couldn't tell the story properly.

Accordingly, it made me sad whenever I listened to him talk. For I could tell just where he went wrong. He never knew the moment at which to knock the ash out of his pipe. He always mentioned his opinion of the Drogevlei School Committee in the wrong place. And, what was still worse, he didn't know what part of the story to leave out.

And it was no use my trying to teach him, because as I have said, this is the thing that you can never learn. And so, each time he had told his story, I would see him turn away from me, with a look of doom on his face, and walk slowly down the road, stoop-shouldered, the last of the Van Barnevelts.

On the wall of Floris's voorkamer is a long family tree of the Van Barnevelts. You can see it there for yourself. It goes back for over two hundred years, to the Van Barnevelts of Amsterdam. At one time it went even further back, but that was before the white ants started on the top part of it and ate away quite a lot of Van Barnevelts. Nevertheless, if you look at this list, you will notice that at the bottom, under Floris's own name, there is the last entry, "Stephanus." And behind the name, "Stephanus," between two bent strokes, you will read the words: "Obiit Mafeking."

At the outbreak of the Second Boer War Floris van Barnevelt was a widower, with one son, Stephanus, who was aged seventeen. The commando from our part of the Transvaal set off very cheerfully. We made a fine show, with our horses and our wide hats and our bandoliers, and with the sun shining on the barrels of our Mausers.

Young Stephanus van Barnevelt was the gayest of us all. But he said there was one thing he didn't like about the war, and that was that, in the end, we would have to go over the sea. He said that, after we had invaded the whole of the Cape, our commando would have to go on a ship and invade England also.

But we didn't go overseas, just then. Instead, our veldkornet told us that the burghers from our part had been ordered to join the big commando that was lying at Mafeking. We had to go and shoot a man there called Baden-Powell.

We rode steadily on into the west. After a while we noticed that our veldkornet frequently got off his horse and engaged in conversation with passing kaffirs, leading them some distance from the roadside and speaking earnestly to them. Of course, it was right that our veldkornet should explain to the kaffirs that it was war-time, now, and that the Republic expected every kaffir to stop smoking so much dagga and to think seriously about what was going on. But we noticed that each time at the end of the conversation the kaffir would point towards something, and that our veldkornet would take much pains to follow the direction of the kaffir's finger.

Of course, we understood, then, what it was all about. Our veldkornet was a young fellow, and he was shy to let us see that he didn't know the way to Mafeking.

Somehow, after that, we did not have so much confidence in our veldkornet.

After a few days we got to Mafeking. We stayed there a long while, until the English troops came up and relieved the place. We left, then. We left quickly. The English troops had brought a lot of artillery with them. And if we had difficulty in finding the road to Mafeking, we had no difficulty in finding the road away from Mafeking. And this time our veldkornet did not need kaffirs, either, to point with their fingers where we had to go. Even though we did a lot of travelling in the night.

Long afterwards I spoke to an Englishman about this. He said it gave him a queer feeling to hear about the other side of the story of Mafeking. He said there had been very great rejoicings in England when Mafeking was relieved, and it was strange to think of the other aspect of it – of a defeated country and of broken columns blundering through the dark.

I remember many things that happened on the way back from Mafeking. There was no moon. And the stars shone down fitfully on the road that was full of guns and frightened horses and desperate men. The veld throbbed with the hoof-beats of baffled commandos. The stars looked down on scenes that told sombrely of a nation's ruin; they looked on the muzzles of the Mausers that had failed the Transvaal for the first time.

Of course, as a burgher of the Republic, I knew what my duty was. And that was to get as far away as I could from the place where, in the sunset, I had last seen English artillery. The other burghers knew their duty also. Our kommandants and veldkornets had to give very few orders. Nevertheless, though I rode very fast, there was one young man who rode still faster. He kept ahead of me all the time. He rode, as a burgher should ride when there may be stray bullets flying, with his head well down and with his arms almost round the horse's neck.

He was Stephanus, the young son of Floris van Barnevelt.

There was much grumbling and dissatisfaction, some time afterwards, when our leaders started making an effort to get the commandos in order again. In the end they managed to get us to halt. But most of us felt that this was a foolish thing to do. Especially as there was still a lot of firing going on, all over the place, in haphazard fashion, and we couldn't tell how far the English had followed us in the dark. Furthermore, the commandos had scattered in so many different directions that it seemed hopeless to try and get them together again until after the war. Stephanus and I dismounted and stood by our horses. Soon there was a large body of men around us. Their figures looked strange and shadowy in the starlight. Some of them stood by their horses. Others sat on the grass by the roadside. "Vas staan, burghers, vas staan," came the commands of our officers. And all the time we could still hear what sounded a lot like lyddite. It seemed foolish to be waiting there.

"The next they'll want," Stephanus van Barnevelt said, "is for us to go back to Mafeking. Perhaps our kommandant has left his tobacco pouch behind, there."

Some of us laughed at this remark, but Floris, who had not dismounted, said that Stephanus ought to be ashamed of himself for talking like that. From what we could see of Floris in the gloom, he looked quite impressive, sitting very straight in the saddle, with the stars shining on his beard and rifle.

"If the veldkornet told me to go back to Mafeking," Floris said, "I would go back."

"That's how a burgher should talk," the veldkornet said, feeling flattered. For he had had little authority since the time we found out what he was talking to the kaffirs for.

"I wouldn't go back to Mafeking for anybody," Stephanus replied, "unless, maybe, it's to hand myself over to the English."

"We can shoot you for doing that," the veldkornet said. "It's contrary to military law."

"I wish I knew something about military law," Stephanus answered. "Then I would draw up a peace treaty between Stephanus van Barnevelt and England."

Some of the men laughed again. But Floris shook his head sadly. He said the Van Barnevelts had fought bravely against Spain in a war that lasted eighty years.

Suddenly, out of the darkness there came a sharp rattle of musketry, and our men started getting uneasy again. But the sound of the firing decided Stephanus. He jumped on his horse quickly.

"I am turning back," he said, "I am going to hands-up to the English."

"No, don't go," the veldkornet called to him lamely, "or at least, wait until the morning. They may shoot you in the dark by mistake." As I have said, the veldkornet had very little authority.

Two days passed before we again saw Floris van Barnevelt. He was in a very worn and troubled state, and he said that it had been very hard for him to find his way back to us.

"You should have asked the kaffirs," one of our number said with a laugh. "All the kaffirs know our veldkornet."

But Floris did not speak about what happened that night, when we saw him riding out under the starlight, following after his son and shouting to him to be a man and to fight for his country. Also, Floris did not mention Stephanus again, his son who was not worthy to be a Van Barnevelt.

After that we got separated. Our veldkornet was the first to be taken prisoner. And I often felt that he must feel very lonely on St. Helena. Because there were no kaffirs from whom he could ask the way out of the barbed-wire camp.

Then, at last our leaders came together at Vereeniging, and peace was made. And we returned to our farms, relieved that the war was over, but with heavy hearts at the thought that it had all been for nothing and that over the Transvaal the Vierkleur would not wave again.

And Floris van Barnevelt put back in its place, on the wall of the voorkamer, the copy of his family tree that had been carried with him in his knapsack throughout the war. Then a new schoolmaster came to this part of the Marico, and after a long talk with Floris, the schoolmaster wrote behind Stephanus's name, between two curved lines, the two words that you can still read there: "Obiit Mafeking."

Consequently, if you ask any person hereabouts what "obiit" means, he is able to tell you, right away, that it is a foreign word, and that it means to ride up to the English, holding your Mauser in the air, with a white flag tied to it, near the muzzle.

But it was long afterwards that Floris van Barnevelt started telling his story.

And then they took no notice of him. And they wouldn't allow him to be nominated for the Drogevlei School Committee on the grounds that a man must be wrong in the head to talk in such an irresponsible fashion.

But I knew that Floris had a good story, and that its only fault was that he told it badly. He mentioned the Drogevlei School Committee too soon. And he knocked the ash out of his pipe in the wrong place. And he always insisted on telling that part of the story that he should have left out.

Source:
Herman Charles Bosman: *Mafeking Road and Other Stories: The Anniversary Edition*, Craig MacKenzie (ed). Cape Town: Human & Rousseau: 1998, written c. 1947.

The Boers of Sundays River

A Boer War story which must finally be told

Pieter Wagener

As we approached Addo my mother started swallowing KPP headache powders. Kirkwood was still half an hour's drive away and by that time her expected headache would be dulled. She had an aversion to oranges and eggs because her entire life alternated between these two products. When not farming with Leghorn chickens, we spent our holidays with my father's relatives in the Sundays River Citrus Valley. I shared her aversion. Every Friday a large number of chickens' heads and feet were chopped off and cooked in a pot to make soup for the farm workers. Two hundred miles further my father's brothers farmed with oranges.

As we stopped among the orange trees on the family farm, my cousins came running out screaming, clutching their boxing gloves. By the time my aunts and uncles had loudly greeted us, my younger brother would have knocked out at least one cousin.

We entered the living room where I sat nervously on a couch and listened to my aunts enthusiastically discussing the regularity of their bowels. Aunt Dollie came in with coffee and thick slices of milktart while I glanced around furtively for the *Huisgenoot* which I had forgotten there the previous year. I had little hope of finding it, for the newly found health of the house's inhabitants would have sealed the fate of that magazine. Uncle Fonnie was busy describing the events on the third day of his prostate operation when he caught sight of me. "Hey, why don't you go and play outside with your cousins?" I wanted to explain to him that I feared for my life when Uncle Karel exclaimed that evidently the boy did nothing else but read books. The only book in the house, *Een Eeuw van Onrecht*

(An Age of Injustice), I had read when I was five. The author of the book had presumably sent it to Grandfather out of gratitude because his commando could hide on his farm from the English forces. Grandfather, however, told everyone that the prickly pears had given the Boers more trouble than the English.

Aunt Dollie put a large, quivering piece of milktart in front of me. I kept chewing on it until it sounded as if my brother had tamed most of the cousins in the yard. I went out through the back door but had forgotten that the screen door was stuck and I cut my fingers yet again on the fine, rusted wire. Next time I would crawl through the space which the Boer mastiffs had torn out of the lower half of the screen years ago.

My brother and I usually slept in an outside rondavel. It was fifty yards from the kitchen but I could creep behind a water tank without my cousins spotting me. By now they would have no fight left in them and were probably trying to persuade my brother to accompany them on a night-time raid with knobkieries on the mission station across the hill.

It was cool in the rondavel and I wanted to lie down and rest. With my bare feet dirty with sand I couldn't do that. A small chest stood between the two beds. Sometimes my aunt, who also ran the farm shop, left each of us a tin of condensed milk on the chest. The previous year my cousins had filled my brother's with urine and left it there, holes and all. He tried to drink it during the night and lay muttering for a long time before falling asleep. Inside the chest there used to be a Dutch Bible but that had disappeared a long time ago.

I heard the screen door at the kitchen scraping on the cement and knew my mother was on her way to the rondavel. She quietly entered the room and sat down on the other bed. Rina would be back later, she said. Rina was one of the cousins but of a different nature to the rest. She was at boarding school in Port Elizabeth and during the holidays worked in the orange packing shed in the village. Although she was ten years my senior, we were great friends.

"Tomorrow is Saturday and we can visit Aunt Gertie," my mother said. She meant that Rina would take us there.

Aunt Gertruida lived alone on a neighbouring farm. Her English-speaking husband had died within a year of their marriage and since then, for almost forty years, she farmed with the assistance of several foremen.

To walk to her, one had to take a short cut through the bush and only Rina could do that without being hemmed in by the prickly pears. No other family member ever ventured there.

It started getting dark and my mother suggested that it would be better if we waited for supper inside the house.

Inside the house it was noisy. My mother asked the aunts if she could assist in the kitchen but as usual they instructed her to sit down in a chair and keep them company. She couldn't do that and sat with pursed lips listening to the loud chatter of the women. The slightest incident was incessantly repeated with loud exclamations and most of the comments referred to a part of the anatomy of certain ladies who believed that the sun was always shining from it.

In the living room there was even more noise. The uncles had got hold of a can of *withond,* a potent brew, which other relatives had sent from Calitzdorp. Under the influence of this liquor the family trait of teasing always came to the fore. My father, especially, was the butt of much jeering, as he got married at an advanced age to a woman much younger than himself. There were references to my blonde hair and my slender body and they choked with laughter as they speculated about my origin. My father then shouted back – fuck you, and after all, whom do you think my other son resembles?

With all the carousing one could never determine when the dinner commenced. The men barged in and out of the kitchen with thick slices of bread spread with greaves. My brother and the cousins sat on the stoep, hitting out at bats with grass brooms. My mother sat stiffly upright next to the kitchen cupboard, fortified with another dose of KPP in her body. I went to stand next to her after I had trodden on a piece of glowing charcoal at the stove. The men stormed back into the kitchen and loudly announced that the following evening we would have kudu and bushpig for the evening meal. Aunt Dollie called out – you drunken bastards will kill each other and the hunting season is closed and I'm not going to skin another bloody buck again. Everyone, with the exception of my mother and I, roared with laughter.

There was another family trait.

Neither the uncles nor the cousins could bear to see any animal walking around alive on the farm, except cattle and even their days were numbered. If the Boer mastiffs' barking indicated that they had trapped a buck against a wire fence, every single man, day or night, would grab a gun and rush towards the barking. This bloodthirstiness was well known to the blacks at the mission station and when there were family gatherings, they always avoided the farm shop. There were dark rumours among the blacks and with my meagre Xhosa I could infer that I was the child of a feared *umlungu*.

My father's pride was a Lee-Metford rifle, which as he told us, had been taken by the Boers from the English and then given to him as a gift. He had received it as an award for guiding the Boers through the thickly overgrown ravines. By the age of ten he was already a crack shot.

The men did go off on the hunting trip early the following morning. There was no sign of hangover and the group sang hymns as they went up the hills. My brother and the cousins went to catch eels and I sat on the stoep and waited for Rina. She arrived at tea time. It was already too hot to walk to Aunt Gertie's and she and my mother decided that we would leave later that afternoon. I looked forward to it. Aunt Gertie always treated me to fruit sweets, pancakes and prickly pear syrup. In her living room there was also a big shelf filled with English and Dutch books. Some of the English books had belonged to her husband but the rest belonged to the foreman. The foreman was a nephew from Matjiesrivier in the Swartberg and he had worked for her for twenty years. He had lost his wife during the influenza epidemic. In the cool living room I spent my time among the books. When the foreman was there he would choose books that I would be able to understand. Sometimes he merely told me what the story was about and then I, inquisitive, would begin reading avidly. He patiently explained the meaning of new words. When I got tired, he would place a small coir mattress on the floor and I would slowly fall asleep to the ticking of the wall clock.

After afternoon coffee, Rina called us to start our walk. Barefoot I ran on ahead along the kudu paths, between noorsdoring[1], spekboom[2] and prickly pear hedges. My mother constantly admonished me to be careful of yellow cobras. Where the paths forked, I waited for Rina to show which direction to take. The path led down a hill to the Sundays River, which we had to cross barefoot, stepping on river stones. Aunt Gertie's claybrick house was a short distance from there.

She embraced Rina and my mother, kissed me and invited us inside. She went to make coffee and brought me some of her fruit sweets. Aunt Gertie was completely grey but fit from working on her own for many years. While she was busy in the kitchen, she asked my mother when I was starting school and if I couldn't stay with her until then. She could still look after me very well but my mother smilingly declined. Her husband would never allow it. Aunt Gertie would become sombre and I felt sad because she couldn't have any children of her own.

While Rina and I paged through the books, the two women sat talking on the stoep. Later the foreman came from the stables, picked me up and playfully complained because I came to visit them so seldom. After he had also teased Rina, he went to sit with the women on the stoep. As dusk fell, their voices drifted further and further away. They spoke in the singing *bry,* the rolling 'r' sound of the Swartberg. They spoke about my mother's youth in the Gamka, the large families who lived there and the large number of children who belonged to the *Strewersvereniging,* a debating society. They were sad about the empty farmhouses which had fallen into disrepair, that only a few farmers were still making pressed figs and that saltbush ash was no longer strewn over raisins. Like mother, son and daughter they sat until Rina came quietly to tell them that we had to leave before it became pitch dark.

My father died shortly afterwards. From the proceeds of the sale of the farm, my mother moved us to Oudtshoorn where later, in her old age, she went to live with a brother. We never returned to my father's family farm. I went to live abroad and all appeals to my mother to come and live with me and my family were declined. My sister-in-law initially kept me informed of their family by means of newspaper cuttings of their sons' boxing achievements. I lost all contact with the rest of the family. Later I wouldn't even know where my brother was living.

When my mother died, I flew to South Africa for the funeral. I stayed for a while to look up old student friends and on the way to one of them, I had to consult a doctor in Somerset-East. The receptionist made some remark about my unusual surname and mentioned that a group of men with the same name were hunting bushpigs on a farm in the district. What was peculiar, she said, was that they were catching the bushpigs with their bare hands. I assured her that those were my relatives and phoned the farmer.

They were my cousins, older but tougher. Rina had been looking for me for years and they insisted that I phone her in Port Elizabeth. I did, whereupon she asked me to come and see her. There were only a few days left before my journey back and I could barely spare the time. However, Rina said that it had to do with a dying wish of Aunt Gertie's. I turned back and drove to her. A day later we arrived in Kirkwood.

The family farm now belonged to strangers but we could leave the car at the restored farm shop. Rina still knew the kudu paths and in the late afternoon we walked down the hill to the river. The noorsdoring and the spekboom were still luxuriant but the prickly pear had been largely decimated by cochineal. We spoke about the things of our youth and about the aunts and uncles who appeared so immortal then. There was a low bridge across the river and we crossed it in silence. Aunt Gertie's house was in ruins. We stood on the stone-flagged stoep and looked around sadly. Along the hill it was getting dark and we would have to walk back in the dusk.

"Aunt Gertie asked me one day to give you something. You were overseas by then and I couldn't trace you. She made me promise that I would give it to you one day."

I looked at the handbag she was holding in front of her.

"Grandfather always told us how the Boer commando had hidden on the farm because they were ill. Well, after they had recovered, two of their scouts crossed the river down here and walked into an English ambush. One of them was caught and executed because he was wearing a Khaki uniform.

"Grandfather wondered how the English could have known of the scouts' plans. He guessed that Aunt Gertie's husband was the only one who could have betrayed the Boers.

"He discussed this suspicion with his sons. The sons had heard of court martials from the general and they decided that the suspected traitor had to be court-martialled."

"Just like that? On their own?"

"Yes. Even Grandfather didn't know about it."

We walked down to the river bank in the direction of a fenced graveyard.

"He was shot near this spot."

"Who did it?" I asked with trepidation.

"One of the boys had been given a rifle by the Boers. They joked and said that he was now also a Boer soldier. So he believed that he had received the right to execute the death sentence his brothers had imposed on the alleged traitor."

I stared at the graves and felt dizziness overcome me. Aunt Gertie lay buried next to her husband. The graves were covered with river stones and here and there thorntrees had pushed through the cement and stones. Below us the river rushed and from the purling I heard the voices of old people and children. I tried to listen to what they were saying but their voices faded and all I could hear were rifle shots, fired over and over again.

Rina held my arm tightly. "Look at this," she said and handed me a book. It was *Een Eeuw van Onrecht*. "She insisted that I give it to you after your mother's death."

With the book in my hands, I sat down and cried uncontrollably. "Read inside," she said softly.

On the inside page were the signatures of the general and my grandfather. At the bottom of the page was a message to me, written in someone else's hand. I read it and until darkness fell I sat and stared at the grave of the foreman.

NOTES

1. *Euphorbia* species
2. *Portulacaria afra*

Source:
Pieter Wagener: *Boereboeddhiste*. Cape Town: Human & Rousseau: 1997.

Homecoming

Peter Wilhelm

December 1902, late afternoon. He rested under an oaktree, towering, twisted. The bole was abnormal, sprouting an immense growth which sagged from one side like a giant's fist pendulous to the ground. He studied the excrescence, and then he touched it, and then he wedged his canvas traveller's bag against its side; and he made the bag a pillow, lay on his back and looked around.

Quite alone he had walked all day. Sensuously he spread himself in coolness under the tree, his body, like his clothes, shabby, dusty, lived-in. He yawned, but revived in a reflex, spilling up into focus: it was almost night and he had a destination.

He took out his pipe. He tapped tobacco into the bowl. He smoked with enjoyment. The smoke coiled into blue sky and breeze-stirred dark leaves.

He was here, in a place he knew.

His own image came to him: long hair black, beard-stubble grainy. Not even twenty, he was a fighting-man off duty, quiescent senses ready for alert.

Pieter van Vlaams had come home from the war in the North. Peace had come at the end of May, but he had taken his time returning, working here and there, seeing the way the world was put together.

Badly, true: but now he was almost relaxed.

There was a quietness here, down between the mountains and the sea. Wild spring flowers sprouted, fiery coloured life prodigal in an outburst with spawning insects shrill in the dry grass: a vivid surface. Decay was underneath, exhaustion feverish in the people and the veld. Pieter felt it bone-deep, beyond optimism or renewal: the unco-ordinated stresses of peace.

The War: the shadow of a remembered childhood serenity. In another century, with Byron.

Spotting the land were the blockhouses and watchtowers, abandoned, dark and sinister in the bright sunlight. The totems of the conqueror. They would be pulled down one day; now they commanded the landscape. Pieter looked at them and went cold: they prefigured a century of misery, and devastation.

That was how he felt.

He had been wounded once and had to carry his left arm in a makeshift sling, tormented for three months. There was no doctor with them and they were driven restlessly like wild dogs; so his arm healed unnaturally. Now he carried an ugly tuft of scar under his shoulder and his hand would never close again. It made a claw around numbness. At first he exercised alone in the bush, giving little calls of savage pain, involuntary, to the mossies in the thorn-tree thickets. And then he gave up. He would take a claw home. One part dead before the rest.

So much defeat. Unending.

He wanted to farm now, as he had before the War with his father and mother and sister.

Helene, his sister.

And he wanted to marry. To burn in marriage. This simple image of a wife, a cook with children, he had held clear in his mind on every foray or patrol or (futile) escape. Near the end, when they had all spoken of what they would do when peace came, he knew that his simple wishes would be enough for life. Some said: now the true war began in councils, in politics, in rebellion. He had seen the burnt fields and the concentration camps: he wanted to go home.

Under the oak he sighed. He tapped the bowl of his pipe against his boot. He stood up and ran his hands down the front of his jacket, brushing ash away; and reached down to shoulder his bag and step regretfully out of shadow.

This place was familiar to him as a child. Grotesque, the tree had been a marker to his father's farm, up ahead. It told him the same now.

An infinitely distant, small sound made him look back the way he had come. He saw a dustpatch, and then a cart drawn by a mule. He waited, still, unblinking. The road ran crookedly over foothills. The mountains swept close to the sea here, half the sky blocked in shadowed purple and green: the road yellow-green, a thin streak at their base. Pieter, facing the oncoming dust, could see leftwards across dunes and scrub to the frothy sea, almost black now under a deep red sun in vast trails of cirrus. The beginnings of a strong wind stirred in the late afternoon.

He could smell the sea: salt in heather: home.

The landscape netted him into an enormous fabric of sensation and image. At the focus of the vision the little cart struggled up the hill. Towards him.

He waited.

Creaking, the cart came alongside. A starving mule sweated in a dust-streaked coat: eyes strained yellow, bulging in a gaunt skull. Only in war had Pieter seen animals equivalently overtaxed, so horrible and inflexible.

Then other eyes touched him, brown, filmed, contemptuous. A drunk Coloured man lay in the back of the cart, thrown this way and that by the movement, grey wiry hair exploding in unruly corkscrews from a powerful lolling head.

The drunkard did not seem to see Pieter and the cart went on slowly. The rise was steepening. Pieter sighed and walked behind, keeping pace easily.

At the top of the rise there was a level stretch of a few hundred yards. Here Pieter spoke first, with his right hand on the wooden cart's side. His voice was unused.

"Hello Adam."

The cart stopped abruptly. The drunk man tried to sit upright, slumped back holding the reins loosely, then turned to look at Pieter, mouth open on yellow-brown ruin.

Suspicion: stewed in wine.

Adam September was old. But he looked older, like a bone shaped by wind. Savage lines grooved his nut-dark face and his flaring hair gave him the cast of insanity. He brought up a bottle of cheap, urinous sherry and drank heavily and messily, spilling it. Pieter remembered he had once had more control.

"Who are you? What do you want?" Adam's voice was acerbic, cruel: it bit through wine-haze.

Pieter said softly: "You remember me, Adam. I came to see you many times before the War. On Sundays, remember, before the War." He gave his name. "My father has the farm in the valley ahead." Pieter gestured with his crooked left hand.

Adam scowled like an ape which has eaten sour fruit. "And I have a cave in the mountain ahead," he jeered. It was true: Adam September lived in a cave. Some said he was a mystic, and could see the future. Of course he only saw it when drunk.

They spoke for a moment. Adam in coarse-grained Dutch: Pieter in fine-grained Dutch.

And then the cart went on. Pieter saw no command from Adam September to the mule. Instinctively, perhaps, it knew what to do; how to do it. Its thin grey legs nudged dust into the cool afternoon.

Without rancour Pieter said, "Don't be unfriendly." He smiled. He walked on with the cart.

"It's my way," said Adam September. He added, head bobbing: "Who did you say you were? You don't look like Pieter van Vlaams to me. Where have you been?"

"In the North. Fighting."

Adam September spat. Wind-swivelled, his gob caught red sunlight. "I remember now. You went away. With all the other fools."

"Old man, why do you call us fools?"

Adam September sputtered over his words. Pieter strained for his meaning.

"Because that is what you are. Because you lost. Fools have no power, and so they always lose." Fighting gravity Adam September sat upright in his cart. He pointed a thin green-veined hand down the road, back where he had come, to where a dark watchtower jutted skyward. He said: "There is power. I saw them come and put it up in a day. In this way they were able to see the whole country. If a hawk moved they could see it."

"But we fought them for many years."

"That's so . . ."

Adam September added: "Your father is dead. And your mother. Did you know that?"

Pieter said nothing. The old man was lying. Surely.

"You don't believe me," said Adam September. "But it's true. Both of them. At the beginning of this year. There was a fire and they both died in bed."

They had reached the end of the level stretch; now the road went uphill again and Adam September stopped the cart. "Get in," he said, "you can't go on walking like that. Do you have any tobacco?" He made the motions of putting a cigarette to his lips and sucking.

"No."

The outrageous news had reached Pieter. "Dead? Both of them?" How could they be dead?

"I told you," said Adam September. "There was a fire . . . Now get up here on the cart. Do you have any tobacco?" He moved his hand and made sucking noises. Pieter, numb, climbed in beside Adam September. One question moved him.

"And my sister, Helene? What about her?"

"Mad."

Pieter articulated slowly: "What do you mean, mad?"

"They found her howling like a dog in the ash, in her nightgown.

She ran from the fire, and then came back; but there was nothing she could do."

"The farm," said Pieter. "What about the farm? Who's looking after the farm?" As he spoke the words the question gained a malign poignancy. Earlier he had felt a shadow; now it spread.

"Only kaffirs like me, little *baas*. You can kick us out – then you can have it to yourself." Adam September snorted in mirth. "The whole place is a mess; if you work for a year you might get some order again, but I don't think so. The birds and the baboons have eaten everything."

Remembering his parents, Pieter said, "Were they buried properly?"

"*Ja*, they were buried properly. The dominee came from the town and fixed that up. We made a very nice grave for them and put them into it together as they would have wanted. But the whole house was gone, and so when the dominee took your sister away all she had was a nightgown. She stood all night watching the house burn down, howling. But I only saw her the next day when we had the burial, and I think she was finished howling then. She just looked around. The dominee put a coat around her and put her up on a cart, and they went off. That was the last I saw of her. I think she's with a good family in the Ceres district."

Pieter nodded dumbly. While Adam September had been speaking a feeling of profound unreality had crept into him. The late afternoon seemed extraordinarily cold – he felt it through clothing and flesh, tight on his bones – and while the sounds and colours and smells were true to memory he felt excluded from them now, a polar distance from his earlier feeling; and he felt his identity swim at the edges. The War had taught him that when men were caught in a machine they became machine-like, implacable, unhuman. But there was a kind of logic in that: the history of his people, told to him by his father, was steeped in blood and movement, machine states. He had understood what he was in. These unheralded deaths and displacements were like lightning from a clear sky. They had no logic; they intimated a senseless universe.

A formless anger made him clench his fist, and at that precise moment the mule collapsed and the cart snapped backwards, half throwing them out. Adam September's wine spilled noisily into the dust and the black gave a great shout of rage when he saw it happening. The two men struggled for equilibrium as the cart inched downhill dragging the harnessed, whinnying mule. Then with unprecedented speed and precision Adam September leapt free and wrenched the brake into position: all movement stopped and Pieter suddenly heard the loud pants of the wretched mule. The beast had its grey muzzle in the dust and little craters had formed under its nostrils. Each breath sent red dust spraying.

Adam September cursed heavily and brought up a whip, a vicious length of thong through which wire had been threaded. He proceeded angrily to lash the mule, which made no sound except to wheeze as it panted. Pieter stepped to the ground to watch, as senselessly enraged as Adam September at the accident. He gave a small inarticulate cry and kicked the beast, kicked it again as from his unconscious came spilling an image of the animal which had carried Jesus into Jerusalem; he kicked at the image of innocence.

Then shame and pity drove him back. He felt the beast's pain and said: "Leave it alone, Adam: it's no use . . . The thing won't move."

"Yes, yes, yes," said Adam September – but to himself, scarcely attending to Pieter. He continued to beat the mule, regular as a machine: *whop whop whop whop whop whop whop,* an infernal rain of punishment.

Fascinated and guilty, stirred by the brutality, Pieter watched the beating. The mule's shanks seemed to be collapsing into themselves: the thing was a bag of dirt and pain.

It was dying. When Pieter realised this he reached out a hand to touch Adam September. Adam swivelled angrily, deflected from violence. He seemed about to say something when both heard a weird sound from the beast, a high shrilling which might have been pleasure.

The animal died in harness, sinking down in chilling relaxation. It began to cough harshly and they saw a black stream erupt from its backside. The stench of its death filled the air, and at that moment the sun finally began to set. The quality of darkness in the air deepened: shadows lost definition.

Adam September sighed heavily; the whip dropped between his knees and he stared angrily at the dead mule. He began to mutter: "You bastard, you bastard, you bastard." His grating voice had rhythms in it like the beating.

"You've killed it," said Pieter. He felt afraid at the sight.

"No," said Adam September, quietly. "It died earlier this morning. It's been walking around dead all day."

This made Pieter want to walk on very quickly, but almost without knowing it he knelt and stared into the beast's dead eyes. They told him nothing.

The stillness of the two men sent eddies of tension into the air. But at last Adam September took up his bottle of sherry, clamped a filthy hat on his head and slung a shapeless sack over his shoulder. Without looking back he tramped up the rise leaving the cart and the dead mule. After a short hesitation, Pieter joined him. But he did not walk alongside; he kept half a pace behind Adam September.

Saying nothing they went on like that for ten minutes. Pieter found himself rehearsing phrases to put to the old man, but they stayed unresolved in words.

Finally he did say: "What about the cart?"

Adam September scoffed obscenely; he did not look back.

"Adam, wait . . . you're going too quickly. I don't remember the way." Pieter felt profoundly unhappy. He wanted companionship as he had known it in the North – men around a fire, soft voices, laughter, coffee. The darkness gave him a feeling of being in a strange country without recognisable landmarks. The distant beating of the sea was ominous. What he wanted to say to Adam September was: Help me. But he said: "I don't remember the way."

Adam September, the drunk seer, paused briefly and Pieter drew level with him. But then he shook his head. "There's only one road; you know the way."

"Won't you come with me? To the farm?"

"What for? It's got nothing to do with me." Adam September finished his bottle and heaved it into the air; it fell and smashed on rocks. Then he walked on. Pieter trailed by a few paces, a few yards, an indeterminate distance. And then Adam was gone in darkness and he was left to walk on alone, dazed, hopelessly lost in uncontrollable thoughts and memories.

He stopped once and looked around: above, a great sweep of blazing stars: below, moving shadows, trees in the wind, whining insects. He felt pressed between two planes.

At the entrance to his father's farm a nameplate banged irregularly; a wooden arch leaned. Pieter walked along a familiar narrow path until he found the ruined house, grey in starlight. A few walls still stood and he made his way over rubble and ash in their desolate framework. He found the scorched remains of an iron bed and a blackened fireplace which stood densely intact.

He slept near the fireplace dreaming interminable remorseless things. That the dead mule was coming through darkness, searching him out.

Source:
Peter Wilhelm: *LM and Other Stories*. Johannesburg: Ravan Press: 1975.

Three Pairs of Yellow Eyes

Christoffel Coetzee

In an attempt to get away from the destruction of war, the black man Jan Witsie and his followers accompanied by the white woman Soph and her family have fled into the Eastern Free State mountains. The commando of General Mannetjies operates in the mountains, taking cruel revenge on English soldiers and forcing unwilling Boers to continue the war.

In this extract from Coetzee's novel Op soek na generaal Mannetjies Mentz (In Search of General Mannetjies Mentz) *Jan Witsie tells of an awesome dog and two foxes that roam through the mountains and gorge themselves on the abundance of human flesh. These animals are symbolic of Mentz and his two closest compatriots, Voss and Niemann, who have abandoned all human feelings in their obsession with revenge.*

On several occasions the Basotho come across a red jackal and two dogs at these scenes of horror. Usually the three pad off, leering back over their shoulders. Occasionally the smaller dog stops in its tracks to make a quick grab at an anklebone. Often they do not even bother to retire to safety, out of the range of the riflemen under disciplinary orders. From within range of the rifles they observe the incineration of human remains, the smaller dog calmly gnawing on the bone held between its front paws and despite being used for target-shooting by the British soldiers.

This association between a jackal and two dogs is in itself enough to make your scalp crawl – a dog and a jackal never hunt together. Even when a jackal cub and a pup suckle on the same bitch and grow up together in the same yard, the end result is always bloody strife.

And, so says Jan Witsie, because he knows the nature of the lion and of the lamb, for the sake of the lamb he would keep it away from the lion, until he himself has seen them lying down together in peace.

Dogs and a jackal together are a new, concocted kind of creature, says Jan Witsie. It is an abomination, the opposite of the lion and lamb lying down together. "A lion is a lion," says Jan Witsie. "That is why people talk about being 'as brave as a lion'." Thinking back on his hunting days, he remembers the lion favouring the oryx with its lethal horns above the submissive klipspringer, and "go ask your Father if you like, Sophie." And a lamb is a lamb. "That is why we say: 'meek as a lamb'," says Jan Witsie.

He knows a dog as something that nips your ankle when you least expect it. And a horned ewe makes a jackal keep his distance, tail between the legs, the coward – "you know this Soph, don't you, because didn't you grow up among sheep?" says Jan Witsie.

Jan does not tell Sophie the story all in one go, from *in the beginning* up to *and that is how it ends;* he tells it to Sophie during the course of many days. Piece by piece, but repeating large parts for Sophie to mull over. And Jan himself is at his wit's end; he does not know where the story will end.

"Sophie," says Jan Witsie distraughtly, "don't we have enough proof of what is happening right here amongst our people? What are we going to do?"

Jan Witsie wants to recruit Soph to act against the strange beast, even though he himself has no clear idea about how to do it. But time is running out, and he needs an ally against Ma.

At that moment Aunt Soph really wants to say she is actually still small and that "Jan musn't ask me what is what", but she just shivers and pictures in her mind's eye those other beasts of which we do not know the names, the *crawling things and detestable animals* that Ezechiel referred to as the *idols*. Perhaps in this way she is trying to exorcise the devils' spawn peering out over the Poorte by summoning up their ghastly brethren; there is always God's Vow, promising that they will finally be ground in the dust by the lamb and the lion. Aunt Soph starts thinking about the trio roaming from Poort to Poort as being the "idols"; that is the closest she gets to naming them.

Apart from describing the composition of the threesome, Jan Witsie tells her, piece by piece and over a period of time, about their appearance, forbidding and repulsive.

The jackal is a splendid creature with a glossy pelt of long hair, but it cowers away (as is its wont) behind its less fortunate companions. The back of one of the dogs is without hair, the result of unsightly scars that sometimes break out into suppurating sores; apart from that, a dog of average size, devoid of any distinguishing features. A real farmyard cur, and as is often with such curs, one you can easily underestimate. Some of the British soldiers under staff orders take pot shots at the brute to put it out of its misery. The dog appears to be the leader of the pack; when he has had enough of something, the jackal and its mate meekly follow him into the hills. The second dog is a gigantic male, the size of a young calf, with a prominent sac and pizzle that become the butt of jokes amongst some of the Basotho. More often, though, they self-consciously turn away uneasily, embarrassed by the tired jokes and sheer size of these genitals, larger even than those of a merino ram. The most striking feature of this creature is its maimed snout. It must have been in a vicious scrap once, although it is difficult to guess what other animal could have done such damage to the snout of a mighty creature like this. Whatever tackled him must have been a fearsome monster. The upper lip has been almost completely ripped away from one side of the snout, right up to the eye, which is swollen half-shut due to an old injury. The brute keeps cocking its massive head to one side to see what is going on. The rent in its lip reveals a huge, yellowed fang.

When the Lee-Metford bullets are whistling around the threesome, striking sparks from the ironstone, the jackal trots out of range. The dog with the injured back doesn't bother to run away or even look up; he keeps staring fixedly at the scene where the Basotho are burning the remains of the prisoners of war and their escorts, keeping to one side and chewing on his human bone. His companion loses all control and runs wild. He circles the other dog, around and around, as if to deflect the sniping bullets by elevating himself to be the target. He growls and flecks of white foam fly from his skew mouth. He manages somehow to bare his other yellow fang as well. It is clear that his injuries hamper his barking, but still the cliffs echo with a spine-chilling yowl – it sounds as if he is painfully hawking up splintered chicken bones.

All this is frightening enough, says Jan Witsie, but what about this: there are seasoned old veterans among the soldiers under punitive orders acting as escorts to the body burners. They come from wars in the Sudan and India, two or three have even seen action in the Second Afghan War of 1878. They have already seen everything, which is why the punitive orders are like a holiday to them. They are feared snipers. Once they have fixed a target in their sights they never miss. But the idol is out to try them and to test their skills, acquired over many years, to breaking point. This why the idol, excepting the jackal perhaps, rarely moves away when the soldiers draw a bead on them. Still the veterans keep missing, despite these tempting, easy targets.

And how about this, says Jan Witsie: when two teams return from different Necks, reeking of smoke, rotten human flesh and ichor, they both swear that the idol has been at two, three other Poorts. They carefully describe the events of the day in this and that Neck to each other, and in each team's report the two dogs and the jackal appear in the finest detail.

And how to explain this, says Jan Witsie on another day, after having spoken to Basotho from the Kom: groups of prisoners and their escorts who succeed in evading Commandant Mentz's commando and cross the mountains, see the idol outlined against the moon, no matter in which Neck they are. From every vantage point you see the idol silently watching the convoy's progress, until the escorts hand over the prisoners to the Tommies on the far side of the mountains, who have to see that they get to the railheads from where they are carried off to the prisoner-of-war camps.

The occasional traveller, desperate or foolhardy enough to cross a Neck alone on a short cut to Basotholand, tells the same story: of being watched all the time by two dogs and a jackal – usually in deathly silence, except on occasion when the giant hound howls through its maimed snout to urge you along and put the road behind you.

The dying in the Poorte is becoming a health risk. Rats the size of cats, covered in sores, have started appearing. The teams work day and night to burn the remains and to prevent an outbreak of plague by means of lime. The corpses are slow to burn, even when soaked in paraffin – frequently the fires go out, hissing in the slime into which the bodies decompose. Only when the teams have managed to let the fire burn down to a bed of coals, and the heart is the last to let go, exploding when red-hot with a report like that of a cartridge, do they know that the rest will also burn away to a coarse, grey gravel of hard bone, shards of wagon ironwork, harness fittings and buttons. It is as viscous as tar, a fatty mass rather than ash. With pick and shovel the teams dig deep trenches in the stony soil, into which they rake the ashes before covering it with a thick layer of lime. Jan says he can predict that for years afterwards, horses will become curiously restless when approaching those places. And, Jan asks, who knows a horse better than a Witsie?

On moonless nights you see three pairs of yellow eyes following you – and as summer approaches and lightning starts lighting up the mountains at night for a fleeting instant, more frequently you can place the pairs of yellow eyes on either side of a jackal's snout and two dog snouts. In the glare of veldt fires in spring you constantly sense their eyes against your back.

At first light, when a day detail relieves the night shift on its incineration excursions, the two dogs and the jackal often lope along some distance behind the wagon, noses so close to the ground that their long tongues, drooling saliva, are almost dragging in the dust. Never is a shift allowed to forget that it is saturated with the miasma with which it occupied itself, all day or night long.

However, the animals never venture too far away from the mountains. The night shift is so exhausted that they do not even notice the dog with the suppurating back lifting its leg against a wheel and disdainfully pissing a heavy, yellow stream against the nave. The cloying stench of sulphur that now suffocates them is the first indication they have of the dog. For the rest of the way back their half-sleep is disturbed, but by now the dog has already dropped back into the road behind them.

Wherever the mule wagon goes now, from one charnel pit in a Neck back to the camp and from the camp in the Kom to a reeking shambles in another Poort, all of that is marked by the leading dog as his territory. Nothing ventures close to this wagon any more – until this shift also runs into the Revenge Commando. Then the first mule wagon in turn gets drenched in paraffin by a second, and afterwards the sticky, greasy mass is raked over in another trench.

Despite threats and promises of extravagant rewards, the British command have difficulty in raising volunteers to burn the bones and remains. It may be the tales of blacks, says Jan Witsie, but by now it is not only the Basotho who are frightened out of their wits.

The old veterans with their years' experience of half-forgotten wars openly say that they would rather serve a term in solitary confinement than perform punitive service in the Poorts across the mountain. They would rather wash down dry bread with thin meat soup, although the mere thought of meat sticks in their throats. They no longer regard working in the Necks, to which courts martial sentence them for minor infringements such as insubordination or drunkenness on watch, as "concessions" for years of service to the Empire.

Even prisoners of war now start looking for all manner of excuses for not having British escorts across the mountains – and this includes those burghers who want to carry on fighting and regard exile as the coward's way out, says Jan Witsie.

And Jan Witsie challenges Aunt Soph once again: if Aunt Soph does not believe him about the Revenge Commando, why doesn't she ask the British scout – and by the way, says Jan Witsie, the last few times that he saw the smaller dog, one foreleg was limping. Look carefully, and Jan Witsie warns Soph that the Commando will come looking for Charlie, because the paw is healing. Its healing will also be more lasting than that of the sores on the back of the yard dog, says Jan Witsie.

No documents are ever found at the scenes of ambushes. No-one can tell exactly who has fallen prey to the Revenge Commando, and who escapes. This is much more so in the later cases, where the Boer prisoners, British escorts and Basotho wagon drivers flatly refuse to visit the scene of an ambush to identify the victims personally (where such an identification is still possible).

Source:
Christoffel Coetzee: *Op soek na generaal Mannetjies Mentz*. Cape Town: Queillerie: 1998.
Translated by Herman Fourie

Pojo's Child

A.H.M. Scholtz

The following is an extract from the novel Afdraai (Turn-off) *by A.H.M. Scholtz, the first major "Coloured" novelist to write in Afrikaans. The scene is set in a concentration camp and, typical of Scholtz, focuses on the senselessness and cruelty of racism.*

One morning Aunt Rosa Kloppers came to the tents with the news that one of the two adult Beyers girls who always went looking for herbs outside the camp, had given birth the previous night. Everyone always went to them to get herbs against illness. Their mother, who had died while they were still children, was believed to be a woman who could cure disease with medicinal herbs.

Rosa Kloppers had been the midwife at the birth. It was Koba, the one with the long yellow plaits, she said, and it's a boy. But I can see it's not one of our people, she added.

A cousin who still had a gold pound and who had lost her own baby, went to give Koba the money in a pillowcase after she had begged her to give her the child and had promised her the earth. Yellow, black, any colour, she had said. As long as I can feel a child again. But Koba didn't want to know.

The child was a strong child and Koba had more than enough milk. People walked into the tent without fuss or shame to see the child.

Koba cried incessantly. She said: Other women also have babies and you don't carry on like this.

But the women kept coming and they wanted to know who the father was.

It's Pojo's child, Koba sobbed eventually. One of those who dig the graves. He always gave me bread and milk when Lena and I went looking for herbs. He is a very good man. He puts his hand on my arm when we talk. His hand is warm and soft even if it is calloused. It doesn't feel black and the callouses are from all the hard work with the spade.

She sighed. He said I must repay him. I asked with what, I have nothing. He said I had a great deal to give. What about that thing between my legs?

Now I've had the child and my own people are angry with me, no, they hate me. Perhaps it's the work of the devil, Koba cried while Lena stood there with the innocent baby. She had loved him immediately.

His name is Krisjan, my father's name, said Lena, and hugged the child against her breast. Krisjan Beyers.

A woman looked at the child, pulled up her nose and said: The English talk about "culled".

No, "coloured", said another. A half-caste.

But Lena became agitated. Koba, let them say what they like. Krisjan will grow up like a Boer boy. Stop crying! Hasn't Krisjan been born into our family?

She passed Krisjan to his mother. Suckle him, she said. You only did what others are used to doing – and only once at that.

An auntie said she wanted to see the child's face.

That was too much for Lena. You, Aunt, you and your sister, Aunt Fransina, who are great-grandparents, you who have such fat behinds, you with your Bushman bums and your fine, frizzy hair! My mother said you're also only halfway white!

That freckled face! said Aunt Fransina when she looked back at Lena for the last time.

Lena sat down next to Koba to watch Krisjan suckling. You great-grandmothers judge an innocent baby, she said. The day will come when the people of this country won't judge a sallow skin any longer.

Later Koba developed the habit of sitting in the furthest corner of the camp with the baby, picking up pebbles which she threw away again. Without looking to see where they fell. As if she wanted to throw her people's tasteless words out of her mind.

Source:
A.H.M. Scholtz: *Afdraai*. Cape Town: Kwela Books: 1998.
Translated by Madeleine van Biljon

The Affair at Ysterspruit

Herman Charles Bosman

It was in the Second Boer War, at the skirmish of Ysterspruit near Klerksdorp, in February, 1902, that Johannes Engelbrecht, eldest son of Ouma Engelbrecht, widow, received a considerable number of bullet-wounds, from which he subsequently died. And when she spoke about the death of her son in battle, Ouma Engelbrecht dwelt heavily on the fact that Johannes had fought bravely. She would enumerate his wounds, and, if you were interested, she would trace in detail the direction that each bullet took through the body of her son.

If you liked stories of the past, and led her on, Ouma Engelbrecht would also mention, after a while, that she had a photograph of Johannes in her bedroom. It was with great difficulty that a stranger could get her to bring out that photograph. But she usually showed it, in the end. And then she would talk very fast about people not being able to understand the feelings that went on in a mother's heart.

"People put the photograph away from them," she would say, "and they turn it face downwards on the rusbank. And all the time I say to them, no, Johannes died bravely. I say to them that they don't know how a mother feels. One bullet came in from in front, just to the right of his heart, and it went through his gall-bladder and then struck a bone in his spine and passed out through his hip. And another bullet . . ."

So she would go on while the stranger studied the photograph of her son, Johannes, who died of wounds received in the skirmish at Ysterspruit.

When the talk came round to the old days, leading up to and including the Second Boer War, I was always interested when they had a photograph that I could examine, at some farmhouse in that part of the Groot Marico District that faces towards the Kalahari. And when they showed me, hanging framed against a wall of the voorkamer – or having brought it from an adjoining room – a photograph of a burgher of the South African Republic, father or son or husband or lover, then it was always with a thrill of pride in my land and my people that I looked on a likeness of a hero of the Boer War.

I would be equally interested if it was the portrait of a bearded commandant or of a youngster of fifteen. Or of a newly appointed veldkornet, looking important, seated on a riempies-stoel with his Mauser held upright so that it would come into the photograph, but also turned slightly to the side, for fear that the muzzle should cover up part of the veldkornet's face, or a piece of his manly chest. And I would think that that veldkornet never sat so stiffly on his horse – certainly not on the morning when the commando set out for the Natal border. And he would have looked less important, although perhaps more solemn, on a night when the empty bully-beef tins rattled against the barbed-wire in front of a blockhouse, and the English Lee-Metfords spat flame.

I was a schoolteacher, many years ago, at a little school in the Marico bushveld, near the border of the Bechuanaland Protectorate. The Transvaal Education Department expected me to visit the parents of the schoolchildren in the area at intervals. But even if this huisbesoek was not part of my after-school duties, I would have gone and visited the parents in any case. And when I discovered, after one or two casual calls, that the older parents were a fund of first-class story material, that they could hold the listener enthralled with tales of the past, with embroidered reminiscences of Transvaal life in the old days, then I became very conscientious about huisbesoek.

"What happened after that, Oom?" I would say, calling on a parent for about the third week in succession, "when you were trekking through the kloof that night, I mean, and you had muzzled both the black calf with the dappled belly and your daughter, so that Mojaja's kafirs would not be able to hear anything?"

And then the Oom would knock out the ash from his pipe onto his veldskoen and he would proceed to relate – his words a slow and steady rumble and with the red dust of the road in their sound, almost – a tale of terror or of high romance or of soft laughter.

It was quite by accident that I came across Ouma Engelbrecht in a two-roomed, mud-walled dwelling some little distance off the Government road and a few hundred yards away from the homestead of her son-in-law, Stoffel Brink, on whom I had called earlier in the afternoon. I had not been in the Marico very long, then, and my interview with Stoffel Brink had been, on the whole, unsatisfactory. I wanted to know how deep the Boer trenches were dug into the foot of the koppies at Magersfontein, where Stoffel Brink had fought. Stoffel Brink, on the other hand, was anxious to learn whether, in regard to what I taught the children, I would follow the guidance of the local school committee, of which he was chairman, or whether I was one of that new kind of schoolteacher who went by a little printed book of subjects supplied by the Education Department. He added that this latter class of schoolmaster was causing a lot of unpleasantness in the bushveld through teaching the children that the earth moved round the sun, and through broaching similar questions of a political nature.

I replied evasively, with the result that Stoffel Brink launched forth for almost an hour on the merits of the old-fashioned Hollander schoolmaster, who could teach the children all he knew himself in eighteen months, because he taught them only facts.

"If a child stays at school longer than that," Stoffel Brink added, "then for the rest of the time he can only learn lies."

I left about then, and on my way back, a little distance from the road and half-concealed by tall bush, I found the two-roomed dwelling of Ouma Engelbrecht.

It was good, there.

I could see that Ouma Engelbrecht did not have much time for her son-in-law, Stoffel Brink. For when I mentioned his references to education, when I had merely sought to learn some details about the Boer trenches at Magersfontein, she said that maybe he could learn all there was to know in eighteen months, but he had not learnt how to be ordinarily courteous to a stranger who came to his door – a stranger, moreover, who was a schoolteacher asking information about the Boer War.

Then, of course, she spoke about her son, Johannes, who didn't have to hide in a Magersfontein trench, but was sitting straight up on his horse when all those bullets went through him at Ysterspruit, and who died of his wounds some time later. Johannes had always been such a well-behaved boy, Ouma Engelbrecht told me, and he was gentle and kind-hearted.

She told me many stories of his childhood and early youth. She spoke about a time when the span of red Afrikaner oxen got stuck with the wagon in the drift, and her husband and the kafirs, with long whip and short sjambok could not move them – and then Johannes had come along, and he had spoken softly to the red Afrikaner oxen, and he had called on each of them by name, and the team had made one last mighty effort, and had pulled the wagon through to the other side.

"And yet they never understood him in these parts," Ouma Engelbrecht continued. "They say things about him, and I hardly ever talk of him any more. And when I show them his portrait, they hardly even look at it, and they put the picture away from them, and when they are sitting on that rusbank where you are sitting now, they place the portrait of Johannes face downwards beside them."

I told Ouma Engelbrecht, laughing reassuringly the while, that I stood above the pettiness of local intrigue. I told her that I had already noticed that there were all kinds of queer undercurrents below the placid surface of life in the Groot Marico. There was the example of what had happened that very afternoon, when her son-in-law, Stoffel Brink, had conceived a nameless prejudice against me, simply because I was not prepared to teach the schoolchildren that the earth was flat. I told her that it was ridiculous to imagine that a man in my position, a man of education and wide tolerance, should allow himself to be influenced by local Dwarsberge gossip.

Ouma Engelbrecht spoke freely, then, and the fight at Ysterspruit lived for me again – Kemp and De la Rey and the captured English convoy, the ambush and the booty of a million rounds of ammunition. It was almost as though the affair at Ysterspruit was being related to me, not by a lonely woman whose son received his death-wounds on the vlaktes near Klerksdorp, but by a burgher who had taken a prominent part in the battle.

And so, naturally, I wanted to see the photograph of her son, Johannes Engelbrecht.

When it came to the Boer War (although I did not say that to Ouma Engelbrecht) I didn't care if a Boer commander was not very competent or very cunning in his strategy, or if a burgher was not particularly brave. It was enough for me that he had fought. And to me General Snyman, for instance, in spite of the history books' somewhat unflattering assessment of his military qualities, was a hero, nonetheless. I had seen General Snyman's photograph, somewhere: that face that was like Transvaal blouklip; those eyes that had no fire in them, but a stubborn and elemental strength. You still see Boers on the backveld with that look today.

In my mind I had contrasted the portraits of General Snyman and Comte de Villebois Mareuil, the Frenchman who had come all the way from Europe to shoulder a Mauser for the Transvaal Republic. De Villebois, poet and romantic, last-ditch champion of the forlorn hope and the heroic lost cause . . . Oh, they were very different, these two men, de Villebois Mareuil, the French nobleman and Snyman, the Boer. But I had an equal admiration for them both.

Anyway, it was well on towards evening when Ouma Engelbrecht, yielding at last to my cajoleries and entreaties, got up slowly from her chair and went into the adjoining room. She returned with a photograph enclosed in a heavy black frame. I waited, tense with curiosity, to see the portrait of that son of hers who had died of wounds at Ysterspruit, and whose reputation the loose prattle of the neigbourhood had invested with a dishonour as dark as the frame about his photograph.

Flicking a few specks of dust from the portrait, Ouma Engelbrecht handed over the picture to me.

And she was still talking about the things that went on in a mother's heart, things of pride and sorrow that the world did not understand, when, in an unconscious reaction, hardly aware of what I was doing, I placed beside me on the rusbank, face downwards, the photograph of a young man whose hat-brim was cocked on the right side, jauntily, and whose jacket with narrow lapels was buttoned up high. With a queer jumble of inarticulate feelings I realize that, in the affair at Ysterspruit, they were all Mauser bullets that had passed through the youthful body of Johannes Engelbrecht, National Scout.

Source:
Herman Charles Bosman: *Unto Dust.* Cape Town: Human & Rousseau: 1963.

Miss Godby and the Magistrate

Karel Schoeman

The following extract from Karel Schoeman's novel Verliesfontein *(Fountain of Loss) focuses on the unjust arrest of the pro-English "Coloured" man Adam Balie. The scene is set in the summer of 1900-1901, in the imaginary town of Verliesfontein in the Cape Colony. The narrator, Miss Godby, is a librarian and part of the English-speaking community in the town.*

It was that same Sunday afternoon that Minnie came to tell me that Adam Balie had been arrested by the Boers.

Only later, when it became possible to speak openly about all these things and to obtain a better overview of the events, we discovered that above all, it was Adam Balie that the Boers were looking for in the location and elsewhere because of the attitude he had adopted during the war, and the words of loyalty and opposition which he had repeatedly uttered in public, were noted and remembered, to be used against him now and above all else, it was maintained that it was he whom the authorities had negotiated with about possible resistance against the invaders and it was to him that the rifles would be given. This was what made feelings run so high at that time. I merely mention what was said or maintained and which some people honestly and with conviction believed, without, however, wanting to express an opinion about it. How would I be able to judge these things? That Adam in his bright scarf had stood in the winter sunshine on the market square on that day, a piece of paper in his hand, that he made a speech in which he professed his and his people's loyalty, that I had personally witnessed, and that elsewhere he also played a part in celebrations and commemorations and had expressed similar sentiments in other speeches was known to all; but that he had received money through Mr Macalister to pay people for information or that rifles had been handed to him, of that I know nothing. The Boers had searched every house in the location, we heard later, and had even climbed up to the loft of the church but found nothing. That that might have been, I accept but as far as I know those rifles were never found, either in the village or anywhere else. Adam Balie, however, disappeared immediately after the occupation of the village and they kept looking for him, invaded his house time after time, in the middle of the night or shortly before dawn in the hope of catching him but he was gone. The coloured people believed that Mr Macalister had taken him to Beaufort West, that it had been decided between them and that he had waited somewhere along the road for Mr Macalister to pick him up and take him along for safety's sake. In actual fact this wasn't so and Adam disappeared of his own accord shortly after the arrival of the Boers, where to I didn't ever hear. I assume he hid himself in one of the kloofs or took shelter in a shepherd's little hut on a remote farm and that the people in the area looked after him as well as possible, I don't know but that is what other men whom the Boers were looking for, did in those days.

However, these are things we only heard about later, information I had gathered in bits and pieces to be able to give an account at the end of the war, and I can't answer for the accuracy, I merely repeat what I was told. But an account about what and for whom, I did not know and I still don't know.

It must have been for a few weeks that Adam Balie remained hidden somewhere in the district but evidently he remained in touch with the village and he was kept informed of what was happening to us and to his people, how and by whom I can't say because no one ever spoke to me about it. However, that Sunday when all the Boers rode into the village from their camp to attend the service in the Dutch church, he walked into the small church in the location where the coloured people congregated for their own service and took up his usual place in the elders' pew: I repeat that I only tell it the way I heard it, I merely repeat what Minnie Colefax heard from the people who were present in the church and closer than that I can't come to what happened in the church that morning. I tell it the way I heard it because if I don't do it, incomplete and inaccurate as my account in all probability is, who else will do it, who else will account for what happened? There is no one.

So let me carry on in my own way.

Adam Balie came back to the village and after the church service he told the people that he had come to surrender to the Boers because in actual fact it was he they were looking for. Of course the people wouldn't accept it and they tried to talk him out of it or stop him, and when they realised he really meant what he had said, the women wailed and shrieked and fainted, so we were told, and his own wife fell on her knees and grabbed his legs; but Adam was a determined young man and he had evidently decided what he wanted to do. Once the Boers had him and could question him about the rifles, they would be satisfied, he said and then all the retaliatory measures against the coloured people would stop; he had nothing to hide or to be ashamed of, he said, and eventually they also let him go even if it would have been better if they had held him back, even violently, if needs be. This is the way it was all told to me later and this is how I remember it. Presumably he himself believed what he had said and they allowed themselves to be convinced because his words were convincing or perhaps only because this was what they wanted to believe. We were all still ignorant, as I've already mentioned and there was a great deal we still had to learn, all of us. And so Adam Balie surrendered to the Boers on that Sunday morning, where and to whom I don't know because the Commandant and his officers were all at Mr Herklaas Fourie's home where they had been invited for a meal.

Minnie Colefax, who rushed into my kitchen late that afternoon to tell me all about it, came in at the back door, as we all did when we visited informally, bare-headed and without knocking ... that I remember, and as quickly as she had appeared, she disappeared again. It was the same evening, Sunday evening, and across the roofs I could hear the ringing of the first bell for the evening service in the Dutch church while I stood in the passage and tried to digest the events: Captain Crossley under house arrest and Mr Savage in jail and young Charles Kleynhans on his knees in the dust of the street and now Adam Balie who had given himself up to the Boers. This is war, I thought to myself, but still had no solution to all these things, feeling my way in this new world in which I found myself as if it were a strange house in which I had to find a path in the dark. How I sat with him by lamplight at the kitchen table, I remembered, and the basket lined with fig leaves.

Adam Balie was tried in jail where he was kept, by the Boers' magistrate, found guilty and sentenced, or that, in any case, was what we heard because it was a closed trial and we were dependent on rumours and deductions for our information. Again I must emphasise in all honesty and fairness that what I relate, rests on nothing more than my own uncertain memories of the rumours of that time, whispered reports from house to house and the additional information I later acquired bit by bit. No one ever knew precisely what the charge was – incitement, perhaps, or the issue of the rifles which people kept going on about at that time – but that he was found guilty is a fact because after the sentence was passed, he was flogged with a whip in the open space in front of the jail under the blue gum trees to serve as an example to everyone, so it was said. The jail stood apart from the village but near the road that led to the location, and there were always pedestrians and passersby whose attention could be drawn by the events and as far as this public punishment went, there were enough witnesses to confirm what happened and to make the evidence credible while others who weren't present, said they could hear him crying out over a distance; when we received this report, we were obliged to believe it, how disbelieving and unwilling we might have been and only a few dismissed it as location gossip and pointed out that the reports only came from coloured people because there were no white people present at the punishment as witnesses. The number of lashes that were prescribed I no longer know, only that he lost consciousness before the sentence was completed. Two of the constables who were also held captive there, were told to take him back to jail, half-dragged, half-carried, and the door was locked behind them again. This was what we later heard from eyewitnesses and which I personally heard from eyewitnesses.

In the first instance it was Mrs Rigby who came to inform me of this, pale and upset, semi-whispering as though these were things that weren't to be bruited abroad and by merely repeating the events, punishment would ensue; in that time suddenly everybody began speaking in low and secretive tones, frightened to be heard, frightened of being caught where they were conversing and when the conversation ended, they quickly dispersed as if they felt guilty, guilty in thought, word or deed, through association or implication. It was then that we realised it really was war and that what was happening around us was serious; that was when we became scared for the first time, I mean our small group of English people who remained in the occupied village. But 'scared' is a word for children, a word with which to frighten; 'scared' is not what I mean. It was the first time, I would like to say more precisely, that we in our sheltered lives had experienced fear. Mrs Rigby and I spoke at the front door, anxiously and hurriedly, our heads close together and when she left I remained in the dusky passage. Mr Savage who had been detained for a few days or young Charles Kleynhans who stumbled and fell, what were these events set against what had happened in front of the jail under the blue gum trees in the sunshine of the summer's day? Groping, my hands in front of me, step by small step in the dark, I felt my way through this new world, and we all moved onward, hesitant and stumbling, in the belief that in time our eyes would adjust to the dark.

In this time a deep silence fell over the village. O, the young Boers still galloped up and down the streets, there was rowdiness, noise, shouting, incidental shots, but these things no longer concerned us, as if we were irrevocably cut off from it all, we handful, I mean. Fear, as I said, anguish, dismay and silence. We had been left in the lurch by our magistrate, our police no longer had any authority, no relieving army arrived to deliver us, no message of hope or encouragement reached us from the outside world, and the magnitude of our helplessness, no, even more, our total impotence, had finally completely penetrated.

It was during this brief time of silence and dejection that Ragel, Adam's wife, came to seek our aid, in her large white sunbonnet with the flounces which she had always worn previously when delivering the laundry, weeping and gesticulating while I tried in vain to soothe or calm her, stormy and unmanageable about her jailed husband to whom she was refused access, whom no one was allowed to see, not even the doctor. She had been to Mr Macalister's house, she had been to Mr Rigby, later I heard that she ran through the village, from one house to the other, where she might possibly have expected help or support without paying any attention to the young Boers who laughed at her in the street or the coloured grooms who shouted after her, sobbing and gesticulating in her large flounced sunbonnet. We had taught these people to look up to us, to listen to us, to seek our guidance, to listen to our advice and to execute our orders and when she turned to us from one house to the other, in her need to seek aid for her husband, there was no one who dared to do something. What could I have done in any case, except to murmur meaningless commonplaces in an attempt to calm her, to comfort her or encourage her? I offered her a cup of tea but even while I was speaking, I realised how absurd the offer was, fiddling with kettle and cups in the presence of that intense sorrow. She, however, paid no attention to what I was saying but jumped up without wasting any more time on me, and stormed out of the kitchen without even saying goodbye, angrily walking through the rest of the village on her hopeless mission.

Was this all on one single day or did it stretch over more days? The Sunday I remember, our little service in the morning and the tolling of the first bell that evening but the days following, I can no longer differentiate and how much time this development took, a day or two or perhaps even as much as a week, that I can't say. That same afternoon, or an afternoon shortly after, old Mr Dalrymple, the headmaster, called on me and spent some time conferring, confidentially and quietly. He was going to ask the district surgeon to insist on permission to see Adam Balie in jail, he informed me; didn't I think that was the correct procedure? After all, it was the man's right, it was his duty as a civil servant, war or no war. It was a terrible time, he sighed and shook his head, at that time one naturally read about the Franco-Prussian War but never had he expected to experience something similar. And Ragel Balie who had lost all control over herself, who berated all the Boers in the street and stood in front of the jail screaming at them – the Boers weren't used to our coloured people, they wouldn't tolerate something like that. Luckily they only laughed at her but if she carried on in the same way they would lose patience and act against her, she was courting danger, she should be warned, it was, after all, war. And still no sign of the relieving army, he added while he walked a little stiffly down the front steps. A terrible time, yes, my dear Miss Godby, who ever thought that we would experience such things? So he went to the doctor's house but if the young man was ever allowed to see Adam in prison, I never heard and in fact I don't even know whether he ever asked permission: he was a young man and for a long time there had been complaints about his carelessness, there was a great deal of talk about him, and possibly he didn't feel a strong need to interfere unnecessarily or to become involved with the Boers. It was a time of silence, as I've said, a time to be still and keep quiet. The young Boers on their horses, young Giel Fourie of Reigersfontein on horseback with all the other young men, a plume in his hat, arm in arm with girls crossing the street, the sound of horses' hooves and voices in the dark at night, the din surrounding us, that I remember clearly enough; and the silence, the muteness, the suppresion and the evasion – the two things next to one another, in tandem, simultaneous. That I lay awake at night I can also remember, that same night or another, I no longer know and it does not matter, it was at that time in any case. In fact, I lay awake like that during many nights and heard the mice behind the skirting-boards, heard the clay plaster breaking off and crumbling, a rustling so soft that it was barely audible in the silence.

The next morning after I'd tidied the house slightly, I hurriedly put on my hat without looking in the mirror and went to the magistrate's office where the Free State flag had been hoisted on the flagpole and there were young Boers standing around on the stoep. Why I went, I can no longer explain today, even if I had known the reason then; but perhaps I wasn't able to articulate the reason for my decision and I don't think there was even anything as purposeful as a decision and that I went merely because there was nothing else I could do, because sometimes life can be very simple, upsetting in its simplicity. I recount what happened and more than that I never undertook; I never promised to try to explain. This is what happened.

Thus the magistrate's office, the strange flag, the Boers speaking Dutch among themselves and the empty place on the wall where the Queen's portrait had always hung. I had already heard that some of the Boers could speak English fluently, men who had gone to school in Bloemfontein or had even attended the College in Stellenbosch, lawyers and civil servants and other educated men, and the young magistrate who gave me a hearing must have been one of them. As I've said, I left the house in such a hurry that I didn't even look in the mirror when putting on my hat, and I wonder what kind of impression I made on that young man when I suddenly appeared, one of the old English aunts in the village, breathless because she had walked too fast, confused because she hadn't given proper attention to, or prepared what she wanted to say, and with her hat pinned on all awry. Why do I remember that so well, that hat which I only discovered when I arrived back at home? What I looked like had nothing to do with the issue, is of no importance. If he found my appearance comical, the young man behind the desk in Mr Macalister's room showed no sign of it and it was only later that I suspected that he, with his irreproachable courtesy and the undivided attention and seriousness with which he listened to me, was perhaps playing the fool with me, a little game with the silly Englishwoman who had popped up in front of him so unexpectedly.

That I had put on my hat all awry that morning, that they had removed the Queen's portrait, I remember well, but no longer what exactly passed between us, only the courtesy, the attention and the seriousness of the young man, listening to me, his concern I almost want to say, looking back. How I had known Adam Balie for many years, how I had taught him, what an honourable member of the coloured community he was . . . yes, now that I look back and remember, I realise how patronising it all sounded and how futile it was but what else was there that I could say, breathless and confused while the young magistrate with his elbows resting on the desk listened attentively? Only when I had nothing more to say and ended my stammering contention, unnerved by that almost exaggerated interest in what I had to say, he replied in his fluent English, in a low, attractive voice without emphasis or feeling, with a slight smile on his lips to show his goodwill, and while he spoke, I remember now, I noticed how well-cared for his hands were, not the hands of a farmer or a horseman, and I instinctively glanced at my own hands, folded on my lap to hide their trembling, and realised that the seam of one glove had split along the forefinger. I was so upset when I saw it, that I forgot for a moment to follow the low, attractive voice and lost the thread of the argument. That it was war, that he represented the authority of the Free State Republic in our village and had to uphold it and that under these cicumstances he was compelled to act vigorously to maintain the general safety ... what else could he say? After all, they were the things in which he also believed, I presume. I objected, balked, tried to express our anxiety and as I became progressively more upset and incoherent, I realised that I was in danger of losing my uncertain control. So clearly did I see these things and so firmly did I believe in them, so sincere were my motives and so good my intentions and yet I expressed them confusedly and haltingly, my awkward behaviour in no way in proportion to the intensity of my convictions or intentions. With unshakeable, smiling courtesy, however, the young man behind the desk allowed me to have my say and replied with the same unshakeability and the same commonplaces in the same fluent and impassive voice, while I stared in confusion at the tear in my glove. There was nothing more to say, there was nothing more I could do here, he held all the authority, he took the decisions for the village and gave orders and was obeyed and for the length of their presence, he had the power over life and death, over Adam Balie and over me and every one of us. He wasn't even obliged to receive me in his office or to listen to my oration and of this fact, I realised with a sudden disquiet, he was entirely aware, the extent of his power, over Adam, over me who sat opposite him and over us all, he had realised and when he felt called upon or simply felt like it, he would not hesitate for a moment to use it. He also hadn't listened to me when I stumblingly addressed him, I realised at that same moment with sudden insight, but for his own amusement had played a private game of feigned courtesy and thoughtfulness with me, smiling to himself behind the desk. That I was so absurd in his eyes, I could understand and it didn't matter; but he hadn't listened, he wasn't even prepared to listen. It had all been in vain.

What precisely was said between us I no longer recall very well, but I remember my consternation clearly when I think back on that morning; not so much that he didn't take the trouble to listen to me, but that he was free to listen or not to listen, as he thought fit, and that his behaviour was dictated by his own judgment and arbitrariness and not by standards of right or wrong . . . is that what I'm trying to explain? I search for words, groping in the dark and cannot find clarity even for myself. That he had so much power in our little village and that he was so young to carry so much responsibility . . . is that what I mean? How old could he have been, four- or twenty-five perhaps. The Boers who had invaded the Colony were largely young men and even more so the rebels who had joined them here, such as young Fourie of Reigersfontein who had turned twenty-one shortly before. My torn glove and the face of the young man smiling opposite the desk without listening to what I was saying, remains after all these years most clearly in my mind when I think back on that morning. How clearly I still see him in front of me even if it were only that one time that we sat opposite one another for ten or twenty minutes because I didn't ever see him again or hear anything about him. How young he was, I remember now, how well-cared for his hands; didn't someone tell me that before the war he had been a lawyer in the Free State? In any case, they weren't a farmer's hands. Young he was, I recall, absurdly young even in the eyes of a middle-aged woman, and his skin was very fair with an inborn paleness which hadn't been touched by the sun and wind and weather on commando. His hair was blonde and cropped short and his eyebrows so pale that they were almost invisible, his pale blue eyes so light that I would rather call them colourless. Do I make him sound peculiar when I describe him in such minute detail? That's not my intention nor did he strike me as peculiar where he sat opposite me, except that he seemed far too young to carry this responsibility, to exercise this power over life and death. I relate what I remember, and that I remember: his face as he sat opposite me.

His youth and the power he possessed: was that what horrified me so much that morning in the magistrate's office and upset me anew after so many years? "Upset", I say and keep to my choice of the word because upset is not too big a word just as "fear" is not too big a word for what reigned in Fouriesfontein at that time. "Upset", I say and "fear" I say and I stay with the words I have chosen, and even if somewhat hesitantly, I would like to use the word "evil". A big word, the biggest of all, and yet the only one which fits here.

"Evil," I say and with the word I express a judgment and take responsibility for that judgment. Of course it's a word we know from the Bible and prayers and repeat without thinking about the meaning, about the evil of man on this earth, the evil from which we pray to be delivered, the power of darkness, the darkness of this age, the invisible acts of the darkness . . . these are the phrases and the concepts I have known since childhood, part of the system in which I was raised and have always lived; but had evil and darkness suddenly acquired a face and a voice? I use big words which express important things, and in the end the only thing I want to apply them to is eventually a smiling young man behind a desk in an occupied village in the Cape Colony one hot summer morning in January.

However, I don't want to become caught up in words, I'm compelled to search for words to try and express what I feel and these are the best available words suited to my purpose but only approximately, no more, because in the end I would say that I'm concerned with values and not about what they are called. So let me go back; let me start anew, try again.

Whether he was from the Free State or a member of the Boer commando, the magistrate of the occupying forces, all this doesn't matter, the Republics and the war are not what it was all about for me that day in the magistrate's office; it is even less important for me today when I think back on that morning. It could just as well have been before or after the war, just as well somewhere else or with regard to another person; quite by chance it was here in Fouriesfontein during the occupation opposite the young Boer magistrate in the magistrate's office where the Queen's portrait had been removed from the wall, and this detail is not important. For me it boils down to his youth, as I've said, and his indifference, his contempt for the silly old Englishwoman opposite him and the opinions she tried to force on him, the values she tried to formulate; it was his power over me where I sat opposite him as well as over Adam Balie in jail. Do I make my meaning clearer in this manner? Probably not, I'm afraid. For me it finally boils down to a question of power I would say, power which doesn't go hand in hand with a fitting sense of responsibility, power exercised without checks and balances, without a system of values which could direct or control it and in consequence is inevitably abused. That is what I mean by "evil" or "darkness" when I use these big and loaded words; power which is exercised in an irresponsible manner with the intent to destroy or annihilate.

I had a sheltered childhood, I fear, without ever realising it, fed with words and concepts from the Bible and the prayer book, and it was only that morning in the magistrate's office that I was confronted with the existence of these things; it was then that the earth in front of my feet gaped and I looked into the abyss, there where I sat at the desk listening to the young man, the fragile crust on which we had all lived and moved cracked, split and tore open, and I became aware of the darkness.

Source:
Karel Schoeman: *Verliesfontein*. Cape Town: Human & Rousseau: 1998.
Translated by Madeleine van Biljon